CLEAN AIR AT WHAT COST?

China's green transition is often perceived as a lesson in authoritarian efficiency. In just a few years, the state managed to improve air quality, contain dissent, and restructure local industry. Much of this was achieved through top-down, "blunt force" solutions, such as forcibly shuttering or destroying polluting factories. This book argues that China's blunt force regulation is actually a sign of weak state capacity and ineffective bureaucratic control. Integrating case studies with quantitative evidence, it shows how widespread industry shutdowns are used, not to scare polluters into respecting pollution standards, but to scare bureaucrats into respecting central orders. These measures have improved air quality in almost all Chinese cities, but at immense social and economic cost. This book delves into the negotiations, trade-offs, and day-to-day battles of local pollution enforcement to explain why governments employ such costly measures, and what this reveals about a state's powers to govern society.

DENISE SIENLI VAN DER KAMP is Associate Professor in the Political Economy of China at Oxford University. Originally from Hong Kong, she received her PhD from UC Berkeley, and has lived and worked in China, Tajikistan, Canada, the United States, and the UK.

CAMBRIDGE STUDIES IN LAW AND SOCIETY

Founded in 1997, Cambridge Studies in Law and Society is a hub for leading scholarship in socio-legal studies. Located at the intersection of law, the humanities, and the social sciences, it publishes empirically innovative and theoretically sophisticated work on law's manifestations in everyday life: from discourses to practices, and from institutions to cultures. The series editors have longstanding expertise in the interdisciplinary study of law, and welcome contributions that place legal phenomena in national, comparative, or international perspective. Series authors come from a range of disciplines, including anthropology, history, law, literature, political science, and sociology.

Series Editors

Mark Fathi Massoud, *University of California, Santa Cruz*

Jens Meierhenrich, *London School of Economics and Political Science*

Rachel E. Stern, *University of California, Berkeley*

A list of books in the series can be found at the back of this book.

CLEAN AIR AT WHAT COST?
The Rise of Blunt Force Regulation in China

Denise Sienli van der Kamp
University of Oxford

CAMBRIDGE
UNIVERSITY PRESS

Shaftesbury Road, Cambridge CB2 8EA, United Kingdom

One Liberty Plaza, 20th Floor, New York, NY 10006, USA

477 Williamstown Road, Port Melbourne, VIC 3207, Australia

314–321, 3rd Floor, Plot 3, Splendor Forum, Jasola District Centre, New Delhi – 110025, India

103 Penang Road, #05–06/07, Visioncrest Commercial, Singapore 238467

Cambridge University Press is part of Cambridge University Press & Assessment, a department of the University of Cambridge.

We share the University's mission to contribute to society through the pursuit of education, learning and research at the highest international levels of excellence.

www.cambridge.org
Information on this title: www.cambridge.org/9781009152648

DOI: 10.1017/9781009152655

First published 2023

A catalogue record for this publication is available from the British Library

Library of Congress Cataloging-in-Publication Data
Names: Van der Kamp, Denise Sienli, 1985- author.
Title: Clean air at what cost? : the rise of blunt force regulation in China / Denise Sienli van der Kamp.
Description: Cambridge, United Kingdom ; New York, NY : Cambridge University Press, 2022. | Series: Cambridge studies in law and society | Includes bibliographical references and index.
Identifiers: LCCN 2022044496 (print) | LCCN 2022044497 (ebook) | ISBN 9781009152648 (hardback) | ISBN 9781009152662 (paperback) | ISBN 9781009152655 (epub)
Subjects: LCSH: Air–Pollution–Government policy–China. | Air–Pollution–Law and legislation–China. | Environmental policy–Economic aspects–China.
Classification: LCC HC430.A4 V36 2022 (print) | LCC HC430.A4 (ebook) | DDC 363.739/ 20951–dc23/eng/20220923
LC record available at https://lccn.loc.gov/2022044496
LC ebook record available at https://lccn.loc.gov/2022044497

ISBN 978-1-009-15264-8 Hardback

For Deirdre van Dijk-van der Kamp and Mak Shui Ping

CONTENTS

FIGURES

TABLES

ACKNOWLEDGMENTS

This book began on the slopes of Mount Diablo in California where, gasping for breath during a much-needed water break, I began to see a thread that could pull together almost a decade of observations. That moment, and this book, would not have been possible without the mentorship of Kevin O'Brien, whose thoughtful scholarship has shaped my approach to Chinese politics, even before I began my doctoral studies at Berkeley. I am grateful for his wisdom, not least in getting PhD students to hike up the hills of Walnut Creek as they work through their tangled thoughts.

This book has also benefited from the intellectual rigor and incomparable guidance of my dissertation committee – Ruth Collier, Peter Lorentzen, Alison Post, Rachel Stern, and Steven Vogel, each of whom challenged me to be a better scholar in their own distinctive ways. I am grateful for the mentorship I have received from them over the years.

I was lucky enough to spend a year as postdoctoral fellow at the University of Pennsylvania's Center for the Study of Contemporary China, which gave me the time to transform my dissertation into a book. I thank Avery Goldstein and Jacques deLisle, the Directors of the Center, for their support and feedback as this project evolved over the years. Wendy Leutert kept me laughing – and drove me to go further – with her incomparable wit, determination, and generosity. Thank you also to Yuanyuan Zeng for her kind assistance and Neysun Mahboubi for drawing me into a wonderful network of scholars on Chinese law and regulation. My book conference – made possible through the Center's generous support – marked a turning point in the writing process. Thank you to the discussants – Matthew Amengual, Cary Coglianese, Roselyn Hsueh, and Andrew Mertha – for drawing out the comparative insights and reminding me of the violence of regulation. Their comments have transformed this project.

I owe a debt to many individuals in China for sharing their expertise and setting me on the right path. I am grateful to Jennifer Holdaway for introducing me to the network at FORHEAD and opening doors for research on Hebei's air pollution. I was also fortunate to work alongside Wang Wuyi and Yang Linsheng at the Institute of Geography and benefited greatly from their guidance. Thanks also to Yang Lichao at Beijing Normal University for sharing her insightful work on the plight of laid-off workers, and the team at FORHEAD for their support and feedback throughout my time in Beijing. Conversations with Cao Mingde at China University of Political Science and Law deepened my understanding of China's environmental law, while Phil Boxell has been a friend and mentor throughout my time in the field. The team at the Centre for Legal Aid to Pollution Victims unlocked some key insights into the role of environmental lawyers, and colleagues at environmental NGOs continue to inspire me with their frontline efforts to combat pollution. Finally, I thank Fan Laoshi and the old team at Forestry for giving me a firsthand experience of campaign-style mobilization, and Samantha Woods and Fan Xianying (Maggie) for their decades-long support in my research and other endeavors.

Unnamed in the list are the many individuals who agreed to be interviewed for this project, whom I reference only by code. I am immensely grateful to them for taking time out of their busy schedules to speak frankly to this outsider about insider matters. These factory owners, entrepreneurs, officials, street-level bureaucrats, journalists, academics, activists, and experts all play an integral part in China's journey to greener growth. I can safely say that this book would not exist if they had not shared their experiences with me. I have done my best to tell their stories fairly – and I hope my musings on this topic may one day be of use to them too.

The fieldwork for this book was made possible by generous funding from the National Science Foundation (SES-1560166), UC Berkeley's Institute for International Studies and Center for Chinese Studies, and the China Times Cultural Foundation. Grants from the Research Grants Council of Hong Kong (project 9048143) and City University (project 7200634) also provided crucial support during the writing of this book. Guo Yihua, Kang Xiaoyan, Lu Ye, and Xu Chengwu offered excellent research assistance through the Undergraduate Research Apprenticeship Program at Berkeley. I also thank my wonderful, hardworking research assistants at City University of Hong Kong: He Miao, Xu Jinghong, Catherine Kwok Mei Ting, Li Qinshi, and Vito Wong Hoi Yi. Portions of Chapters 3, 4, and 6 of this book originally appeared as articles in *Governance* and *Comparative Politics*. I thank the editors for allowing me to include excerpts from those articles here. Kelley Friel provided excellent copy editing under a tight deadline, while Joe Ng and Gemma Smith at Cambridge ensured that the publication process went smoothly. Three anonymous readers offered exceptionally valuable comments and critiques. Of course, all errors contained in this book are strictly my own.

Over the years, my research has flourished under the advice and support of senior colleagues: Genia Kostka, whose groundbreaking work on China's environment continues to inspire me; Andrew Mertha, who always steers me to the bigger story behind the data; Roselyn Hsueh and John Yasuda (of the so-called Berkeley school of regulation), who break new ground and offer such pithy insights as I shape my own thoughts on these issues. I also thank Rachel Stern for inspiring this line of work and being a staunch ally throughout the project, and Ruth Collier, who keeps me on my toes with her unerring ability to identify the heart issue – even on topics where I am supposedly the expert. A special thanks to Peter Beattie, Iza Ding, Jessica Teets, Rory Truex, Benjamin van Rooij, and Boliang Zhu for their written feedback on earlier drafts. I am also grateful to Yue Hou, Junyan Jiang, Thomas Johnson, Pierre Landry, Ning Leng, Yifei Li, Lizhi Liu, Carlos Lo Wing-Hung, Dan Lynch, Dan Mattingly, Sara Newland, Samantha Vortherms, Alex Wang, Xuehua Zhang, Guobin Yang, Yu Zeng, and my colleagues at AIS at CityU for their comments and feedback on this project over the years (and apologies to anyone I have left off the list).

A special mention goes out to Iza Ding, Coraline Goron, and Deborah Seligsohn, my fellow travelers in this past decade of research on China's environmental governance. Thanks also to Ji Yeon (Jean) Hong and Franziska Keller for folding me into a vibrant network of China scholars in Hong Kong and providing crucial support during the upheaval of 2019 and beyond. I also owe a great debt to Rhea Myerscough, the sharpest writing partner I have come across, for her uncanny ability to divine what I am trying to argue and then show me how to get there.

Finally, I thank my family and friends for their unerring, unconditional support throughout this process. A special thanks to Elsa Massoc, Rhea Myerscough, and Christian Dyogi Phillips for all that OLC wisdom. Also to Donghyun Danny Choi, Mathias Poertner, and Molly McKay for being on call to share stories and provide advice whenever, and wherever. To Komaresan, for bringing me back to what matters in life. To my parents Jake and Mei Chi, for giving me their passion for politics and the courage to embrace big change. To my siblings Jess, Luke, John, Thea, to little Jude, Naomi, and all my Hong Kong family, thank you for keeping me going with coffee, ice cream, beach time, and moments of magic during the long days of writing. And finally, to my grandmothers, Oma and 婆婆, for teaching me patience and giving me a sense of history. This book is dedicated to them.

ABBREVIATIONS

APEC	Asia-Pacific Economic Cooperation
BFR	blunt force regulation
CCDI	Central Commission for Discipline Inspection
CCP	Chinese Communist Party
DENR	Department of Environmental and Natural Resources (Philippines)
EPA	Environmental Protection Agency (USA)
EPB	Environmental Protection Bureau (China)
FDI	foreign direct investment
GDP	gross domestic product
KME	key monitored enterprises
MEE	Ministry of Environment and Ecology
MEP	Ministry of Environmental Protection (old name for MEE until 2018)
MIIT	Ministry of Industry and Information Technology
NBS	National Bureau of Statistics
NGO	nongovernmental organization
NRDC	National Reform and Development Commission
PITI	Pollution Information Transparency Index
RMB	renminbi (Chinese Currency)
SME	small and medium firms
SO_2	sulfur dioxide
SOE	state-owned enterprises
USD	United States dollars

CHAPTER 1

INTRODUCTION

Clean Air at What Cost?

In February 2015, officials at China's central Ministry of Environmental Protection[1] summoned the mayor of Linyi, in Shandong Province, to discuss his city's pollution crisis. Environmental inspectors had recently uncovered major pollution violations in 13 of its 15 largest companies.[2] Five days after the summons, city leaders ordered 57 of Linyi's largest factories to stop production. At the stroke of midnight, authorities cut off electricity to an entire industrial park without notice, even though some factories were in the midst of production; even companies that regulators had verified as compliant were forced to cease operations indefinitely.

In the ensuing weeks, local authorities ordered 412 more factories in Linyi to reduce their output and dismantled several smaller, older factories whose chances of cleaning up their operations had been deemed "hopeless." These orders to stop production lasted for several months, until a looming debt crisis forced local authorities to lift the ban. A high-ranking official in Linyi later estimated that these measures had cost the city 60,000 jobs and led to the default of 100 billion RMB in business loans (approximately 15 billion USD).[3] Yet the city's air quality did improve: Between January and May 2015, the level of harmful airborne micro-particles ($PM_{2.5}$) dropped by 25%.[4]

In this book, I argue that the measures undertaken in Linyi characterize what I call a "blunt force" approach to regulation. This approach has three distinct features. First, the state applies crude, one-size-fits-all restrictions to regulated entities – even those that are complying with the law. Second, the state authorizes bureaucrats to use highly coercive means – such as forcibly destroying regulated entities – to ensure that regulatory action produces immediate change. Third, the state acts arbitrarily, suddenly imposing restrictions on companies without explaining why they are targeted.

Blunt force regulation has allowed the Chinese government to achieve noticeable improvements in pollution levels. According to the data I gathered for this study, between 2010 and 2015, thousands of factories in 11 highly polluting Chinese industries were forced to halt or reduce their production in 269 of the country's 287 prefecture-level cities (地级市) – the highest-level city administrative unit in China, ranking above a county. Further analysis demonstrates that these measures improved air quality across the country, and reduced pollution to a greater degree than conventional regulatory measures. These findings suggest that blunt force regulation allows governments to deliver policy outcomes that might otherwise take years to achieve if implemented through more conventional approaches.

However, blunt force regulation is an enormously costly strategy: It reduces pollution by interrupting production, violating property rights, and indiscriminately punishing both compliant and noncompliant firms. It is an inefficient strategy, because it deprives polluters of the chance to adapt to new regulatory standards while continuing to contribute to growth. It is also counterproductive because it devalues compliance, discourages firms from investing in abatement, and fosters adversarial relations between the regulators and the regulated.

Blunt force regulation is also politically risky: Widespread factory closures decimate local government revenue and increase the risk of unrest from workers who have lost their jobs, and from entrepreneurs who have lost their businesses. The state's outright disregard for property rights can also dissuade foreign companies from investing in local businesses and discourage local companies from expanding their ventures. In short, the rise of blunt force regulation raises three questions:

1) Why would governments choose such a costly solution to reduce pollution? Why destroy businesses, decimate jobs, and depress an area's economy just to clean up the air?
2) If a government can coerce polluters – even compliant ones – to shut down, why not force them to comply with legally enforceable pollution standards? Why shut down the economy if a more reasonable, sustainable alternative is available?
3) What are some realistic alternatives to blunt force regulation? Will China use them?

This book addresses each question in turn. With each answer, I explain why China – a state with the necessary will, resources, and political authority to develop more efficient regulatory solutions – nevertheless resorts to a costly, clumsy blunt force solution. This book also offers answers to some broader questions, such as, can governments enforce complex regulations even when lacking in resources and institutional capacity? Can states enforce regulations arbitrarily and still evade the consequences of heightened market uncertainty?

1.1   THE ARGUMENT IN BRIEF

I argue that blunt force regulation is, at its core, a response to principal–agent problems within the state apparatus. It emerges when political leaders (the principal) want to regulate, but lack sufficient control over local authorities or bureaucrats (the agents) to ensure the regulation will be enforced.

Blunt force regulation solves this problem by standardizing – to an extreme – the actions that local authorities are ordered to take against regulated entities. This makes it easier for central leaders to identify and punish local authorities who deviate from higher-level governments' implementation orders. For instance, central leaders who order local officials to enforce blanket production bans will find it easier to confirm that total bans have been imposed than to check whether local regulators are correctly policing emissions from a variety of factories in different regions.

Blunt force regulation also reduces the number of stages between enforcement action and outcomes. A citywide forced reduction in industrial capacity, for instance, will improve air quality much faster than introducing stricter pollution standards over time. This one-shot approach to delivering outcomes increases the chances that local officials will be discovered – and punished – for disobeying central orders, as central leaders only need to check once to see if a city's air quality has improved. In short, blunt force regulation improves implementation outcomes by temporarily increasing central leaders' ability to monitor, motivate, and sanction local state actors.

This argument – that blunt force regulation is a response to weak bureaucratic control – challenges a longstanding perception that the Chinese state has immense enforcement powers and coercive capacity. After all, this is a state that has managed to control birth rates, censor the Internet, defuse collective action, and deliver decades of economic

3

growth – all of which would have been impossible without bureaucrats who respected and responded to central orders.

In the following sections, I reexamine China's reputation as a strong state. Through investigating the three research questions outlined earlier, I show how blunt force regulation reveals that, in the sphere of environmental governance, the Chinese leadership faces a new set of challenges that is weakening its fabled bureaucratic control. Thus, blunt force regulation represents much more than a leadership's attempts to bring pollution under control.

1.2 WHY SUCH A COSTLY SOLUTION?

When I describe the scale of blunt force regulation in China, people often ask "But what about the risk of social unrest?" and "What about the risk of economic slowdown?" or "Why would the state choose to disrupt the economy on such a large scale?"

These questions are amplified in China's case because authoritarian regimes are more vulnerable to social unrest. Without regular elections to create the appearance of political responsiveness, authoritarian leaders are much less likely to withstand sustained, concerted challenges to their authority (Gandhi and Przeworksi 2006; Haber 2006; Huntington 1991; Nathan 2003). This is why China puts so much effort into repressing or segregating contentious actors, making it impossible for them to organize and breach the collective action barrier (Cai 2010; Deng and O'Brien 2013; Lee 2007; O'Brien and Li 2006; Walker 2008). Why, then, would the regime allow thousands of workers with shared identities, locations, and grievances to be laid off without compensation, over a short period of time, effectively creating the conditions for coordinated labor unrest? Further, why would the state disregard property rights and shut down businesses, sowing resentment and distrust in the business class on which it depends to maintain economic stability?

One possible explanation is that the Chinese government is driven to blunt force regulation out of a sense of urgency. Widespread contamination of the groundwater has made drinking water a serious public health concern (Han et al. 2016). Air pollution is contributing to a decline in life expectancy (Ebenstein et al. 2015; Rohde and Miller 2015). This scarcity of clean air and water will increase the public health burden, overwhelming an already overstretched health system.

Moreover, China's environmental degradation has galvanized pro-tests among wealthy, well-connected urban elites (van Rooij et al. 2016; Wang 2016; Wang and Jin 2007), on whom top leaders depend for regime support, and are therefore reluctant to repress or silence. Thus, for all the talk of authoritarian long-term horizons (Beeson 2010; Wright 2010), China's leaders are finding that – like their democratic counterparts – they must take immediate action to appease popular demands to control pollution.

However, unlike their democratic counterparts – and in contrast to the vast majority of states – China's leaders wield enormous coercive power. The regime is adept at discouraging or demobilizing labor unrest, and can use its concentrated political authority to control even the most powerful industries (Dickson 2003; Friedman 2014; Fu 2017; Gallagher 2006; Lee 2007; Pearson 2011; Tsai 2011; Naughton and Tsai 2015). In one northern Chinese county I visited, blunt force measures against the local cement industry led to the loss of 90% of the township's tax revenue and more than 50% of local employment. However, instead of uniting in protest against the government, laid-off workers despondently drifted home to wait for new jobs to appear or sought jobs in other cities.[5] Business owners accepted small sums of compensation from the government and took on the Herculean task of turning hollowed-out cement factories into more acceptable green businesses, such as agrotourism ventures.[6] News reports[7] and my inter-views with factory owners around China[8] suggest that acquiescence to blunt force regulation is the norm.

A regime that can bring about this level of acquiescence is unlikely to be deterred by the social costs of blunt force regulation. Thus, previous research suggests that China's leaders accept concentrated short-term risks because the problem is urgent, brutal implementation efforts will yield immediate results, and the regime commands tried and tested tools for neutralizing social resistance (Josephson 2004; Shearman and Smith 2007).

This is why some outside observers perceive China's blunt force pollution regulation as a lesson in authoritarian efficiency, and praise the government for its "authoritarian environmentalism" (Gilley 2012). In a short space of time, the Chinese state reduced pollution, contained dissent, and drove entrepreneurs to invest in cleaner indus-tries. In Japan, the same process took a decade, and required protracted negotiations with businesses and expensive compensation schemes for workers (Peck et al. 1987; Tilton 1996). Not so in China.

China's success in reducing pollution through blunt force regulation could lend credence to theories that the regime's centralized, top-down governance model makes it more resilient. A group of scholars led by Heilmann and Perry (2011a) argue that the leadership's concentrated authority enables an ad hoc governance style characterized by a lack of binding rules, stable norms, or clearly specified policies. This institutionalized ambiguity allows the regime to respond quickly and inventively to urgent policy issues such as pollution. It also enables it to implement policies decisively, even when formal enforcement institutions are lacking (Ang 2016; Heilmann and Melton 2013; Heilmann and Perry 2011a; Strauss 2009; Zhi and Pearson 2017).

To an extent, blunt force regulation illustrates the advantages of this flexible mode of governance. When stock markets go into free fall, Beijing can suspend trading and ban securities houses from short selling to prevent shares from bottoming out, as occurred in an infamous case in 2015.[9] When air quality soars to dangerous levels, local officials can order factories to cease production and force cars off the roads.[10] And if the state cannot enforce complex regulatory measures, it can simply apply punitive sanctions to all possible violators. Elsewhere in the world, governing bodies – out of respect for property rights or the legislative process – must work within the law, and apply compromise solutions until more drastic regulatory measures are approved. Not so in China.

1.3   THE LONG-TERM CONSEQUENCES

However, a deeper look at the aftermath of blunt force regulation reveals at least three long-term consequences that may be harder for the regime to overcome.

First, the extralegal nature of this type of regulation has contributed to a highly unstable business environment. Constant uncertainty over when governments will stop production or seize factory assets has increased businesses' fear of state interference. Business owners are also reluctant to make new investments or expand their ventures due to fears of arbitrary closures in the next anti-pollution campaign.

Second, by applying sanctions so indiscriminately, blunt force regulation discourages businesses from complying with the law. Instead of incentivizing polluters to adhere to environmental standards, the state imposes compliance via production bans. Rather than reward firms that reduce pollution *and* generate local revenue, the state closes them down and then tries (during an economic slowdown, no less) to rebuild the economy anew. Why would any company comply with emissions standards amid this level of uncertainty?

This risk became apparent during my interviews with factory owners in a southern Chinese county after blunt force regulation decimated a 40-year-old waste recycling industry. Months after the crackdown, local officials were urging a few remaining factories to move into the "cleaner" industrial parks. Some factory owners stoically resisted government orders, choosing instead to risk a further crackdown. As one surviving factory owner retorted, "why should I move into that industrial park? Why should I pay higher rent to go to that place? Even if I do move into that industrial park, will that really make me clean enough? I don't trust these people [the government]!"[11] His concerns were justified. When I later interviewed the owner of one of these designated industrial parks, he revealed that at that point, only the most basic infrastructure was available.[12]

The third long-term consequence is that blunt force regulation fails to address the deeper problem of regulatory capture because it simply sidesteps the issue of corrupt bureaucrats. High-profile, one-off campaigns may reduce pollution, but they do not improve the regulatory apparatus or make the threat of punishment more credible in the long term. Instead, bureaucrats and regulators can easily revert to their old habits of shielding firms from environmental regulation once blunt force measures have ended. As a result, months after local officials obey Beijing's edicts to curb production, polluting industries revive their production, and industrial output recovers (and surges).[13] Or months after Beijing sends in teams of inspectors to uncover violations, provincial officials revert to protecting noncompliant cadres (Tian and Tsai 2020), and pollution returns to prior levels (van der Kamp 2021). Moreover, it is these old habits – regulatory capture, shirking policy implementation, and protecting noncompliant firms – that give rise to China's frequent regulatory crises. Time and time again, when chemical spills poison rivers,[14] schools collapse in earthquakes,[15] or chemical explosions rip apart city districts,[16] reports reveal it is because bureaucrats have turned a blind eye to ongoing regulatory violations.

These problems suggest that China's coercive powers may be misapplied. If the state can force companies to stop production indefinitely, why not use this power to make them obey pollution laws? If leaders can order local officials to shut down their economies, why not order them to enforce existing pollution regulations, which could address China's pollution crisis more effectively and sustainably in the long term?

1.4   WHY NOT REGULATE THROUGH THE LAW?

One possible explanation for states choosing blunt force regulation over standard enforcement procedures is the need to overcome resource limitations. According to this explanation, the state *intends* to act through the law; it even builds the institutions and enforcement mechanisms to do so. However, local agencies lack the necessary personnel and funds to adequately implement the law, which leads to prolonged lapses in enforcement. To prevent further lapses, the state initiates concentrated waves of enforcement – known in the literature as "campaigns" – in the hope that one "big push" implementation effort can scare actors into compliance and quickly close the gap between the leadership's ambitious goals and their inadequate implementation resources (Biddulph et al. 2012; Dutton 2005; Liu et al. 2015; Manion 2004; Tanner 2000; Strauss 2006; Zhu, Zhang, and Liu 2017). The problem is that this idea of a resource-poor Chinese state with limited monitoring powers is increasingly at odds with the reality of China's modern, data-driven governance.

The Chinese state is wealthy. Its control over key sources of revenue (including land and state-owned industrial sectors) has given it a share of revenue that constitutes over 20% of the country's GDP – comparable to that of the Organization for Economic Co-operation and Development countries (Naughton 2017, 56). Local governments may have limited resources, but this is because Beijing uses fiscal policy to keep local authorities on a short leash by controlling decisions on how much revenue can be collected and disbursed (Wang and Herd 2013, 9–14; Wu and Wang 2013, 179; Ong 2006; Huang 2008; Kennedy 2013, 1010–11; Tsui 2005; Zhang 1999). When the central government is committed to a policy issue – such as pollution control – the leadership can (and does) disburse money to local governments to fund its implementation.

For instance, Figure 1.1 tracks the resources that Beijing has invested in the country's formal environmental enforcement apparatus over the past two decades. It illustrates a steady increase in the number of environmental personnel and enforcement organizations, which has vastly enhanced local governments' monitoring and enforcement capabilities.

The Chinese state is also becoming known (or even notorious) for its information-gathering capacities. Its sophisticated surveillance

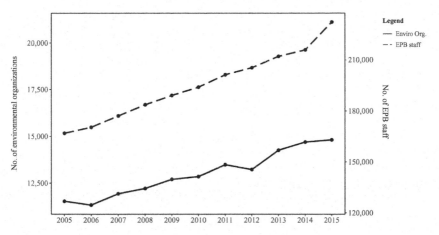

Figure 1.1 Growth in institutional resources for conventional regulation, 2005–16.
Data Source: China Environment Yearbooks, MEP

technology, use of citizen feedback though protest, and online posts to preempt unrest all demonstrate the regime's rapidly expanding ability to monitor society (Distelhorst and Hou 2017; King, Pan, and Roberts 2013; Kostka 2019; Lorentzen 2014; Truex 2017). These information-gathering efforts extend deep into the environmental sphere. Figure 1.2 illustrates that there has been a major spike in spending on environmental inspections since 2012. This increase can be attributed to the widespread installation of continuous emissions monitoring systems, automated devices that measure, in real time, the level and type of pollutants that factories emit – a technology on par with what is used in the United States. They have been installed in all major industrial sources of pollution, including power plants, wastewater treatment plants, and large industrial factories, making it easier for regulators to quickly identify key culprits.

In certain respects, China's use of technology to enforce regulation even outpaces America's. For instance, a US Environmental Protection Agency (EPA) regulator who had recently returned from an official visit to China in 2018 was struck by the ubiquity of mobile app usage in everyday life there. He noted that "China is so far ahead of the US in some systems," and pondered:

> If everyone is on this platform for sharing information [WeChat], why can't the regulatory agencies use it to share data quickly from local to

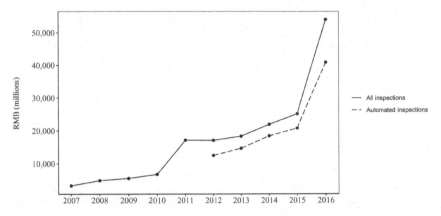

Figure 1.2 Growth in expenditure for conventional regulation – inspections, 2007–16. *Data Source:* China Environment Yearbook, MEP

national levels? They could use a barcode to scan a company's emissions data and upload it directly to a national system. . . Then central agencies could crosscheck the uploaded data with business registration data to see if all sources had been reported.[17]

Once upon a time, China's environmental agencies were derided as "retirement bureaus" – irrelevant, underresourced agencies where aging cadres were put out to pasture. Thus, blunt force regulation (a regular occurrence throughout the 1980s and 1990s) did seem like a necessary corrective to the ineffectual actions of weak, poorly trained local enforcement agencies.

But today's environmental agencies are increasingly well staffed and sophisticated. In my fieldwork I came across municipal regulators who use complex quantitative models to identify and target specific sources of pollutants,[18] as well as county regulators who use high-tech monitoring techniques to catch secret sources of emissions.[19] Some of China's most prestigious universities are also consulting with regulators, sending teams of graduate students to assist them in their monitoring efforts.[20]

Since 2015, Beijing has armed regulators with a strict new environmental law that gives polluters clearer rules to follow and provides bureaucrats with a stronger toolkit of formal, legal mechanisms with which to sanction rule breakers. For the first time, these sanctions include a provision to criminally prosecute company owners and local officials – an added deterrence against falsifying emissions data. Punitive sanctions have doubled in some localities,[21] and powerful firms that previously defied standards now face crippling fines. An industry insider in Jiangsu Province half-jokingly explained to me in an interview in 2019:

> I have come across factory owners who say that nowadays, if you want to put your competitor out of business, you just stand outside his factory and call in pollution complaints one after another. This will force environmental regulators to investigate, which is guaranteed to shut [that factory] down at least for some period of time... Beijing is serious about these enforcing pollution standards now![22]

Thus, while China's environmental enforcement apparatus may not be on par with those of advanced industrialized countries, its resources and supervisory capacity would be the envy of many developing countries.

But these improvements in China's conventional enforcement apparatus only bring the puzzle into sharper relief. Here is a state with considerable coercive power, administrative capacity, and an increasingly sophisticated monitoring apparatus. Surely a state this strong should be able to enforce existing pollution regulations once it sets its mind to the task?

I argue the opposite. In this book, I show that blunt force regulation is a response to *weak* state capacity. It emerges when states lack "infrastructural power" – that is, when state leaders cannot enforce binding rules across a territory (Mann 1984, 188; Berwick and Christia 2018, 79). Studies of weak infrastructural power often concentrate on a state's limited information-gathering or administrative capacity. They analyze how more resources or better monitoring can help leaders identify when subjects or state officials subvert their rules (Duflo et al. 2013; Goldstone 2006; Lee and Zhang 2017; Slater 2008). I argue that China's core problem is not its ability to *gather* information, but its struggle to *use* the information it gathers to credibly punish local officials.

1 5 ENVIRONMEN1AL POLICIES AND CREDIBLE PUNISHMENT

China's problems with credible punishment are most noticeable in the environmental sphere, where the leadership struggles to align national goals with local government interests. In the past, when economic growth was the country's main priority, this divergence between central and local interests was less apparent. Bureaucrats implemented national economic policies not just out of loyalty to central leaders, but because Beijing set up a performance-based system in which local officials were awarded cash bonuses based on the amount of revenue generated in their area (Landry 2008; Li and Zhou 2005; Xu 2011). The system also worked because it was compatible with corrupt officials' interests. Local authorities who preyed on businesses for kickbacks knew that under-the-table earnings would be higher if the economy was thriving (Naughton 2016).

Yet as Beijing's focus switches to environmental protection, there are signs that local officials are increasingly disregarding central orders (Cao, Kostka, and Xu 2019; van Rooij et al. 2017; Ward, Cao, and Mukherjee 2014). Beijing may issue forceful instructions to control pollution, but implementing these orders depresses growth, which eats into local officials' revenue streams and diminishes the rents they collect from protecting polluting industries. This discourages local officials from implementing such policies, especially when they can exploit the regime's information failures to misreport performance.

As the gap widens between leaders' goals and local authorities' interests, Beijing has resorted to punitive instruments to force compliance. These include formal, institutional mechanisms (such as criminal punishment through the courts) as well as more informal, party-based mechanisms (including ideological and normative appeals or threats of disciplinary action) (Mertha 2017; Mei and Pearson 2014; Pei 2017; Strauss 2009). Yet, as I show throughout this book, the institutions for enacting such punishments are porous and subject to leaders' discretion. Thus, bureaucrats can seek protection through high-level connections, which weakens the threat of punishment, even for persistent rule breakers.

Political scientists argue that this lack of credible punishment is why even in systems in which political leaders enjoy absolute power, they will eventually delegate bureaucratic oversight to "referees" or independent third parties – such as the courts – which have interests that are separate from (and may conflict with) those of leading politicians or political parties (Levistky and Ziblatt 2018; McCubbins and Schwartz 1984, 166, 172; North and Weingast 1989). But in single-party regimes, how many leaders are willing to delegate punitive powers to an independent judiciary, knowing that they might be personally implicated in enforcement failures? How many leaders are willing to put party members before independent courts, knowing that they depend on their loyalty to stay in power? On the other hand, how many leaders, lacking credible threats of punishment, can convince their subordinates to act against their material interests based on ideological and normative appeals alone? This is the age-old dilemma that China's authoritarian leaders face when implementing policies that go against powerful local interests (Minzner 2015; Stern 2013; Wallace 2016; Wang 2015).

Blunt force regulation offers a temporary solution to this dilemma in two ways. First, the visible, verifiable nature of enforcement actions – such as using industry-wide shutdowns to control pollution – makes it easier for central authorities to quickly detect noncompliance, even in far-flung localities that normally evade close observation. Second, the one-off nature of blunt enforcement actions makes it easier for central authorities to check and punish local implementation failures than to monitor performance based on complex, incremental enforcement actions over many years. Thus, blunt force regulation drastically simplifies the enforcement process by allowing central authorities to directly punish local officials for noncompliance. Central leaders can thus avoid delegating the job of punishment to independent powers, and minimize the degree to which political discretion corrupts the enforcement process.

1.6 OBSERVABLE IMPLICATIONS AND SCOPE CONDITIONS

This theory has three observable implications. First, it suggests that blunt force regulation is most likely to occur in places with weak infrastructural power, or in policy areas in which bureaucrats have a long history of disobeying central orders. It will therefore be most intensively employed in areas and sectors where political leaders have lost control over local implementation. Indeed, as I show in Chapter 4, blunt force regulation in China is directed *not* at the most polluted localities, but at those in which local officials have consistently under-implemented environmental policies.

Second and more broadly, this suggests that blunt force regulation is most likely to be used in developing countries because they are more vulnerable to the institutional problems described earlier. While leaders of developed countries also encounter shirking in enforcement, this is largely due to regulatory complexity: In some issue areas, the risks

are highly variable, and require expert knowledge and complex procedures to enforce the standards (Black 2010; Paoli and Wiles 2015, 5–8).
Pollution regulation is a classic example of such an issue area, because
the standards vary widely depending on the type of pollutant or the
process a factory uses. This makes it easier for corrupt regulators to
elude scrutiny by the average layperson or politician who lacks expertise on these topics (Carrigan and Coglianese 2011, 120–1; Downs
1967, 145; Niskanen 1971; Wilson 1980).

But for developing countries, compliance problems stem from weak
institutions in addition to regulatory complexity (Blackman 2009).
Leaders lack strong courts and independent accountability structures
that can credibly oversee and punish noncompliant officials and companies. Instead, they resort to cruder monitoring and punishment tools
that are more easily corruptible. This leads to compliance problems
even for less complex, less controversial regulatory issues (as I explain
in Chapter 3).

Finally, my theory proposes that blunt force regulation *does* achieve
noticeable improvements in regulatory outcomes, even in countries or
regions with a long history of weak enforcement. This is because its
indiscriminate, one-shot nature allows political leaders to temporarily
sidestep principal–agent problems in the bureaucracy, regardless of how
underdeveloped the regulatory apparatus might be. Thus, as I show in
Chapter 5, cities in China with notoriously poor compliance records
experienced clear reductions in pollution levels following blunt force
regulation. This finding suggests that this method is effective at overcoming Chinese leaders' problems with credible punishment.

I focus on evidence of blunt force regulation in China, but examples
can be found from across the world. In India, central authorities
imposed a blanket closure of Delhi's heavy polluting industries to halt
rising pollution levels (Dasgupta 2000). In the Philippines, the president imposed a 6-month lockdown on a popular tourist region, using
blunt force regulation to fix festering sewage problems.[23] In Chapter 8,
I show how in all of these cases leaders turned to blunt force regulation
following prolonged compliance failures, and did succeed in improving
regulatory outcomes. However, China's unusual combination of high
coercive power (leading to more severe measures) and weak infrastructural power (which necessitates more frequent interventions) means
that China may be distinctive in the severity, breadth, and length of its
blunt force campaigns.

1.7 WHAT ARE THE ALTERNATIVES, AND WILL CHINA USE THEM?

This book demonstrates that blunt force regulation is effective at temporarily overcoming China's weak bureaucratic compliance, yet the strategy's long-term effectiveness is uncertain. I concentrate on China's war on pollution (approximately 2010–18), but examples of blunt force pollution regulation date back to the 1980s. Time and time again, swift, brutal campaigns have eliminated vast swathes of China's polluting industries, only for them to crop back up again a few years later (van Rooij 2002). Meanwhile, local officials continue to shirk emissions reduction orders, or resort to absurd, one-off measures such as closing factories or switching off heating in schools, offices, shopping malls, and residential homes to meet looming reduction targets.[24] Even the successes of the recent war on pollution seem to be eroding: Smog levels have risen in some years,[25] and industrial output has rebounded.[26] Meanwhile, Beijing has rolled back binding pollution targets to accommodate the vicissitudes of the trade war[27] and the COVID-19 pandemic; it has revived investments in coal-fired power plants and reopened closed coal mines,[28] taking a backward step in its policy to reduce coal and meet its pledge to become carbon neutral by 2060. Li Ganjie, the Minister of the Environment, acknowledged in 2019 that "the importance of environmental protection has weakened in some regions, and momentum has slowed."[29] This suggests that the achievements of blunt force regulation are fleeting, and are unlikely to provide a lasting solution to China's pollution problems.

As I have presented this story about China's war on pollution over the years, people have often asked: But what is the alternative? If China lacks the institutional means to punish bureaucratic noncompliance, then perhaps this is the best solution? If regulatory capture is so pervasive, how else can you get polluters to reduce pollution levels?

The experience of other developing countries has demonstrated that there *is* an alternative – one that leverages civil society's ability to punish noncompliers. Studies from Southeast Asia and Latin America (Blackman et al. 2004; García et al. 2007; Neaera Abers and Keck 2009; O'Rourke 2004; Pargal and Wheeler 1996) find that even when courts are weak and regulatory agencies lack teeth, social norms and the fear of public activism can drive polluting firms to go "beyond compliance" (Gunningham et al. 2004).

I call this approach "bottom-up enforcement" – what van Rooij, Stern, and Furst (2016) refer to as "regulatory pluralism" and O'Rourke (2004) labels "community-driven regulation." According to this approach, the state turns to communities, activists, nongovernmental organizations (NGOs), and the media to boost its monitoring capacity. Citizens are encouraged to use institutional channels such as lawsuits, petitions, investigative reporting, and even protests to report noncompliance, acting as a "fire alarm" for regulatory capture (McCubbins and Schwartz 1984). It is precisely because traditional regulators are so weak that non-state actors have begun to play such an important role in enforcing regulation in the Global South (Braithwaite 2006, 891; Dubash and Morgan 2012; Hochstetler 2013; Tilt 2007).

Michael Mann – the original theorist on state infrastructural power – also argues that strong infrastructural power can evolve through a strong civil society (Mann 2008, 356). If citizens proactively gather information to put pressure on local companies, or if they consistently demand improvements from political leaders, these interactions slowly build up into semi-institutionalized means of monitoring bureaucrats. Effective institutions do not have to be developed entirely by the state; they can also coevolve from repeated feedback between the state and society (Ang 2016; Migdal, Kohli, and Shue 1994; Wang 1997).

In sum, these theories suggest that in states with weak infrastructural power, governments can use bottom-up enforcement mechanisms to overcome bureaucratic noncompliance. Rather than resort to costly blunt force measures, the state can deploy collaborative, citizen-driven approaches that are less damaging to the economy, and that outsource monitoring costs to civil society. Crucially, bottom-up enforcement operates within the law, buttressing the power of conventional regulatory institutions. This approach is therefore more effective at improving compliance in the long term, because it follows pre-agreed rules and incentives, giving polluters a sense of certainty.

China has demonstrated that it recognizes the advantages of enforcing through the law and using public participation to strengthen regulatory institutions. In addition to enhancing its environmental laws, Beijing passed new laws on public interest litigation in 2015 that allowed NGOs to file lawsuits against polluters on behalf of the public. The Ministry of Environmental Protection (MEP) has also established a central hotline that encourages citizens to report polluters.

A central government official from the MEP interviewed for this study in 2016 cited the two most important issues in environmental governance in China as: 1) improving public trust in the government and 2) using public activism to strengthen enforcement. He argued that trust is needed to stop the trend in environmental protests, in which fearful citizens obstruct environmentally sound infrastructure projects due to fears that it might poison their localities. But activism, he noted, was essential in helping the central government police polluters.[30]

Yet the regime maintains an ambivalent attitude towards bottom-up enforcement. It wants citizens to raise the alert, but only through supervised, predictable channels. It wants NGOs to assist in public interest litigation, but then stops them from suing government agencies that violate the law.[31] And it wants lawyers and journalists to do their part, but then arrests or threatens those who push the boundaries (Pils 2014; Repnikova 2017; Stern and Hassid 2012; Stern and Liu 2020; Stern and O'Brien 2012). Thus, as I show in Chapter 6, which discusses a case of citizen protest, the regime's ambivalence to public participation – and its insistence on controlled, supervised citizen input – is weakening the potential for bottom-up enforcement. What explains this ambivalence? Why support citizen enforcement, only to constrain it? And why revert to blunt force regulation after investing in more sustainable, rules-based alternatives?

1.7.1 Force of Habit
One possible explanation is that China reverts to blunt force regulation out of habit. Studies of comparative regulation show how states that struggle to shake off institutional legacies (such as socialist planning) can fall into suboptimal patterns of regulation. They start off intending to regulate at arm's length, but then find that the "state-as-regulator" model requires strong courts capable of enforcing contracts and a sophisticated bureaucracy that can extract information in order to monitor market actors (Levi-Faur 2009; Polanyi 1957; Pearson 2015, 36–7; Vogel 1996). Governments that lack these capabilities sometimes find it easier to nationalize or control businesses directly (Sappington and Stiglitz 1987; van de Walle 1989, 607; Chaudhry 1993; Wengle 2015, 123–30).[32] In sum, state ownership provides an attractive short term solution to crises because it reduces the information and coordination costs of direct ownership.

A similar logic seems to be at work in regulating China's polluters. While the state cannot nationalize all polluting companies in order to better regulate them, Beijing's blunt force pollution reduction demonstrates two characteristic features of this response: 1) direct state control of market actors and 2) administrative shortcuts that minimize the state's reliance on dysfunctional bureaucracies and weak judicial institutions.

To some, then, China's repeated use of blunt force regulation reflects a broader pattern of "pervasive short-termism" in economic governance (Naughton and Tsai 2015, 28). The state employs an available, immediate solution to a problem that subsequently undermines the steps it is taking to create more lasting, effective institutions. In the sphere of market regulation, for example, the Chinese state often turns to old management bodies (such as former economic ministries) to control firms when newly minted regulators have failed. While this might force China's financial institutions or airline industries to meet necessary global standards (Naughton and Tsai, 2015; Pearson 2015), it also prevents regulatory bodies from ever building up the authority to control these sectors.

These theories suggest that China returns to blunt force regulation again and again because the state cannot shed its role as a planner, or its habit of solving problems through direct control. This instinct is amplified in times of crisis when, instead of acting as an independent regulator and allowing the markets to resolve the crisis naturally, the leadership responds by intervening and fixing problems directly. However, this perspective also holds out hope that blunt force regulation is just a transition phase, and that the state will shake off these bad habits and acquire new, more efficient ones as markets and regulatory institutions continue to evolve.

1.7.2 Authoritarian Compromise

The examples and evidence in this book point to another perspective. They suggest that blunt force regulation is undertaken not just out of habit, or out of urgency, but by *choice*. This choice stems from the authoritarian leadership's preference for governing loosely by the rules and for evading direct accountability to citizens.

The regime prefers to avoid clearly stated rules not only because this increases its flexibility, but because clearly specified rules could be turned against the leaders themselves. As O'Brien and Li (2006) show, the more a regime uses the law to legitimate its rule, the more easily citizens can use these laws and institutions to challenge discretionary authority and expose abuses of power.

The regime's reluctance to institute binding rules has led to a unique "adaptive governance" and "guerilla policy style" (Heilmann and Perry

2011a) in which policies are implemented with a high level of discretion, the rules governing society and the bureaucracy are fluid, and the leadership controls bureaucrats by constantly catching them off guard. In other words, the regime replaces the rule of law with rule by discretion, and trades credible commitments for ad hoc implementation (Birney 2014; Zhi and Pearson 2017, Zhu et al. 2019). However, the absence of binding rules also makes it harder to force everyone in the ruling apparatus – from leaders down to local cadres – to follow through on their commitments (North and Weingast 1989; Olson 1993; Ostrom 1990). This trade-off between offering subjects certainty through rules and allowing leaders to be constrained by rules captures a compromise at the heart of Chinese governance.

Blunt force regulation encapsulates this authoritarian compromise. The Chinese leadership wants to fix pollution through institutionalized channels. It is using every tool in its arsenal to strengthen sanctions and construct binding terms that could improve regulatory enforcement. It has introduced high-priority bureaucratic targets for reducing pollution and passed stricter laws – backed by criminal sanctions – to punish violations of these pollution regulations. It has also centralized the administration of environmental regulators so that agents on the ground report directly to ministries in Beijing.

However, the analysis in this book shows that enforcement through institutionalized mechanisms is weak. Case studies demonstrate how high-level officials use their discretionary power to shield polluters, thwarting even the "most likely" cases of institutionalized enforcement. Quantitative tests show that conventional regulatory measures have only a fraction of the effect of blunt force regulation on reducing pollution.

As long as the regime preserves the option to govern loosely by the rules, then the rules are unlikely to be respected. Instead, it must use forceful, extralegal blunt force regulation to overcome systemic non-compliance in order to reduce pollution. From this perspective, blunt force regulation is likely to persist; it is not just a transition phase.

1.8 COMPARATIVE IMPLICATIONS

Studies of regulation in weak institutional environments typically focus on how to control the state's coercive power. They examine how state leaders can reassure investors that their assets will be protected from arbitrary seizure, even in the absence of independent courts or effective legislatures that can constrain executive power (Badran 2013; Helmke and Rosenbluth 2009; Hou 2019; Jensen 2008; Jensen et al. 2014; North and Weingast 1989; Staats and Biglaiser 2012; Wang 2015). Alternatively, when a state's coercive powers are weak and firms are powerful, past research investigates how to force firms to comply with laws issued by an ineffectual state (Cao et al. 2021; Chaudhry 1993; Lee 2017; O'Rourke 2004). But what happens when a state has strong authority over firms, and *does* want to enforce regulation? Would compliance be automatic under such conditions?

This book examines what happens in such a scenario. It focuses on a state (China) that is known for its coercive power, and on an issue (the environment) on which leaders *do* want to uphold regulatory laws and *do* have the authority and resources to implement these regulations. Nevertheless, leaders fail to make polluters comply with these laws. China's case therefore illustrates that obstacles to enforcement stem not just from a lack of will, resources, or coercive power, but from the deeper challenge of weak infrastructural power. Before leaders can rectify noncompliance in polluters, they must first address noncompliance within the state itself. Moreover, China's struggle to sustain outcomes through blunt force regulation shows that imposing compliance through coercion alone is suboptimal. Coercive powers can only temporarily make up for gaps in infrastructural power. In sum, this book offers a more complex conception of China as a powerful state with a porous, highly fractious policy implementation process. In so doing, it forces us to rethink what it means to be a "high-capacity" state.

By highlighting the arbitrary nature of blunt force regulation, this study also offers an insight into how governments and polluters manage situations of high regulatory uncertainty. In developing countries, businesses are accustomed to operating in markets without credible commitments. However, prior studies have shown that such an environment can be intensely frustrating for market actors, who find it difficult to plan amidst the chaos of corruption or irregular enforcement (Dasgupta 2000; de Soto 2001; Dubash and Morgan 2012; Wang 2015). These studies document how states and businesses develop informal cooperative mechanisms to mitigate institutional weakness and build resilience against constant uncertainty (Amengual 2016; Chen and Hollenbach 2022; Post 2014). By contrast, I describe an alternate, much more adversarial pathway in which the state abandons all pretense of cooperation, subjecting firms to the full force of that uncertainty. Moreover, I show that even governments with long-term horizons that expect to pay the costs of such adversity in the future will engage in this kind of scorched earth response. This study investigates the causes of such deliberately suboptimal actions to expand our understanding of why states or market actors act "irrationally" in conditions of high uncertainty.

1.9 METHOD OF INQUIRY

This book applies a mixed-methods research design that uses both quantitative and qualitative data (which I collected over 20 months of field research) to generate theories, test hypotheses, and develop my argument. The origins of this study of blunt force regulation can be traced back to my site visits to Hebei Province (in the North) and Guangdong Province (in the South), where I heard rumors of extreme government campaigns to address pollution problems.

I started out by collecting qualitative data to investigate these phenomena. I conducted a total of 98 interviews in Guangdong, Hebei, and Jiangsu provinces and covered a range of administrative levels including municipalities (直辖市), urban districts, and rural counties. I interviewed state officials, factory owners, industry experts, citizen activists, and local academics to gain a range of perspectives on what was happening. I use this data in Chapters 2–4 to illustrate the logic of blunt force regulation.

However, as this research advanced, I began to ask myself: Why does the state use such an extreme form of regulation? While my qualitative data suggested several hypotheses, I decided to use quantitative data to test these hypotheses, and to see if I could identify a regime-level logic that was independent of the idiosyncratic characteristics of specific cases or political groups. I compiled an original dataset on the environmental enforcement measures undertaken in each of China's prefectural-level cities, taking care to distinguish between conventional measures (such as inspections and fines) and extralegal, blunt force measures (such as shuttering factories and forcibly reducing production). I also employed NASA satellite data to develop city-level measures of pollution. Using these three datasets, I exploit within-country variation across China's cities to assess whether blunt force regulation is essentially a method of bureaucratic control, and whether it reduces pollution levels.

Finally, I gathered qualitative data to examine the social and economic costs of blunt force regulation in more depth. These case studies allow me to delve into the complex, long-term effects on different groups and actors that might be obscured by large-n, cross-sectional data. To capture the diversity of affected groups in China, I selected cases from different regions with contrasting political economies: some cases involved blunt force regulation of export industries, where small and medium enterprises are engaged in cutthroat competition, and are prepared to sacrifice the environment for marginal returns. Other cases focus on blunt force regulation of large, established firms, including state-owned enterprises that were accustomed to being insulated from the effects of market competition. In addition to interviewing key stakeholders, I gathered details from local, provincial, and national news reports to clarify the timing of events, and to map out local officials' tactics in their interactions with firms and citizens.

1.10 PLAN OF THE BOOK

This book was conceived during my fieldwork, where in multiple towns and suburbs I stumbled across a drastic approach to pollution enforcement that simply did not fit existing categories of regulatory enforcement. This drove me to: 1) clarify why blunt force regulation looked so different from other types of regulation; 2) explain why the Chinese state would pursue such a scorched earth solution; and 3) assess why this approach was so ubiquitous, despite the consolidation of new laws and institutions to support more stable, conventional regulation. In the ensuing chapters I elaborate my findings on these three points.

In Chapter 2, I begin by clarifying exactly why blunt force regulation is so distinctive. I compare this approach to two established conceptions of how regulation should operate ("rules-based" and "risk-based" regulation) to illustrate how it fits into neither category. Instead, blunt force regulation represents an unusual combination of ambiguous but inflexible regulation, which makes it unusually costly (by increasing business uncertainty and regulatory distrust) and counterproductive (by discouraging companies from complying with future regulation). This raises the question: Why blunt force regulation?

In Chapter 3, I propose that governments choose this suboptimal approach because they seek, first and foremost, to overcome principal–agent problems in the enforcement process. Drawing on case research and interviews with government officials around China, I illustrate how blunt force regulation creates shortcuts that allow political leaders to increase the credible threat of punishment, temporarily scaring bureaucrats into compliance. Finally, I offer some observable implications of my theory, which I test in the ensuing chapters.

The next section of the book (Chapters 4 and 5) tests the observable implications of my theory. In Chapter 4, I use process tracing on a case of blunt force regulation from southern China to show that two common explanations for such measures – deterring excess pollution and reducing industrial overcapacity – fail to fully account for their occurrence. Instead, I show how blunt force regulation represents local officials' response to sudden scrutiny from higher-level officials. I then use quantitative methods to test this theory on a national scale. I demonstrate that cities in which local officials were underenforcing pollution regulations were more likely to be subjected to high levels of blunt force pollution regulation than those with high levels of pollution or industrial overcapacity. These findings reveal that blunt force regulation is a form of bureaucratic control.

In Chapter 5, I conduct further quantitative analysis to determine how blunt force regulation affects pollution levels. By regressing pollution levels on blunt force measures, I show that this type of regulation is effective at overcoming enforcement failures; indeed, it is associated with much greater reductions in pollution than conventional regulation. These findings challenge a common conception that blunt force regulation is mere political theater, in which the government uses highly publicized spectacles to convince the public it is doing something about pollution. Drawing on interviews with national and local regulators, I show that, far from mere performance, blunt force measures are the result of high-level government planning, enlist the efforts of several government agencies, and constitute part of a concerted, multi-year strategy to reduce pollution levels across the country.

Some might interpret the findings from Chapters 4 and 5 as evidence that China has devised a creative and innovative solution to its pollution problem. Others, dismayed by the costs, might suggest that blunt force regulation is merely a transition phase, and that more stable forms of regulation will appear as the country's markets and institutions mature. In the final part of the book (Chapters 6 and 7) I assess these interpretations, examining what blunt force regulation reveals about China's governance structures.

In Chapter 6, I explore whether blunt force regulation is merely a transition phase. I provide evidence that the Chinese government has invested heavily in conventional regulatory institutions and recognizes that they offer more lasting solutions. I also show how the Chinese government has promoted bottom-up enforcement to strengthen these institutions. Using a case study of anti-pollution protests in a wealthy Chinese city – a case that, at the outset, appeared likely to succeed at improving government enforcement – I then examine how the state's ambivalence to civil society activism closes off channels for effective bottom-up enforcement. I draw on further interview evidence to show that as an authoritarian state, Chinese officials fear the accountability mechanisms (such as a free press, independent judiciary, and community activism) that make bottom-up enforcement so effective in other countries. These limitations have pushed the leadership to repeatedly return to blunt force solutions, suggesting that it is not just a transition phase.

In Chapter 7, I probe the short- and long-term costs of blunt force regulation, which are seldom documented in local media reports. Through case studies and local news reports, I illustrate that workers do protest, businesses do resist, and local bureaucrats do publicly criticize the short-term nature of these solutions. How does the state guard against the political risks of blunt force regulation? Using two cities as case studies – one wealthy and developed, and the other poor and industrial – I show how the state concentrates the costs of blunt force pollution reduction on the groups that are the least able to push back. It targets smaller, private firms or industries that rely on temporary, transient labor. I provide further evidence to support this theory by showing that of the approximately 6,000 firms targeted by blunt force regulation in the last 5 years, a disproportionate number were privately owned and employed informal workers. These strategies are effective at preventing unrest, but they exacerbate inefficiencies in the economy and may complicate efforts to reduce pollution in the future.

In Chapter 8, I broaden the scope of the analysis to assess whether blunt force regulation is unique to China. The findings reveal that it is a widespread political phenomenon found in both advanced industrial environments (like the UK) and weak institutional environments (like India and the Philippines). When political leaders confront urgent or overwhelming enforcement problems, they sometimes resort to unreasonable, one-size-fits-all measures to ensure that enforcement actions are effective. Blunt force regulation is one of a set of potential responses to principal–agent problems that inevitably emerge during regulation. However, the character of blunt force regulation – including how forceful or indiscriminate it is – is shaped by institutional features such as a state's enforcement and coercive capacity.

Blunt force regulation is neither ideal nor just. It relies on the naked authority of the state and can be painful for groups and individuals that are powerless to resist outright coercion. Amid the developing world's struggle to mitigate governance crises, are such solutions worthwhile? This book examines the negotiations, trade-offs, and everyday violence of local pollution enforcement in China to unpack how states approach the problem of enforcement. It sheds light on the political compromises that underpin China's choices, as well as the logic that drives governments around the world to settle for suboptimal approaches to regulation.

NOTES

1 Renamed the Ministry of Environment and Ecology (MEE) in 2018. However, this book will use the name Ministry of Environmental Protection (MEP) as it was the MEP for the study period.

2 China Central Television, "From 'supervising enterprises' to 'supervising the government'" (《焦点访谈》从"督企"到"督政"), March 1, 2015, http://news.cntv.cn/2015/03/01/VIDE1425211015378282.shtml.

3 *The Paper*, "Linyi's pollution control rapidly turns a corner" (临沂治污急转弯), July 2, 2015, www.thepaper.cn/newsDetail_forward_1347676.

4 *South China Morning Post*, "60,000 jobs: the cost of one Chinese city's cleaner air," July 2, 2015. www.scmp.com/news/china/policies-politics/article/1831846/60000-jobs-cost-one-chinese-citys-cleaner-air

5 For an excellent study on the impact on local workers, see L. Yang, *Analysis of the Impact of Firm Closures on the Livelihood the Local Informal Workforce* (企业关停对当地临时就业人员的生计影响研究), 2015.

6 For more details on this case, see *Economic Daily* (经济日报), "Farewell to the 'Cement Corridor'" (告别"水泥走廊"), December 17, 2014, www.ce.cn/xwzx/gnsz/gdxw/201412/17/t20141217_4138023.shtml.

7 See, for example, *The Southern Daily* (南方日报), "The transformation of a 40-year-old e-waste industry in Qingyuan, Guangzhou" (广东清远 40 年电子拆解业转型 垃圾焚烧污染重), July 26, 2016, www.chinanews.com/sh/2016/07-26/7951598.shtml.

8 Interviews X4050316, X4120316, X7a190416b, X7a190416d with entrepreneurs in factory owners around Guangdong province from March–April 2016.

9 *The Guardian*, "China bans major shareholders from selling their stakes for next six months," July 9, 2015; *New York Times*, "Chinese shares tumble again," July 27, 2015.

10 *New York Times*, "Beijing imposes traffic rules ahead of Olympics," July 21, 2008. www.nytimes.com/2008/07/21/world/asia/21iht-21beijing-traffic.14658075.html.

11 Interview X7a190416a with factory owner (April 2016).

12 Interview X7b200416 with industrial park manager (April 2016).

13 *Financial Times*, "Surging China steel output defies Trump pressure," April 17, 2018, www.ft.com/content/1dc206ac-4160-11e8-803a-295c97e6fd0b.

14 *New York Times*, "Spill in China brings danger, and cover-up," November 26, 2005, www.nytimes.com/2005/11/26/world/asia/spill-in-china-brings-danger-and-coverup.html?_r=0.

15 *New York Times*, "China admits building flaws in quake," September 4, 2008, www.nytimes.com/2008/09/05/world/asia/05china.html.

16 *South China Morning Post*, "Has China failed to learn the lessons of deadly Tianjin explosions?" August 12, 2016, www.scmp.com/week-asia/politics/article/2002987/has-china-failed-learn-lessons-deadly-tianjin-explosions; *South China Morning Post*, "Devastation at blast site after China chemical plant explosion leaves at least 64 dead, 640 injured," March 22, 2019, www.scmp.com/news/china/society/article/3002772/jiangsu-chemical-plant-explosion-death-toll-reaches-44-32.

17 Interview Y11110418 with US EPA regulator (April 2018).

18 Interview X2110815a with provincial environmental official in Hebei province (August 2015) and X6210116 with municipal environmental officials in Guangdong province (January 2016).

19 Interview X4a270116a with district environmental official in "District X" (January 2016).

20 Interviews X2110815b in Hebei province and X6210116 in Guangdong province with city- and provincial-level environmental regulators (August 2015 and January 2016).

21 *South China Morning Post*, "Chinese companies fined US$154 million for environmental offense," December 6, 2017.

22 Interview X10291019 with chemical industry insider in Hong Kong (October 2019).

23 Mark Thompson, *South China Morning Post*, "Is there more to President Rodrigo Duterte's Boracay closure and drug war than meets the eye?," May 1, 2018, www.scmp.com/comment/insight-opinion/article/2144058/there-more-dutertes-boracay-closure-and-drug-war-meets-eye.

24 Nector Gan, "China turns off the lights in 'Christmas town' as officials race to meet energy targets," CNN, December 26, 2020, https://edition.cnn.com/2020/12/25/business/china-power-shortage-intl-hnk-dst/index.html.

25 Centre for Research on Energy and Clean Air, "Analysis: China's carbon emissions grow at fastest rate for more than a decade," May 21, 2021, https://energyandcleanair.org/analysis-chinas-carbon-emissions-grow-at-fastest-rate-for-more-than-a-decade/; Reuters, "Northern China smog worsens in October-November as pace of restrictions eases: Greenpeace," December 13, 2018, www.reuters.com/article/us-china-pollution/northern-china-smog-worsens-in-october-november-as-pace-of-restrictions-eases-greenpeace-idUSKBN1OC05S; *China Dialogue*, "Is China returning to old, polluting habits?" December 26, 2018, https://chinadialogue.net/en/pollution/10995-2-18-is-china-returning-to-old-polluting-habits/.

26 Centre for Research on Energy and Clean Air (CREA), "China key regions meet modest winter air quality targets, as cleaner heating offsets

swelling industrial emissions," May 6, 2021, https://energyandcleanair.org/
china-winter-2021-air-quality/; *Financial Times* 2018.

27 *China Dialogue*, "China releases 2020 action plan for air pollution," July 6,
2018, https://chinadialogue.net/en/pollution/10711-china-releases-2-2-
action-plan-for-air-pollution/; Greenpeace, "Greenpeace warns of high
risk for further waves of new coal plant approvals in China: data,"
March 29, 2021, www.greenpeace.org/eastasia/press/6470/greenpeace-
warns-of-high-risk-for-further-waves-of-new-coal-plant-approvals-in-china-
data/.

28 *China Dialogue*, "Will recent power shortages slow China's progress to
carbon neutrality?" November 3, 2021, https://chinadialogue.net/en/
energy/will-recent-power-shortages-slow-chinas-progress-to-carbon-neu
trality/.

29 *South China Morning Post*, "China's smog battle losing 'momentum' in
some regions, environment minister says," January 28, 2019, www.scmp
.com/news/china/politics/article/2183967/chinas-smog-battle-losing-mome
ntum-some-regions-environment.

30 Interview X1120516 with MEP official, Beijing (May 2016).

31 An amendment in 2017 clarified that only People's Procuratorates are
allowed to use administrative public interest litigation (Article 25 of
China's modified Administrative Procedure Law). *China Dialogue*,
"Yunnan chemical factory becomes testing ground for citizen lawsuits,"
August 23, 2017, https://chinadialogue.net/en/pollution/9983-yunnan-
chemical-factory-becomes-testing-ground-for-citizen-lawsuits/.

32 For instance, Chaudhry (1993) argues that foreign and domestic assets in
the Middle East were nationalized in the 1950s and 1960s because states
lacked the necessary bureaucratic coherence to construct financial institutions or prevent monopolies as an independent regulator. Similarly,
Wengle (2015) finds that the Russian state defaulted to nationalizing
the energy industry in the East of the country because it could not figure
out how to dissuade strikes, resolve payment disputes, or prevent blackouts
while regulating at arm's length (Wengle 2015, 123–30).

CHAPTER 2

BLUNT FORCE REGULATION

Imagine you are the owner of a medium-sized ceramics factory in one of China's major industrial centers. Local government officials have recently been grumbling about pollution in the city center, occasionally shutting down one or two major polluters. At their urging, you relocate your factory 40 km outside the city. You could have moved to another city that was more lenient on polluters, but your suppliers and buyers are all nearby, and the cost of building a new network would be prohibitive. You invest 60 million RMB (approximately 9 million USD) in relocating and building new factory infrastructure. This sum will take 5 years to pay off, but it is worth the investment if it helps you meet the government's increasingly stringent pollution standards.

Then 6 months after you begin operations at the new factory, city officials inform you that you have been added to a list of factories designated for closure by the end of the year – a list that includes approximately three-quarters of the city's ceramics industry, as well as textiles and dying factories. You ask the government why you've been targeted, or what environmental standard you've failed to meet, so you can take measures to avoid being closed. But the government simply says this is a measure to restructure polluting industries, and that closure is inevitable.

Local authorities threaten to destroy your equipment and cut off electricity if you resist closure. Buyers see you on the list of factories designated for closure and stop placing orders for new goods, leaving you with heavy debts in addition to the 60 million you spent to relocate your factory. Your workers also begin to desert you. There is talk of compensation from the government, but you know it won't come close to the 5 years of income you will need to pay off your debts. By the end of the year, you, along with over 300 of the city's ceramics factories, have been shuttered.

This was the fate of a ceramics factory owner in the southern Chinese city of Foshan in 2007–8,[1] a period dubbed the city's "great manufacturing freeze." It is also a classic example of blunt force regulation.

What is blunt force regulation? In this chapter, I show that it represents a distinctive combination of inflexible, coercive, and arbitrary enforcement. Media accounts often highlight the coercive nature of this approach. They show how it quickly eliminates pollution but severely disrupts the economy and society.[2] This trade-off has led to comparisons with similar forms of regulation that are also perceived as effective but economically inefficient – such as command-and-control regulation.

Contrary to this prevailing view, I argue that blunt force regulation is not only inefficient, it is also ineffective in the long term because (unlike command and control) it is arbitrary. The state applies a combination of indiscriminate *and* unpredictable enforcement, which causes businesses to distrust the state and devalue compliance. Clean air is achieved at both great economic cost and great risk to future regulatory compliance. I use comparisons to related regulatory styles to show why this distinguishes blunt force regulation from even the most heavy-handed forms of enforcement found elsewhere. I further show that while US regulators may envy their Chinese counterparts, who can simply shut down polluters, the Chinese leadership recognizes that US-style regulation – based on clear rules and transparent enforcement – is a more sustainable and effective way to regulate in the long term. In sum, this chapter explores the problematic aspects of blunt force regulation, setting the stage to investigate (in the ensuing chapters) the book's central puzzle: Why use blunt force regulation?

2.1 WHAT IS BLUNT FORCE REGULATION?

Blunt force regulation is a one-size-fits-all approach. In the sphere of pollution regulation, it usually takes the shape of blanket production cuts or regulatory bans. A well-known example is China's winter production bans: The state orders entire regions or industries to shutter factories for months at a time to keep pollution levels manageable,[3] or to control an unexpected risk. In 2015, for instance, the state ordered chemical companies throughout the country to suspend operations after a major chemical explosion ripped apart the Port of Tianjin.[4] The state typically enforces these bans by announcing suspension orders and then immediately sending inspectors to factories to determine whether they are in compliance. However, authorities sometimes engage in much more coercive tactics to enforce these bans, such as switching off electricity or gas to an entire industrial area.[5]

Blunt force regulation also comes in more extreme forms, such as when the state permanently shutters entire industries to control pollution. This version is designed to produce more lasting outcomes, though on a smaller scale. It is much more likely to take place in a single city or province than to be applied throughout a region or across the country. The case of Foshan (described earlier) is a striking example. The state will order targeted industries to close down or leave the area by a set deadline and will destroy all factories that do not comply by that date.

Blunt force regulation has three distinctive characteristics. The first is *inflexible* enforcement. The state stipulates the necessary compliance procedures and refuses to adapt them, even when enforcement exacerbates other risks. In early 2019, for instance, factories across China's Jiangsu Province were ordered to suspend production to reduce air pollution in the area. Representatives from China's chemical industry complained that these sudden stop orders actually *increased* pollution because they "caused a huge amount of carbon monoxide to burn in flare and be released, ironically resulting in increased carbon emissions."[6] Nevertheless, the state forced them to stop operations in the name of pollution control. For more drastic, long-term compliance orders (such as closing or relocating factories) authorities may grant a few months or longer for factories to comply, but the outcome is nonnegotiable. Thus, as I show in Chapter 4, an entire city's cement industry that had been designated for closure by February 17, 2014 was promptly dynamited to the ground on that day, despite multiple entreaties from factory owners to spare their facilities.

Second, blunt force regulation is characterized by *arbitrary* standards and enforcement justifications: Firms lack information on when (or why) the state imposes restrictions. This happens because political leaders determine *ex ante* which categories of polluters might pose a risk to the environment, and then force uniform restrictions on that entire category, irrespective of individual compliance levels. For instance, the managing director of a foreign-owned company in

Suzhou recalls being ordered to shutter his factory for 15 days soon after the Tianjin chemical explosion in August 2015. Regulators told him this was necessary to control the risk of "chemical dust" – the cause of the Tianjin explosion 1,000 km away – even though his factory did not produce explosive chemical dust and was held to very high standards by its American parent company. In fact, the same inspectors who insisted on closing the factory had previously seen and approved its safety standards.[7]

Third, blunt force regulation is *coercive*. The state achieves compliance in regulated entities by intervening directly in production processes. For instance, regulators use forceful, sometimes extralegal measures such as seizing and destroying factory equipment, cutting off utilities, or forcibly dismantling industrial sites to reduce pollution quickly. These methods contrast starkly with conventional approaches to regulation, which require the state to respect firms' independence and use "arm's-length," incentive-based tools (such as penalties or rewards) to get factories to stop polluting. Recall the case of Linyi, mentioned in Chapter 1, where the government suddenly cut off electricity to an entire industrial park to ensure that all companies (including compliant ones) reduced their emissions immediately. This intervention was so abrupt that in one glass factory, the unexpected electricity outage caused 2,000 tons of molten glass and tin to flood into a furnace, causing irreparable damage.[8] Interviews with environmental regulators in the United States confirm that this manner of direct enforcement would be anathema in countries where the law protects property rights and leaves the decision to comply in the hands of regulated entities.[9]

Though inflexible, coercive, and arbitrary, blunt force regulation is sometimes portrayed as a much more effective way to regulate than the conventional, arm's-length regulatory approach. This is because arm's-length regulation requires governments to work within pre-agreed laws, respecting property rights and using standards and incentives to nudge companies towards the desired behavior (Rothstein et al. 2013). By contrast, as an official from China's Ministry of Environmental Protection explained to me,

> In China, we can get rid of small polluting companies very quickly because we can just close them down. In America, they have to give small companies the chance the clean up first or wait for them to move away after they have failed to meet compliance standards. All of that takes much longer.[10]

Similarly, when probed on why a city had undertaken blunt force regulation, a Chinese municipal official explained to me,

> Forced reductions are so much more effective at reducing emissions because they can completely restructure industries and target the source of pollution. When we do 'end-stage' enforcement, first we have to find evidence of pollution, and even then we can only recommend closures. Regulating after pollution has happened is so much more costly and ineffective.[11]

Indeed, adhering to set rules and refraining from direct intervention can take a long time to deliver the desired outcomes. In the United States, for example, almost a decade after the Clean Air Act was passed in 1970, one-quarter of all major sources of industrial pollution (such as power plants) were still found to be openly violating pollution standards (Cole and Grossman 2003, 927). Recent studies find that large, publicly owned entities in the United States are more likely to violate pollution standards than private entities, and to escape punishment for these violations (Konisky and Teodoro 2016).

However, blunt force regulation also ends up being less efficient because it is so costly. The disproportionate nature of sanctions, especially when applied so indiscriminately, can lead to employment and economic losses far greater than what might be considered reasonable for controlling pollution or containing a risk. As one Chinese provincial official mused (soon after presiding over one such blunt force exercise), "the sky is blue but we have nothing to eat."[12]

Yet this criticism is true of all regulatory bans, seen in both China and countries like America. Likewise, the criticism that blunt force regulation disproportionately harms small businesses is also true of command-and-control regulation practiced around the world. What, then, makes blunt force regulation so distinctive? Below, I argue that what sets it apart is that it is both economically inefficient in the short term *and* ineffective at reducing risks in the long term.

2.2 WHY IS BLUNT FORCE REGULATION DISTINCTIVE?

Regulation often entails a trade-off between efficiency and effectiveness (Bardach and Kagan 1982) because decision-makers must choose between minimizing social and economic costs (efficiency) and minimizing potential regulatory risks (effectiveness). For instance, a government could roll back certain regulations to protect jobs and increase market competition, but this could increase society's exposure to potential harms. Alternatively, the state could make regulations so severe that it eliminates all possible risks, but this will place a heavy burden on regulated entities. Consider, for instance, the tortuous debates around COVID-19 restrictions in 2021–2 where governments faced the unenviable choice between increasing restrictions to protect public health and reducing them to sustain economic activity.

Attempts to manage this trade-off have led to two broad approaches to regulatory enforcement. The first approach is "risk-based" or "problem-solving" regulation, which aims to be more efficient by calibrating restrictions to the level of risk (Gunningham and Holley 2016, 278–9; Paoli and Wiles 2015, 5–7). Rather than applying the same blunt solution to many different scenarios, regulations are written broadly, and enforcement agents are granted considerable discretion to adapt the rules to specific scenarios or emerging risks (Paoli and Wiles 2015, 7–8). This strategy allows the state to use regulators' expertise to develop more targeted, proportionate interventions against firms (Black 2010).

Risk-based regulation is often deemed preferable to the second approach, rules-based regulation, because it avoids the unfairness of one-size-fits-all regulation. Moreover, this approach allows regulated entities to participate in the formulation of regulatory plans (as seen in management-based regulation), which can grant firms a sense of empowerment or ownership in delivering socially desirable outcomes (Ayres and Braithwaite 1992; Coglianese and Lazer 2003). In its most ideal form, risk-based regulation can lead to self-regulation, where industries voluntarily formulate standards that go beyond what governments require and then hold each other accountable, lessening the need for constant surveillance from regulators (Haufler 2013). However, risk-based regulation also increases the risk of under-enforcement or regulatory capture, because flexible rules and enforcement discretion make it difficult for central officials to detect when local regulators might be shirking their duties (Bardach and Kagan 1982, 39–40).

The second approach, "rules-based" or "prescriptive" regulation, privileges enforcement effectiveness and takes a more uncompromising approach to risks (Black 2010; Paoli and Wiles 2015, 7–8). Rules-based regulation is characterized by clear, specific standards, coupled with a low level of flexibility in the enforcement stage. Politicians pass laws that dictate exactly how regulators should inspect and punish firms, and regulators are required to implement such laws "by the book," even when interventions seem excessive or absurd (Kelman 1981; Revesz 1992; Scholz 1984b). This strategy requires enforcement agents to adhere to clearly stipulated rules so that central authorities (and the public) can detect when regulators are failing to do their jobs (Coglianese and Kagan 2008, 19; Bardach and Kagan 1982, 44–5, 74). A commitment to by-the-book enforcement also ensures that companies are treated equally under the law and are aware of why they are being sanctioned (Carrigan and Coglianese 2011, 115; Rothstein et al. 2013). In sum, rules-based regulation entails a straighter path to implementation because "discretion denying rules are one way in which upper-level officials can seek to protect the policy they make from disagreement by lower levels" (Weinberg 2017, 1106). However, controlling risks through formulaic responses can be highly inefficient and extremely punitive for smaller, less profitable companies (Thornton et al. 2008).

Blunt force regulation is striking because it does not conform to either logic. At first glance, it seems like an extreme form of rules-based regulation. The state prioritizes effectiveness, using indiscriminate rules to eliminate pollution despite the high political, social, and economic costs. And yet, a closer look at the enforcement mechanics reveals that it lacks the transparency and by-the-book character of rules-based regulation. Instead of specifying the enforcement standards to give fair warning to regulated entities, government officials set broad parameters for regulation and then issue justifications after specific enforcement measures are carried out. This is why firms often accuse the government of arbitrary enforcement. And yet, despite the state's use of broadly written enforcement standards, blunt force regulation also lacks the proportionate, targeted nature of risk-based regulation. Instead of calibrating enforcement to match the level of risk, restrictions are imposed in a nonnegotiable, one-size-fits-all manner – increasing the cost to society.

In sum, blunt force regulation combines the inflexible *and* discretionary aspects of rules-based and risk-based regulation, which makes it both *more* costly and *less* likely to reduce risks in the long term. Some analysts may disagree with this portrayal, and argue that blunt force regulation is effective at reducing risks. Indeed, as I show in Chapter 4, it can be very effective at reducing pollution in the short term. However, regulatory effectiveness also entails long-term risk reduction. The state imposes restrictions not just to reduce immediate risks but to instigate changes in company behavior to prevent future risks. In this

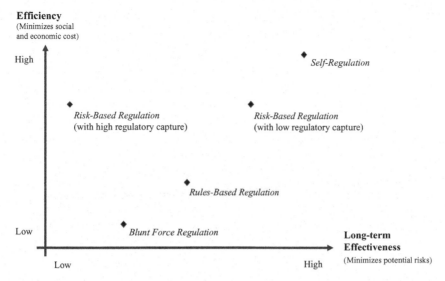

Figure 2.1 Efficiency and effectiveness of blunt force regulation vs. other regulatory approaches

chapter, I argue that blunt force regulation falls short on controlling future risks, which is why it is considered ineffective in the long term. It thus encapsulates the disadvantages of *both* approaches, as I illustrate in Figure 2.1.

In the following sections, I compare blunt force regulation to similar heavy-handed enforcement approaches – such as command-and-control regulation and regulatory bans – to clarify exactly why its combination of inflexible and arbitrary enforcement is so distinctive.

2.2.1 Command and Control

Blunt force regulation is often likened to command-and-control regulation for its inflexibility. Under the command-and-control approach, the state requires regulated entities to comply with uniform, categorical rules by a certain deadline, or risk fines and closure. For example, the 1970–90 US Clean Air Act required all polluting firms, regardless of their size, income, or infrastructure, to install fixed types of pollution control devices on their smokestacks (Cole and Grossman 2003, 910). The state did not tailor the standards to accommodate the limited budget of small companies, or extend deadlines to give companies in high-polluting industries more time to catch up to their less-polluting counterparts (Carrigan and Coglianese 2011; Cole and Grossman 2003).

Thus, command and control can seem like a deliberate purge of small firms and heavy industry – as seen with blunt force pollution regulation in China.

However, while command and control can seem unduly inflexible, the state still operates within the law. Politicians might impose strict performance standards that disproportionately affect small firms or heavy polluters, but they are still required to state these standards clearly. Moreover, regulators can only sanction firms if they have clear evidence of noncompliance (Carrigan and Coglianese 2011, 115). Thus companies are aware of why they are being sanctioned and can use this information to adapt to new standards.

By contrast, under blunt force regulation, the state keeps the rules opaque and the compliance standards ambiguous, so companies sometimes do not know why they are facing restrictions. In 2013, for example, government officials in the central Chinese province of Anhui suddenly forced all firecracker companies – including compliant ones – to dismantle their production equipment and shutter their businesses. Officials stated vaguely that these measures were necessary to "upgrade and standardize the fireworks industry," but they did not explain why firecracker companies were targeted while other polluting industries were left untouched. Nor did they explain what standards would constitute "upgrading."[13] This meant that surviving companies were offered zero information on what they should do to avoid future closures.

In sum, blunt force regulation is distinct from command and control because it is enforced in such an arbitrary way. The state withholds information on expected behaviors, which sends conflicting signals to regulated entities. Rather than operating "by the book" or justifying its actions in written rules, the state keeps the rule book ambiguous and its reasons opaque, giving local officials the flexibility to deliver outcomes by unexpected means. This echoes China's longstanding practice of policy implementation through "adaptive governance" (Heilmann and Perry 2011a), in which the state deliberately keeps rules vague and maintains high levels of bureaucratic discretion to allow greater flexibility in policy implementation (Ang 2016; Heilmann 2008a; Strauss 2009).

2.2.2 Regulatory Bans
Blunt force regulation is also likened to regulatory bans – where the state subjects regulated entities to sudden, one-size-fits-all restrictions to

rapidly control an unexpected risk. As with blunt force regulation, regulatory bans can seem arbitrary and unfair, leading to accusations of "regulatory unreasonableness" (Bardach and Kagan 1982).

For example, following the deadly foot-and-mouth epidemic in the UK in 2001, the EU issued a directive banning farmers in the UK from burning or burying livestock carcasses. Farmers were required to pay contractors to collect and dispose of dead livestock, or take carcasses to specialist disposal centers, at considerable additional cost. The ban came into force on June 1, 2003, and farmers caught burying or burning livestock faced heavy fines.[14]

Famers' groups complained that these measures – introduced by the EU to contain the outbreak – were "totally unnecessary," and that burning or burial was "the safest, most hygienic and environmentally friendly method of disposing of carcasses."[15] Moreover, when the ban came into force, the number of specialist disposal centers fell far short of what was necessary to process carcasses. Farmers were faced with the unenviable choice of leaving carcasses out to rot while awaiting disposal services or burying them and risking a heavy fine.

Like blunt force regulation, a regulatory ban can seem unfairly indiscriminate. It fails to take into account firms' varying capacities to comply, and subjects compliant entities to the same sanctions as their less compliant counterparts. For instance, livestock farmers in the UK were asked to comply with a uniform ban by a set deadline, with little advance warning and with little concern for their differing abilities to accommodate the additional cost. The ban, imposed by bureaucrats from afar, lacked transparency and treated farmers with brutal uniformity – ignoring the efforts that many had taken to mitigate the risk of infection. Finally, like in Foshan, the ban failed to account for problems on the ground, such as inadequate disposal centers. It is no wonder that farmers across the country claimed they had no choice but to "break the law."[16]

But the UK ban on livestock burial to combat foot-and-mouth disease differed from blunt force regulation in two important ways. First, the UK authorities employed a more flexible approach to enforcement. Acknowledging the absurdity of banning farmers from burying carcasses when no alternatives were in place, the Department for Environment, Food, and Rural Affairs announced it would apply a "light touch" to enforcement in the first few months.[17] This reflects a common practice in advanced regulatory environments[18] where states use flexible or "cooperative" enforcement to ease the initial shock of stricter regulations (Ayres and Braithwaite 1992; Hawkins 1984; Scholz 1984b). For instance, enforcement agents might offer a grace period to allow companies to adjust to new compliance standards or educate company owners to help them meet new requirements. Thus, while a ban may seem highly unreasonable on paper, authorities can use flexible or cooperative enforcement methods to implement it more reasonably in practice.

Second, UK farmers could still choose to "break the law" in response to this "unreasonable" regulation. The government could deter law breaking with fines, but could not coerce farmers to deliver carcasses to disposal centers, or forcibly extract payments for third-party disposal services. In other words, the UK government could only control farmers' behavior at an *arm's length*, regulating their behavior indirectly through incentives or penalties – as is the norm in advanced, industrialized countries (Levi-Faur 2009; Viscusi, Vernon, and Harrington 2000).

By contrast, under blunt force regulation, the state violates regulatory independence to enforce bans. Local officials use outright coercion to ensure that specific goals are achieved, even if their actions defy the law, disregard property rights, or cause unnecessary damage to infrastructure (Kostka and Hobbs 2012; van Rooij 2006; Wang 2013). For instance, in the northern Chinese city of Handan, the government issued a directive in 2014 ordering all seventy-seven factories with coal-fired furnaces that used 10 tons of steam or less to demolish and replace them with gas-fired furnaces within 100 days. Rather than wait for factories to complete these actions by the deadline, the government sent teams of enforcement officers to factories in the area to forcibly tear down the furnaces. In one case, as a factory owner tried to lock the gates of his compound to prevent the team from entering, enforcement officers streamed in and proceeded to tear down his furnace. When the owner protested, officers declared, "The demolition of furnaces is part of the nationwide responsibility to protect the environment! No one individual can obstruct this process!"[19]

In sum, blunt force regulation is distinct from regulatory bans because it is both inflexible and coercive. Instead of making allowances for glaring compliance difficulties, the state uses violent or forceful methods to ensure that companies comply.

2.2.3 Campaign-Style Enforcement
Scholars of Chinese politics are well acquainted with the phenomenon of blunt force regulation — often referred to as "campaign-style

enforcement" in the literature. Campaigns are centrally initiated enforcement efforts with four distinct features: 1) a sudden influx of fiscal and administrative resources from the center; 2) an unusually high degree of coordination between normally combative local government agencies (Liu et al. 2015, 87; Shen and Ahlers 2019); 3) clearly defined short-term enforcement targets — such as doubling inspections and penalties against polluting firms (Biddulph et al. 2012, 383–5; Dutton 2005; van Rooij 2006, 67); and 4) widespread national media coverage to encourage public participation in monitoring noncompliant actors (van Rooij 2009; Biddulph et al. 2012). Blunt force regulation displays all of these characteristics.

However, campaigns do not always exhibit the same level of indiscriminate or inflexible enforcement as blunt force regulation. Sometimes, they simply entail an intensification of formal enforcement measures, such as inspections. Known as "regulatory enforcement campaigns" (Biddulph et al. 2012), these measures are designed to ratchet up the threat of punishment but refrain from outright coercion, allowing regulated entities to take the initiative on how to respond.

A good example of a regulatory enforcement campaign is China's nationwide pollution inspections campaign in 2016 and 2017. Beijing sent teams of central inspectors around the country to investigate pollution violations. According to data from the Ministry of Environment and Ecology, these inspections led to a twentyfold increase in central pollution inspections over 2 years. However, companies were only punished if inspectors could show evidence of violations,[20] and polluters were given 6 months to rectify any problems. In other words, the state maintained an arm's-length approach, focusing on improving behavior instead of using indiscriminate punishment to produce immediate change.

Regulatory enforcement campaigns can take on the more coercive, extralegal characteristics of blunt force regulation. Beijing sets inflexible enforcement targets that force local officials to achieve certain policy outcomes, irrespective of the conditions on the ground (Shapiro 2001; Strauss 2009). The Great Leap Forward (1958–62) is a famous, disastrous example of this style of outcome-focused campaign. A more recent example is forestry reform in the 1990s. In a push to prevent deforestation, Beijing issued a directive requiring all forest land to be reclassified according to a strict 70:30 ratio of ecological to commercial land use: 30% could be logged and sold, but the remaining 70% would have to be preserved. This made it easier for the Central

Ministry of Forests to police and prevent overuse. But the brutal uniformity of this command failed to account for the diversity of forest land across China, or the variation in local communities' dependence on forests for their income (Strauss 2009).

Amid the pressure to fulfill top-down targets, local officials sometimes "sacrifice[e] the implementation of due process procedures for the sake of swiftness and severity" (van Rooij 2009, 26), as occurred in the anticrime "Strike Hard" campaign in the 1980s and 1990s. Beijing set local government quotas for arrests and convictions to stamp out crime (Dutton 2005), resulting in skyrocketing numbers of arrests and executions – some without due process (Tanner 2000).[21] In one case, a suspect was arrested, prosecuted, and then executed in 15 days. Campaigns most closely resemble blunt force regulation when they take on these indiscriminate, coercive characteristics.

2.3 UNINTENDED CONSEQUENCES

The comparisons made illustrate that blunt force regulation is distinctive because it combines inflexible, arbitrary, and coercive enforcement methods. In this section, I draw on qualitative evidence to show why this combination makes pollution enforcement more problematic in the long term.

2.3.1 Deterring Investment

Blunt force regulation increases uncertainty costs. The state's reluctance to specify when, how, and why restrictions are enacted leads to a highly unpredictable business environment. Firms become reluctant to invest or expand their businesses for fear that they might be closed down or have their assets seized. Consider the case of factory owner that I interviewed in an industrial county in southern China: The owner had been operating a waste recycling factory in a nearby town, but after a year of being subjected ad hoc "stop production" orders he decided to move his entire business to a city known to be more "relaxed" about pollution. Yet soon after arriving to this new city, he found himself, once again, facing arbitrary sanctions from the government:

> We come here, we buy the land, invest in our factories, we even invest in this pollution reduction technology because there is pressure to comply with emissions standards. But then local leaders decide they

don't want us anymore. It may be for environmental reasons, it may be because they want to focus on tourism, but suddenly we are forced to stop production for one out of ten days, then one week a month, then two! Eventually it doesn't make sense for us to stay anymore...[22]

When I asked him why he didn't push back, he shook his head and said, "It's easier just to move away." This factory owner, like a number of his colleagues I interviewed, was considering moving his business to Vietnam or Southeast Asia, exclaiming, "It is so much easier to do business in foreign countries because the government can't boss you around in that way!"[23]

For small and medium sized enterprises (SMEs), the uncertainty costs are especially acute because blunt force regulation has become part of the everyday repertoire of regulation. In addition to the crisis-driven regulation experienced by large firms, SMEs can expect, almost on a yearly or monthly basis, to face some intrusive ban, closure, relocation, or severe disruption to their economic activities. Some SME owners I interviewed claimed that this constant uncertainty had made them consider leaving China altogether. Labor and startup costs might be higher elsewhere, but at least they could expect less government interference.[24]

Moreover, due to the inflexible nature of blunt force regulation, a firm cannot keep this uncertainty at bay simply by increasing its compliance. In recent years, an accident or major violation by one chemical factory in China could lead to an entire industrial park being shut down, even if other factories in that park were compliant.[25] It has become so difficult to guard against this risk of blanket closures that in 2018, the management of an industrial park in Jiangsu Province boasted that their park had shut down 35 chemical companies (Pflug 2018) – an apparent effort to entice companies to set up in their park amid the atmosphere of regulatory uncertainty. By pursuing a record number of closures, the park management signaled its resolve to screen out and punish noncompliers, thereby ensuring "good citizens" a lower risk of being dragged down by noncompliant neighbors.[26] While such stringent enforcement is to be applauded, it is unlikely that all industrial parks in the country can achieve these monitoring standards or provide this level of guarantee against enforcement unpredictability. The manager of an industrial park in a tier 2 Chinese city told me they only tested 4 of the 26 factories in the park for pollution because it was too expensive to test them all. He argued that because factories were randomly sampled for testing, it would achieve the same deterrent effect.[27]

To be sure, even transparent, arm's-length regulation can be costly to businesses because it is so inflexible. Stricter standards or heavier penalties can quickly put companies out of business – especially small firms that operate at the margins. However, as a local university professor (and ceramics industry expert) mentioned at the time of the closures, if the government clarifies standards and acts within the rules, it can reduce these costs to businesses over time because combining positive incentives with enhanced regulatory strength spurs innovation and strengthens a new norm of "clean" production.[28] Firms develop new, cleaner technologies to stay in the business or increase their market share (Blackman 2000, 1079–80), and governments reward firms with subsidies and special certifications for taking a lead in setting new standards (Carrigan and Coglianese 2011, 115–17; Yasuda 2016, 8). Instead of a zero-sum game in which clean air is achieved through painful economic slowdowns, firms eventually learn to stay profitable while minimizing the damage to the environment (Thornton, Kagan, and Gunningham 2009, 406). For example, California's economy grew stronger even as its environmental regulations became stricter (Vogel 2005).

However, businesses only move towards these virtuous cycles of compliance when they believe that compliant behavior will be rewarded. This is especially true in pollution regulation, where reducing emissions or changing polluter behavior can be a lengthy process requiring high up-front costs and concentrated, short-term sacrifices. Without clear rules, stable expectations, and predictable policy implementation, companies lack the guarantees that make long-term investments seem worthwhile. Local officials defect from enforcing regulations, and businesses make no effort to comply, because neither side expects the other to abide by the written regulatory rules. The result is a vicious cycle of weak enforcement and poor compliance, followed by stopgap solutions to regulatory crises that fail to solve problems in the long term (Amengual 2016; Savedoff and Spiller 1999). Indeed, recent studies from China show that polluters are less likely to invest in compliance when policies and standards are ambiguous (Liu et al. 2018). In the absence of stable laws or credible commitments, actors will favor short-term returns – such as quick-fix pollution payouts – over actions that might lead to higher long-term payoffs, such as investments in new infrastructure (Baker et al. 2016; Chen et al. 2017; Zhu and Zhang 2017), because they fear that their investments might be for nothing if the factory is forced to close down anyway.

2.3.2 Devaluing Compliance

Blunt force regulation also exacerbates distrust. The government's use of coercive, strong-arm tactics causes business owners to resent and evade regulation. For instance, a study of street-level environmental officials in China found that inspectors who focused on educating or persuading polluters, rather than sanctioning them, were more effective at changing attitudes and improving compliance (Liu, van Rooij, and Lo 2018). Indeed, past research has found that such "cooperative" regulatory approaches – which focus on building compliance through mutual respect and repeated interactions – are much more effective at generating future compliance (Ayres and Braithwaite 1992; Hawkins 1984; Scholz 1984a).

However, when regulators violate established rules of enforcement – whether informal or formal – they exacerbate distrust, causing businesses to resent and evade regulation in the future (Braithwaite 2006; Carrigan and Coglianese 2011; Dasgupta 2000; Hawkins 1984; Mascini 2013; Short and Toffel 2010). Companies may temporarily change their behavior when faced with a direct regulatory threat, but seldom take independent action to fix pollution in the long term. For instance, Chinese firms reportedly often install pollution infrastructure during strict enforcement campaigns, but then stop operating it the minute government attention wanes.[29]

By punishing compliant firms, blunt force regulation devalues compliance, making it harder for governments to convince polluters to upgrade their infrastructure. In 2019, for example, a group of large chemical companies that belong to the European Chamber of Commerce released a position paper condemning the Chinese government's "sudden stop policies." They were disgruntled by the government's insistence on "a one size fits all approach to the chemical industry" and state officials' failure to recognize "key differences between multinational corporations and domestic companies with respect to their maturity on health, safety and environment matters."[30] After years of being undercut by noncompliant domestic competitors (who shirked antipollution measures to offer cutthroat prices), these multinational companies believed their investments in pollution abatement would finally be rewarded during China's war on pollution.

Instead, they were subjected to the same "sudden stop" policies as their noncompliant counterparts.

2.4 THE PUZZLE OF BLUNT FORCE REGULATION IN CHINA

The Chinese government seems to recognize the shortcomings of blunt force regulation. In 2018 and again in 2019, the Ministry of Environment and Ecology announced that it would be ending its policy of blanket production cuts in that winter's antismog campaign. The ministry acknowledged that these measures were unfair to companies that were already complying with pollution standards.[31] At the second session of the 13th National People's Congress in March 2019, Premier Li Keqiang further emphasized the need for a more stable, legal approach to regulating pollution. His speech touched on the advantages of arm's-length regulation, noting that letting firms respond independently to incentives (instead of being coerced into compliance) would lead to more sustainable regulation. He also proposed giving noncompliant firms a grace period to encourage their efforts to comply. Shortly after this speech, Li Ganjie, the Minister of the Environment, condemned the use of one-size-fits-all measures in environmental policy implementation. He stated that amid China's pursuit of stable environmental regulation, these disruptive measures were like "one mouse dropping ruining a whole pot of soup."[32]

By 2020 the Politburo was also condemning local governments' use of campaign-style emissions reductions – in which local leaders would use stop production orders to temporarily meet emissions reduction targets, causing blackouts or sudden energy shortages across China's coastal regions. The Politburo stated that these efforts were reckless and did little to improve energy structures in the long term.[33]

Yet there are signs that the Chinese leadership was already committed to investing in more stable, transparent approaches to regulation long before these condemnations. In the past decade, central government leaders have made considerable efforts to shift to a more stable, legal, incentive-based approach to regulating pollution. In 2012, to improve its surveillance of polluters, the government established a highly sophisticated automated system to measure emissions from all major sources of pollution. In 2015, it passed stricter environmental laws to raise the costs of noncompliance; regulators can now punish persistent violators with consecutive fines and criminal sanctions instead of one-off fines. Finally, the government has increased the number of staff in regulatory agencies, funded regular training for field-level regulators,[34] and centralized the administration and funding of these agencies to improve regulatory independence (Mertha 2005; van Rooij et al. 2017; Zhang 2017).

The state's investments in conventional regulation make sense. As China moves towards a more complex stage of environmental regulation, policing polluters has become more technically complicated. In the 2000s, pollution levels improved quickly because the government could focus on the most direct interventions with the highest payoffs (Liu et al. 2015; Seligsohn 2018). In 2005–10, at the height of enforcing this policy, China experienced a 3.9% annual reduction in sulfur dioxide (SO_2) emissions (Itahashi et al. 2012). This was achieved through retrofitting power plants (one of the biggest sources of pollution) and closing down the most inefficient firms that were unlikely to attain the new standards. However, once governments have exhausted the quick fixes presented by this low-hanging fruit, pollution regulation becomes a complex management problem. Demands related to information gathering, technical knowledge, and enforcement begin to intensify. If the state intends to balance continued economic development with environmental goals, then its focus needs to switch to improving compliance among the surviving actors rather than shutting them down.

Yet, despite these investments in a conventional, incentive-based regulatory apparatus, the Chinese state has continued to apply costly, one-size-fits-all blunt force regulation. Moreover, despite denouncements from the top-level leadership, orders to engage in blunt force regulation can still be traced back to the central government (which I discuss further in Chapters 3 and 4). This leads to the core puzzle of this book:

> Why would the Chinese state risk such concentrated economic and social disruptions just to punish polluters? Why undermine stable regulatory norms with blunt force regulation, sacrificing higher long-term payoffs for such meager short term gains? More broadly, why do governments choose such costly, counterproductive regulatory approaches when more reasonable solutions are possible?

In the following chapters I develop my answer to this puzzle. I show how blunt force regulation is a calculated response to weak bureaucratic control. It is a strategy that political leaders use to overcome underlying institutional weaknesses and address longstanding enforcement prob-lems. I further demonstrate that, contrary to common narratives, China *does* show signs of weak state capacity in environmental enforcement. This is why Beijing persists with blunt force regulation, despite recog-nizing the inefficiency and ineffectiveness of this approach.

NOTES

1 Xinhua net (新华网), "Can closures bring about economic transform-ation?" (关停能否带来转型?佛山整治传统陶瓷业引发震撼), May 7, 2008, http://news.xinhuanet.com/energy/2008-05/07/content_8121660 .htm; Xinhua net (新华网), "Guangdong, Foshan: A traditional manufac-turing city 'Green Upgrade'" (广东佛山：一座传统制造业大市的"绿色升级), November 25, 2016, http://news.qq.com/a/20161126/014317.htm.

2 See, for instance, *Forbes*, "China shuts down tens of thousands of factories in widespread pollution crackdown," October 24, 2017, www.forbes.com/ sites/trevornace/2017/10/24/china-shuts-down-tens-of-thousands-of-factor ies-in-widespread-pollution-crackdown/.

3 See, for example, Reuters, "China's Hebei imposes 'special emission' limits on steel mills," October 15, 2015, www.reuters.com/article/china-pollu tion-steel-idUSL4N1CL03W.

4 *South China Morning Post*, "Has China failed to learn the lessons of deadly Tianjin explosions?" August 12, 2016, www.scmp.com/week-asia/politics/ article/2002987/has-china-failed-learn-lessons-deadly-tianjin-explosions.

5 *South China Morning Post*, "60,000 jobs: the cost of one Chinese city's cleaner air," July 2, 2015, www.scmp.com/news/china/policies-politics/art icle/1831846/60000-jobs-cost-one-chinese-citys-cleaner-air.

6 European Chamber of Commerce, Petrochemicals, Chemicals and Refining Working Group, *European Business in China Position Paper, 2019/2020*, 248.

7 Interview X10170120 with a former managing director and long-time insider in the chemical industry in China (January 2020).

8 *South China Morning Post* July 2, 2015.

9 Interview Y11110418 with USEPA regulator (April 2018); interview Y11120418 with USEPA environmental lawyer (April 2018).

10 Interview X1120516 with official from the Ministry of Environment and Ecology (May 2016).

11 Interview with city-level environmental enforcement official (January 2016).

12 Interview X2140515a with provincial economic official (May 2015).

13 Anhui Provincial Government Notification to Firecracker industry 《关于烟花爆竹生产企业 整体退出意见的通知》; Qianjiang Evening News, "Anhui firecracker companies win sue provincial government and win case" (安徽花炮企业状告省政府胜诉), April 24, 2015, http://qjwb.zjol .com.cn/html/2015-04/24/content_3027030.htm?div=-1.

14 *The Telegraph*, "Farmers may leave carcasses to rot after burial ban," March 13, 2003, www.telegraph.co.uk/news/uknews/1424452/Farmers-may-leave-carcasses-to-rot-after-burial-ban.html.

15 *Wales Online*, "Angry farmers will 'break the law'," May 10, 2003, www.walesonline.co.uk/news/local-news/angry-farmers-will-break-law-2484180.

16 *The Telegraph* 2003; *Wales Online* 2003.

17 Department official quoted in *Wales Online* 2003.

18 Interview Y11110418 with USEPA regulator (April 2018).

19 See *China Environment News* (中国环境报), "Wei county's excess boilers are stopped to bring air pollution under control" (冬病夏治几多疗效?魏县乘锅炉停运督促大气污 染企业抓紧整治), August 6, 2014, www.scaes.cn/detail/?mid=2708.

20 A'yu, "yu ge luren maisaipao de huanbao ducha" [The Environmental Inspectors That Race Against Passers-By], *The Livings (renjian)*, October 10, 2019.

21 Amnesty International, *The Death Penalty in China: Breaking Records, Breaking Rules*, 1997.

22 Interview X7a190416c with owner of large recycling factory, Guangdong Province (April 2016).

23 Interview X7a190416b with owner of SME, Guangdong Province (April 2016).

24 Interviews X7a190416b, X7a190416c, X10080416, X4050316 with factory owners in Hebei and Guangdong provinces (2015–2016).

25 Interview X11171219 with long-time chemical industry manager, Shanghai (December 2019). See also *China Business Review*, "The Chinese Province of Jiangsu: Shutdown of Nine Chemical Parks," February 10, 2019, www.chinabusinessreview.com/navigating-the-aftermath-of-the-jiangsu-chemical-plant-explosion-four-months-on/.

26 Interview X11171219 with chemical industry consultant, Shanghai (December 2019).

27 Interview X7b200416 with industrial park owner, Guangdong Province (April 2016).

28 See Xinhua net (新华网), "Can closures bring about economic transformation?" (关停能否带来转型?佛山整治传统陶瓷业引发震撼), May 7, 2008, http://news.xinhuanet.com/energy/2008– 05/07/content_8121660.htm.

29 China Energy News, 中国能源报, "MEP launches strong attack against excessive emissions from thermal power stations," June 29, 2015, http://paper.people.com.cn/zgnyb/html/2015-06/29/content_1582287.htm; Chai Jing, "Under the Dome" (《穹顶之下》), February 28, 2015; Interviews X4161215; X1120516; X1130516.

30 European Chamber of Commerce, Petrochemicals, Chemicals and Refining Working Group, *European Business in China Position Paper, 2019/2020*, 248.

31 *Reuters*, "Exclusive: in bold bet, China may let provinces set own winter output curbs for heavy industry," September 11, 2018, www.reuters.com/

article/us-china-pollution-winter/exclusive-in-bold-bet-china-may-let-prov inces-set-own-winter-output-curbs-for-heavy-industry-idUSKCN1LR083; *Caixin Global*, "China won't push 'one-size-fits-all' production cuts in upcoming smog season, ministry says," August 21, 2019, www.caixinglo bal.com/2019-08-21/china-wont-push-one-size-fits-all-production-cuts-in-upcoming-smog-season-ministry-says-101453249.html.

32 See Caixin, 李干杰解读重污染天气成因 回应"一刀切"等问题, March 11, 2019, http://topics.caixin.com/2019-03-11/101391008.html.

33 See Xinhua, 新华热评：坚决纠正运动式"减碳"(Resolutely correcting campaign-style "coal reduction"), www.xinhuanet.com/politics/2021-07/31/c_1127717063.htm.

34 These details emerged during an interview with a county-level environ-mental officer in a less developed county of Hebei Province (Interview X3a240615a, June 2015).

CHAPTER 3

WHY BLUNT FORCE REGULATION?

In the spring of 2008, as I cycled through the streets of Beijing, I began to notice a change in the air. Where once my commute had been hazy and smog ridden, I now raced down wide, sunlit avenues under blue skies. Around me, vehicle owners complained that they could no longer drive to work because odd and even license plate numbers were banned on alternate days. Reports filtered through of mass factory shutdowns around the city. We soon found out that, determined to clean up Beijing's pollution in the lead-up to the 2008 Olympics, the Chinese government had resorted to restricting traffic, closing indus- tries, suspending construction, and shuttering power plants. These efforts succeeded. For the commuting cyclists and residents – and the international athletes who later swarmed the city – Beijing's spring and summer were beautiful that year. Since 2008, the government has repeated this strategy again and again, for the 2010 World Expo (Shen and Ahlers 2019), the 2014 Asia–Pacific Economic Cooperation (APEC) summit (later dubbed "APEC blue"),[1] for mili- tary parades, and major party conferences.[2]

The Chinese government's ability to produce sparkling blue skies at will is often interpreted as a sign of its immense capacity and commit- ment. The state sets its mind to a difficult but important task and executes it, regardless of the cost. Democratic governments seeking to enforce groundbreaking policies must contend with legal constraints and multiple competing interests, which can result in "piecemeal solutions" (Gilley 2012, 289) or protracted court processes (Bardach and Kagan 1982) that delay much-needed interventions. By contrast, authoritarian leaders enjoy a degree of insulation from the interest group lobbying or institutional deadlock that delays or undermines solutions elsewhere.

Thus China's leaders see the looming problem of industrial overcapacity and promptly demolish steel and cement factories (Kostka and Hobbs 2012); Beijing decides China's economy needs to be upgraded and accelerates this process by forcibly shuttering polluting factories (Wang 2018); a high-profile event such as the Olympics calls for blue skies and the state delivers it (Shen and Ahlers 2019); or major environmental problems come to the fore and the state launches nationwide regulatory campaigns to address them (Yang 2017; van Rooij 2009, 14–16; Wang 2017, 898). To date then, blunt force regulation has largely been explained in terms of the outcomes produced. Yet these explanations never fully address why the Chinese government resorts to such costly, disruptive measures when it could use more proportionate measures.

To be sure, policy implementation is complex and is influenced by multiple overlapping motivations. Government officials *do* shut down industries to restructure the economy, to scare polluters into compliance, and to appease public concerns. But by describing blunt force regulation in terms of the outcomes produced, these explanations skate around China's problems with bureaucratic accountability. In short, they fail to account for the government's struggle to implement policies amid weak institutional capacity.

I take weak capacity as the starting point. In this chapter, I argue that blunt force regulation is also a response to principal–agent problems in the enforcement process. In weak institutional environments, political leaders (the principal) lack the oversight to ensure that local bureaucrats (the agents) enforce costly environmental policies. In a bid to increase their oversight capacity, leaders use direct enforcement tactics that drastically reduce bureaucratic discretion, making it easier to observe and ensure that local officials are complying with their orders.

I develop this argument in three stages. First, I show how Beijing's increased attention to environmental protection has led to a loss of central control over local policy implementation. Faced with contradictory orders from Beijing to both protect the environment *and* promote economic development, local officials have begun to shirk their duties, responding with selective policy implementation. Second, I explain how, amid this decline in local compliance, the party-state's promise to punish bureaucrats lacks credibility. Apart from a few campaign-style witch hunts, which have increased significantly since 2015 (Shen and Jiang 2021), weak courts and high levels of bureaucratic discretion continue to allow local officials to shirk enforcement orders with impunity. This suggests that the regime cannot force the bureaucracy to reduce pollution by implementing environmental laws. Finally, I demonstrate how blunt force regulation enables political leaders to temporarily sidestep the problem that its threats of punishment are not credible, forcing local officials to deliver long-awaited environmental outcomes, albeit through drastic means.

Thus, in contrast to the theories of authoritarian environmentalism advanced above – which assume that extreme measures are a sign of efficient action – this chapter investigates a different question: What powers and institutions do states *lack* that they must turn to the extreme solution of blunt force regulation?

3.1 STATE CAPACITY AND ENVIRONMENTAL ENFORCEMENT IN CHINA

China is often classified as a high-capacity state capable of "penetrat [ing] society and implement[ing] its actions across its territory" (Mann 2008, 1). The leadership's success at delivering rapid growth, controlling birth rates, and (more recently) its use of high-tech surveillance to shape citizen behavior (Kostka 2019; Xu et al. 2021) all portray a strong central government that can get the bureaucracy to act according to its plans.

In China, the concepts of "local authorities" and "bureaucrats" tend to overlap. Like bureaucrats, China's local officials (almost all of whom are unelected) are governed in hierarchical systems, act primarily on orders issued by the central leadership, carry out specialized functions, enjoy a high degree of discretion, and are only minimally accountable to the populations they serve.

One striking feature of this bureaucracy is its high levels of discipline, which the Chinese government has been able to maintain without an independent judiciary or democratic accountability. Instead, central leaders motivated bureaucrats to follow orders and fulfill government functions through a combination of performance targets and material rewards. Local officials were assessed on their ability to deliver targets across a spectrum of policy areas and then promoted (or punished) based on the results of their performance evaluation (Landry 2008; Li and Zhou 2005; Lieberthal and Oksenberg 2020). Recent research has shown that this arrangement worked, not only via formal targets and promotions, but through an informal system of cash for compliance: Lacking third-party institutions to monitor bureaucrats, the leadership developed a practice in which the more revenue local bureaucrats generated from local fees and services, the more they could keep in cash bonuses (Ang 2016; Naughton 2017). This combination of clear targets and cash rewards convinced bureaucrats to report revenue and facilitate growth, rather than abuse their powers for petty corruption (Naughton 2016; Tsui and Wang 2004).

Safe in the knowledge that bureaucrats would adhere to the center's key priorities, Beijing also encouraged bureaucrats to innovate through a process of "directed improvisation" (Ang 2016) and "policy experimentation" (Heilmann 2008b). Central leaders would issue ambiguous mandates and then grant bureaucrats considerable discretion to adapt policies to local needs and conditions, thereby fostering a steady but flexible approach to economic development (Birney 2014).

Yet as growth slips down the list of Beijing's priorities, and as non-revenue-generating policies (such as environmental protection or social welfare) come to the fore, scholars note that the system of closely aligned central–local incentives has begun to unravel (Fewsmith and Gao 2014; Heilmann and Melton 2013, 35–6). Instead of receiving cash for compliance, local officials find that central orders now conflict with local interests: Either local governments have to spend their hard-won revenue to implement central directives or, in the case of pollution regulation, slow down industrial growth to meet new environmental standards.

China's bureaucratic structure also exacerbates this trade-off between growth and environmental protection. Short tenures (averaging approximately 3 years in one city) drive bureaucrats to prioritize short-term, countable outputs (such as revenue and GDP growth) over activities (such as pollution control) that require high up-front investments but generate little immediate payoff (Eaton and Kostka 2014; Economy 2014). To be sure, not all bureaucrats experience these short-term promotion pressures. The vast majority (including street-level environmental regulators and their department heads) tend to remain in one locale throughout their careers, and face less rigorous scrutiny of their performance. At the city level, only local leaders (such as the mayor and party secretary) and the elite bureaucrats in charge of powerful bodies (such as the courts, Organization Department, or disciplinary arms of the party) face such stringent evaluation and promotion metrics (Ang 2016; 108–9). Theoretically, this means that local environmental agencies (with their lower-ranked bureaucrats) should be able to enforce their pollution control mandates without the pressure of short-term targets or competing policy priorities.

However, China's bureaucratic structure also concentrates authority in the hands of local leaders, depriving environmental agencies of their regulatory autonomy. For instance, while city-level environmental regulators are responsible for the everyday business of inspecting and monitoring polluters, city or provincial governments directly control the budgets and staffing of Environmental Protection Bureaus (EPBs) (Mertha 2005). Moreover, while local regulators can recommend sanctions against polluters, only city leaders or their superiors have the authority to close down polluting entities or approve legal sanctions against larger polluters (Ding 2020, 537; Shen and Jiang 2021, 44). Finally, while the central Ministry of Environmental Protection (MEP) can instruct city or provincial leaders to improve their environmental enforcement, it cannot force local leaders to increase funding to regulatory bodies or punish them for failing to implement policies – though this has changed somewhat under recent reforms initiated by Beijing.[3] In sum, it is not local regulators or the environmental ministry, but local *leaders* who decide whether environmental policies will be implemented on the ground.

These local leaders are also in charge of funding and implementing city-level economic policies. In this way, the party-state's concentrated decision-making structure gives local leaders the power to choose between prioritizing economic growth or environmental protection in their locality. And while local officials may choose to "selectively implement" environmental policies when they become a priority (O'Brien and Li 1999; Heilmann and Melton 2013, 34–3; Strauss 2009, 1178), after years of being rewarded for generating revenue, they are reluctant to invest in environmental protection, especially when it threatens local employment and revenue streams (Economy 2014).

Thus, Beijing made reducing emissions a "high-priority" target in 2006, but more than a decade later it still struggles to get cadres to try to achieve it (van Rooij et al. 2017). Instead, local officials have developed an entire repertoire of techniques to shirk this responsibility: They take advantage of the regime's information failures to shield powerful companies from environmental sanctions (Cao et al. 2021; Eaton and Kostka 2017; Lorentzen et al. 2014); they falsify data on emissions and sanctions, defying central government attempts to

53

improve pollution through quantifiable targets (Mei and Pearson 2017; van der Kamp et al. 2017; Zhou et al. 2013); or they engage in "performative" governance, using high-profile interventions to signal compliance while avoiding substantive measures that actually deter companies from polluting (Ding 2020; Tian and Tsai 2020).

In recent years, Beijing has tried to overcome these institutional flaws by reasserting central authority in local implementation. It has increased the practice of political signaling, in which central leaders use internal orders and short-term campaigns to force local officials to drop everything and act on central priorities (Mertha 2017; Pei 2017; Wang and Minzer 2015).[4] However, constant signaling and clear instructions go against the party's instinct to keep policy implementation ambiguous and malleable, because over-specifying policies prevents the leadership from maintaining its ad hoc, "guerilla" style of governance (Heilmann and Perry 2011a; Naughton 1995, 31). Thus, despite the rise in the number of campaigns, Beijing keeps its policies vague and its regulations ambiguous, abrogating the responsibility to resolve conflicting policy orders to local officials (Kostka and Nahm 2017; Zhi and Pearson 2017).

In sum, the bureaucratic discretion that once led to highly successful policy experimentation is now enabling bureaucrats to shirk central orders (Cai 2010; Heilmann and Melton 2013; Hillman 2010; Kung, Cai, and Sun 2009), most noticeably by investing in economic growth at the expense of the environment (Cao et al. 2019; Jia 2017; Lorentzen et al. 2014; Ward et al. 2014). Where once the state could rely on incentives to generate bureaucratic compliance, incentives are now weakening, institutional problems have been exposed, and bureaucratic principal–agent problems have reemerged.

3.2 INFORMATION ASYMMETRIES AND CREDIBLE PUNISHMENT

China is not unique in this respect. Principal–agent problems are universal in regulatory enforcement due to unavoidable information asymmetries: Political leaders (the principal) cannot guarantee that their instructions will be implemented because they lack the expertise to detect when local bureaucrats (the agent) are defying their orders. Without specialized knowledge to assess the appropriateness of enforcement actions, central authorities – however powerful they might be – cannot easily identify when bureaucratic discretion has crossed over into capture (Downs 1967, 145; McCubbins and Schwartz 1984; Weber 1978). It may take an outbreak of citizen protest or a serious regulatory crisis for central authorities to identify and punish regulatory capture – especially in issue areas (such as pollution control) for which the risks vary widely and enforcement is complex and highly technical (Thornton et al. 2009).

Information asymmetries force leaders to offer external motivations – such as rewards or fear of sanctions – to encourage bureaucrats to enforce the rules, even when they contradict their own interests (Geddes 1996; Klitgaard 1988). Thus, successful implementation rests not only on central leaders' power and authority, but on the carrots and sticks they use to motivate the actors tasked with implementation. In the United States, for example, local bureaucrats enforce environmental standards even when they hurt the local economy because they fear being discovered by federal inspectors or being taken to court.[5] Over time, social norms and public surveillance have encouraged both firms and bureaucrats to comply as a matter of course (Gray and Shadbegian 2005; Gunningham et al. 2005; Kagan et al. 2003), which eases the burden on central leaders to doggedly monitor compliance.

In developing countries, however, governments face two institutional weaknesses that exacerbate the problem of information asymmetry. First, central governments often lack the resources to monitor local performance, which increases the chances that bureaucratic capture will go undetected (Duflo et al. 2013; Olken 2007). Moreover, even if central leaders are able to improve monitoring, they must also be able to use this information to sanction bureaucrats; otherwise the threat of detection is hollow. This leads to the second problem – that governments lack the necessary institutions to credibly punish bureaucrats for sustained noncompliance. In small countries with small governments, central leaders may be able to monitor and punish misdemeanors directly. However, in large states with vast bureaucracies, there are limits to leaders' capacity to process and act on the information they receive (Soifer 2008, 234). Other than occasional purges or high-profile punishments to temporarily scare bureaucrats into compliance (Meithă 2017; Mei and Pearson 2014), leaders must eventually delegate this oversight function.

In developed countries, leaders often delegate bureaucratic oversight to the courts. By specifying the actions expected of state officials or regulated entities, and by empowering an independent judiciary to punish violations of these rules, political leaders can create a pervasive sense of monitoring and certainty of punishment, even in large states (North and Weingast 1989; McCubbins and Swartz 1984, 166, 172).

In developing countries, however, legal institutions are often weak or compromised. Local officials can buy off the judiciary to rule in their favor or draw on high-level political connections to protect themselves from retribution (Moustafa 2014; Stern 2013). This undermines the independent functioning of the courts, making it harder to sustain a credible threat of punishment. Without support from an independent judiciary, central leaders may entrust oversight to loyal officials, but this is a less credible form of punishment that relies on the vagaries of personal loyalty (Geddes 1996; Migdal 2001).

In short, political leaders in developing contexts often lack "state infrastructural power," that is, the ability to monitor and compel local officials to consistently implement policies across a state's territory (Mann 2008). In this situation, even leaders who are highly committed to enforcing pollution regulation cannot effect changes on the ground.

China's success in reforming and rapidly growing its economy suggests that states can still generate some form of bureaucratic compliance even without strong oversight institutions or independent courts. As long as local leaders' personal interests are (more or less) aligned with national interests, central leaders can be confident that policies will be implemented without policing bureaucrats' actions too closely (Ang 2017). Indeed, theorists have argued that even corrupt bureaucrats will respect property rights and refrain from plundering the local economy if they believe this restraint will stimulate economic growth and lead to future monetary gains (Olson 1993). But what happens when this fortuitous alignment of interests erodes? As the Chinese leadership's focus shifts from promoting rapid growth to managing the externalities of this growth (such as pollution, social inequalities, and government debt), what do China's failures in environmental policy implementation tell us about the country's infrastructural power?

3.3 INFRASTRUCTURAL POWER IN CHINA

China's leaders appear to be aware that the country's central and local interests are no longer well aligned. As markets mature, regulation becomes more complex, and information asymmetries become more pronounced, Beijing is taking major steps to combat information failures. In the past decade, China's leaders have stepped up environmental monitoring to detect where local officials may be underenforcing pollution regulations. Chinese cities are now awash with air quality monitors, and major polluting facilities are required to install real-time emissions monitoring systems. Beijing has also leveraged grassroots activism as a form of monitoring, encouraging nongovernmental organizations and citizens to engage in petitions, protests, lobbying, and lawsuits to expose noncompliant officials (Hesengerth and Lu 2019; Mertha 2014; Teets 2018). Yet, recent studies find that increased monitoring has not translated into improved air quality (Goron 2021; Karplus et al. 2018; Kostka and Li et al. 2012; Seligsohn et al. 2018; Zhu et al. 2022).

China's struggle to improve compliance suggests that when central orders conflict with local interests, the state's sophisticated information-gathering capacities (King et al. 2013; Lorentzen 2014; Roberts 2018; Truex 2017) may not be enough to overcome bureaucratic principal–agent problems. The leadership has to be able to do more than simply detect noncompliance; it must also have the capacity to punish bureaucrats who consistently defy orders (Chan and Lam 2018).

The regime currently relies on top-down internal party mechanisms (known as "hold-to-account" orders), in which party leaders punish corruption or disobedience among cadres (Shen and Jiang 2021). However, two features undermine the credibility of this punishment. First, the threat is greatest when it comes directly from the central leadership, but Beijing can only sustain its attention on each case for a short period. Follow-up on cadres is delegated to provincial or lower-ranked officials, leading to a more corruptible process in which punished officials are often restored to their original career path a year later (Mei and Pearson 2014, 90). The second feature undermining the credibility of the current punishment system is that the use of arbitrary punishments can alienate cadres, which conflicts with Beijing's desire to maintain a stable and loyal bureaucracy (Mei and Pearson 2017, 2). Both features temper the threat from the central authorities, which is why leaders in other countries have (reluctantly) introduced independent judiciaries to increase control over local authorities (Ginsburg and Moustafa 2008; Rosberg 1995). They recognize that independent courts demonstrate to economic actors that the rules will be uniformly enforced, and to local bureaucrats that they are under constant surveillance.

While China initially took major steps towards developing a national legal system, it has increasingly rolled back the independent function of its judiciary in recent years (Ang and Jia 2014; Liebman

57

2007, 2014; Minzner 2011; Wang 2015). Constant political interference in legal procedures indicate that the regime is unwilling to relinquish power to allow genuine rule of law to prevail (Hurst 2016; Minzner 2015; Nathan 2003; Pils 2014; Stern and Liu 2020; Su and He 2010). Thus, even if citizens were able to prove bureaucratic or polluter misconduct in a court of law, the constraints on independent judges erode their chances of success.

Instead of legal institutions, the regime has focused on improving governance by strengthening "internal" accountability mechanisms – such as institutionalized leadership turnover and explicit promotion criteria for bureaucrats (Naughton 2016). This shift to internal, party-based accountability over the rule of law is especially evident in environmental governance. Rather than using the independent power of the courts to sustain a credible threat, the regime has applied a combination of fiscal transfers and increasingly stringent targets to incentivize local officials to address environmental problems (Stern 2010; Wong and Karplus 2017; Yang 2017).

However, keeping legal institutions weak makes it harder for the government to police lower-level bureaucrats who shirk their duties or abuse their powers (Moustafa 2007). The central government presides over a vast bureaucracy, but it relies exclusively on the weaker tools of promotion incentives and occasional high-powered campaigns to keep lower-level bureaucrats in check. Thus, local officials can always fall back on erecting a protective information barrier that hides their true actions from their superiors (Fewsmith and Gao 2014; Naughton 2014, 407).

In effect, China's self-imposed limits on institutional accountability have created a credible commitment problem: When external pressures to comply with rules are limited, compliance depends largely on the will and interests of the individuals involved (North and Weingast 1989). The inadequacy of internal, hierarchical surveillance mechanisms to enforce compliance was revealed in 2017 when Beijing conducted a nationwide inspection of regulators. In addition to discovering data tampering by 3,100 enterprises, these surprise inspections also uncovered cheating by local officials. In the city of Xian, for example, regulators were caught stuffing cotton wool into air quality detectors to manipulate the readings. These regulators were only discovered because the MEP conducted random spot checks on 18 of China's most polluting northern cities.[6] As one former EPB cadre confessed: "The *only* thing we fear are random spot checks from the MEP."[7]

Thus, the Chinese leadership's struggles with credible punishment suggest that in certain policy spheres in which central and local interests are misaligned, the state *does* lack infrastructural power. Although leaders are highly committed to enforcing a policy, they cannot effect changes on the ground. How, then, can China make bureaucrats comply with urgent environmental policies?

3.4 THE LOGIC OF BLUNT FORCE REGULATION

I argue that in states with weak infrastructural power, leaders use blunt force regulation as a top-down solution to bureaucratic noncompliance. Recall the two key problems that governments face. First, political leaders lack the expertise and monitoring capacity to verify whether bureaucratic behavior has crossed from compliance into capture. I propose that blunt force regulation solves this problem through indiscriminate, one-size-fits-all sanctions. For instance, political leaders, knowing that steel factories have high emissions, choose to forcibly stop production in *all* steel companies in an area, even if some are complying with pollution standards.

This type of blunt regulatory action (banning production) is far more visible and verifiable than incentive-based mechanisms (such as pollution penalties): It is easier to check if an entire industrial park has stopped producing than if an individual factory is paying a penalty. This increases the chances that noncompliance will be detected, which raises the risk of punishment for local officials. In other words, blunt force regulation makes the regulatory process more "legible" to central authorities (Scott 1998, 45), which in turn makes it easier for them to implement changes across the territory.

The second challenge that political leaders face is the problem of credible punishment. Even if regulatory capture has been detected, central leaders will have a hard time sustaining the threat of punishment if independent monitoring mechanisms are compromised. Blunt force regulation solves this problem through extreme, one-shot regulatory interventions, such as ordering local officials to forcibly shutter or relocate factories.

Moreover, in contrast to the ordinary regulatory actions of monitoring, fining, and negotiating with polluters – which are more opaque, and which require consistent pressure on local bureaucrats to succeed – under blunt force regulation the state reduces pollution through forced interruptions in productive activity. The distance between state action

59

(shutting down firms) and outcomes (improved air quality) is immediate. This limits bureaucrats' ability to shirk implementation or corrupt the regulatory process. This means that political leaders only need to inspect local bureaucrats once to ensure the job has been done, and they only need to sustain the threat of punishment for a short period of time. In short, the one-shot nature of blunt force regulation suddenly makes the threat of punishment credible, even from a leadership that ordinarily lacks oversight.

In sum, to answer the puzzle introduced at the end of Chapter 2, I argue that China's leaders persist with blunt force regulation, even while recognizing its inherent problems, because they need it to overcome deep-seated institutional obstacles to enforcement. By temporarily enabling leaders to monitor, motivate, and sanction local bureaucrats, blunt force regulation increases the odds that regulatory outcomes will actually improve on the ground.

3.5 WHAT ABOUT REGULATORY COMPLEXITY?

This chapter argues that blunt force regulation is a story of bureaucratic fragmentation and weak state capacity. It shows that when central and local interests are misaligned, pockets of bureaucratic noncompliance will arise. This explains why we also see such varying levels of policy implementation (and occasional blunt force regulation) on issues where central and local interests tend to be misaligned, such as *hukou* (household registration) reform (Chan and O'Brien 2019; Vortherms 2019; Yang 2021), social welfare (Solinger and Jaing 2016), labor rights (Yang and Gallagher 2017), food safety (Yasuda 2017), and rural land reform (Looney 2020).

However, these are also issues known for regulatory complexity, which increases opportunities for bureaucratic noncompliance. When enforcement is highly complex and places extensive technical demands on regulators, it becomes harder to prove corruption in court or to use social pressure to bring about compliance (Carrigan and Coglianese 2011, 120–1; Gunningham et al. 2005).

Pollution, in particular, is notoriously complex to regulate. Consider, for instance, a study of pollution regulation in the heavy-duty trucking industry in the United States (Thornton et al. 2008). When calculating what level of diesel emissions were acceptable, regulators had to consider the year and model of a truck, the kind of fuel it used, how long a truck was idling for, the incline it drove on, and the ambient temperature. Moreover, because each trucking company had a diverse fleet, regulators had to assess individual trucks for compliance instead of just examining company-level compliance practices. This heavy regulatory burden led to "low regulatory and social visibility," which contributed to weak compliance levels in the trucking industry (Thornton et al. 2008, 284–5). In response, the state did occasionally use direct, indiscriminate mandates (such as forcing all trucking companies to scrap or upgrade their diesel engines) to bring about changes in compliance, echoing China's blunt force pollution regulation. This happened in California, where enforcement institutions are well resourced and well established (Thornton et al. 2008, 285), suggesting that blunt force pollution regulation is not just a story of weak bureaucratic control in China. In fact, it is a necessary response to regulatory complexity.

Regulatory complexity undoubtedly does drive Beijing to apply blunt, direct mandates to regulate fast-growing industries. For instance, in his study of food safety regulation in China, Yasuda (2017) shows how the government uses blunt force regulation because technical complexities make arm's-length regulation of the sector impossible. The export food sector requires very close monitoring of site-level production processes to ensure that products meet global safety standards. However, the central state does not trust regulators to oversee the process properly, because they lack training and because the bureaucracy is too fragmented to ensure compliance. Thus, Beijing has set up a central agency – AQSIQ – to regulate the sector directly. Unusually, the state also allows foreign importers to directly control production processes at the farm and factory levels, even for Chinese producers. Moreover, AQSIQ sometimes resorts to complete bans on certain products when there is any hint of a risk in the supply chain, even if this threatens to decimate the entire export food sector (Yasuda 2017, 62). Thus, as with polluting industries, the state acts as both manager and regulator of factories to eliminate risks and achieve the desired outcomes.

Yet if blunt force regulation is merely a response to regulatory complexity, how do we explain its emergence in issue areas that do not require much technical knowledge? Consider, for instance, a case of blunt force regulation in the textiles industry in the 1990s. At the time, Beijing was concerned that local governments' undisciplined lending to the textile sector would lead to overproduction, which would undermine the industry's competitiveness. The Bureau of Textiles therefore issued policies to retire spindles and reduce investments in the industry, but local officials – desperate to protect high employment rates – ignored these instructions and the number of spindles continued to grow (Hsueh 2016,135). In 1998, Beijing initiated a nationwide closure of textile factories. To ensure that production would be discontinued, central bureaucrats were sent around the country to cut the spindles in state-owned textile enterprises. These measures resulted in the destruction of 10 million spindles and the loss of 1.16 million jobs in the textile sector (Hsueh 2016, 137).

Retiring spindles and imposing limits on bank loans are both relatively straightforward policy interventions that would not require much training to implement. The fact that the Bureau of Textiles still had to intervene directly to ensure implementation suggests the issue was not inadequate training, but inadequate *oversight*. Hsueh even argues that central and provincial leaders used blunt force measures against the textile industry to reassert their authority in industrial sectors where it has lost control over local implementation (Hsueh 2016, 135–7). In other words, the use of blunt force regulation is not just a matter of regulatory complexity; it is also motivated by local disobedience to central commands.

3.6   SUMMARY

Blunt force regulation is suboptimal. In more advanced regulatory environments, governments only resort to such costly punitive measures after firms have repeatedly failed to comply (Ayres and Braithwaite 1992; Hawkins 1984). Governments also take pains to identify and punish individual violators, and refrain from harsh, indiscriminate regulation for fear of discouraging future compliance. However, improving outcomes through routine inspections or incentive-based mechanisms requires considerable administrative resources and committed (or coercible) bureaucrats – both of which are lacking in developing countries. I argue that blunt force regulation sidesteps these limitations by simplifying regulatory interventions to the extreme.

In the next two chapters, I use empirical evidence to test this argument. In Chapter 4, I use a case study from Southern China to illustrate how blunt force regulation works, and to address alternate hypotheses. I then use quantitative data to test this theory on a nationwide scale. I demonstrate that cities with higher levels of bureaucratic noncompliance are more likely to be subjected to blunt force regulation, even after controlling for rival explanations such as high levels of pollution or industrial overcapacity.

In Chapter 5, I use quantitative evidence to test the impact of blunt force regulation on regulatory outcomes. My theory predicts that this approach not only targets noncompliant bureaucrats; it is also more likely to overcome principal–agent problems than other regulatory measures. Through quantitative analysis, I illustrate how blunt force regulation is associated with noticeable changes in pollution levels across China. By contrast, conventional regulation has a far weaker effect on reducing pollution. These findings suggest that blunt force regulation is effective, even when enforcement institutions fail and efforts to regulate through conventional channels are weak.

NOTES

1 *The Guardian*, "Beijing attempts to cut air pollution for APEC summit," November 4, 2014, www.theguardian.com/world/2014/nov/04/beijing-smokescreen-hide-pollution-apec.
2 CNN, "Blue sky vanishes immediately after Beijing's massive parade," September 4, 2015, www.cnn.com/2015/09/04/asia/china-beijing-blue-sky-disappears-after-military- parade/index.html.
3 Around 2015, the State Council created central-level environmental inspection bodies that are empowered to liaise with two powerful central departments, the Central Commission for Discipline Inspection and the Organization Department, to recommend investigations against local leaders (Shen and Jiang 2021).
4 A sample list since 2007 includes short-term campaigns such as: 1) a special enforcement program to rectify illegal polluters and protect the health of the masses (整治违法排污企业保障群众健康环保专项行动); 2) the great 100-day safety inspections; midnight operations (安全百日大检查；零点行动); 3) regulating pollution with an iron-fist campaign (铁腕治污行动); and 4) special actions to strike down illegal behavior on waste imports (打击进口废物环境违法行为专项行动).
5 Interviews Y11110418 and Y11120418 with USEPA regulators (April 2018).
6 See *Caixin*, "Northern China chokes on fake emissions data," April 6, 2017, www.caixinglobal.com/2017-04-06/101075101.html.
7 Interview X4151215 with former EPB cadre, Guangdong Province (December 2015).

CHAPTER 4

BLUNT FORCE REGULATION AND BUREAUCRATIC CONTROL

To industries operating in China, local governments' attitudes to environmental policy can seem absurd, even contradictory. One day they turn a blind eye to violations, and allow polluting companies to outcompete their more compliant counterparts with cutthroat prices. The next day, they overregulate, shutting down even those that comply to the highest degree. A frustrated employee at a foreign-owned chemical company in Jiangsu Province explained:

> A few years ago, my bosses would complain that we were being undercut by local companies because they wouldn't comply with pollution regulations. Now they complain that government enforcement is too strict! ... All those years we would follow regulations hoping that the government would reward us eventually. Our compliance was not perfect, not to an A+ level, but still a B+ or A−. But then the government starts to enforce fiercely and anyone who doesn't comply to the top standard is punished. So now we're treated as if we are no better than those C or D grade companies, the ones who were making no effort to comply the whole time.[1]

And yet, as I interviewed factory owners around China, I also came across an air of resignation. "This is the cost of doing business in China," they would say, or, "It is hard being a factory in China now, since pollution has become a big priority." "The government in China is very powerful," they pronounced. "It can do whatever it wants."[2] But none of this tells us why local officials would subject factories to this fate.

Why shut down a factory that is trying to comply with environmental standards? Why shut down entire industries in just a few months, plunging the city into an economic crisis? And if pollution prevention is so important, why withhold information on the environmental standards driving these shutdowns, thereby preventing other industries from learning what might be expected of them in the future?

To date, studies of blunt force regulation in China – usually from the literature on China's regulatory enforcement campaigns (see Chapter 2 for more details) – have offered three possible explanations for this kind of arbitrary enforcement behavior: 1) it is a deterrence campaign, designed to scare firms into compliance; 2) it is a form of industrial policy, designed to restructure rather than to regulate industry; or 3) it is a form of political theater, initiated by local officials to signal loyalty to party leaders or to appease public concerns about pollution.

By contrast, I argue that blunt force regulation, especially in its most extreme and indiscriminate form, is directed first and foremost at coercing bureaucrats into compliance. Central and provincial leaders who have lost control over the policy implementation process will use blunt force regulation to force local officials to finally implement tough policies.

In this chapter, I test this argument using a mix of qualitative and quantitative evidence. First, I use process tracing on a case of blunt force regulation from southern China to develop my theory. I illustrate how the extreme measures used against polluters cannot be explained in terms of deterrence, industrial upgrading, or political signaling. I further reveal how higher-level orders prompt local officials to suddenly decimate the polluting factories they previously protected. This is why companies see enforcement change from one day to the next, from local officials turning a blind eye to pollution to a sudden zero-tolerance policy.

I then employ quantitative data to test this logic on a nationwide scale. Original data on blunt force measures, collected over 20 months of field research, indicates that between 2010 and 2015, authorities in 269 of the country's 287 prefectural-level cities were ordered to forcibly reduce or halt production in dozens of highly polluting industries. My quantitative analysis demonstrates that localities with a history of bureaucratic noncompliance are more likely to be subjected to blunt force regulation, even after controlling for rival explanations such as high levels of pollution or industrial overcapacity. This suggests that blunt force regulation *is* used to reassert top-down bureaucratic control.

4.1 BLUNT FORCE REGULATION IN QINGYUAN

The city of Qingyuan is located just 70 km north of Guangzhou in the wealthy coastal province of Guangdong. Nestled between green hills and a wide river, Qingyuan has been dubbed the "garden suburb" of Guangzhou. Yet for 40 years, it has also been the site of one of China's biggest e-waste and electronic recycling industries. Since the 1980s, these factories have turned imported waste into recycled copper, aluminum, and plastic. Most factories are small, operating with basic technology on slim profit margins. However, their combined production output is high: in 2013, approximately 38% of China's recycled copper and 14% of its total copper production came from two counties in Qingyuan.[3]

In 2012, China's Ministries of Finance and Environmental Protection issued notices ordering all local governments to conduct an audit and cleanup of e-waste industries.[4] This sounded the death knell for Qingyuan's e-waste industry. The Guangdong provincial government quickly identified Qingyuan as one of two key cities (along with Shantou) that needed an "e-waste pollution rectification plan," prompting it to launch a 2012–20 program to "rectify" the industry.

However, on-the-ground enforcement remained haphazard. Despite mounting pressure from middle-class homeowners – newly arrived from Guangzhou, and outraged at the pollution on their doorstep – Qingyuan's local Environmental Protection Bureau (EPB) adhered to former (weaker) enforcement standards, which had little visible impact on industry practices.[5] In contrast, in nearby Shantou, city officials acted promptly on provincial orders; they shuttered 2,028 e-waste factories in 2013 and subjected a further 3,141 to direct supervision by the environmental, tax, and commerce bureaus.[6]

In early 2014, Qingyuan's government suddenly changed tack, cracking down on 696 small e-waste factories. Factories were forced to either close or move to a new industrial park. City officials then initiated the first stage of a central-government-funded project to clean up soil polluted by stockpiled e-waste. On April 16, the provincial vice governor visited Qingyuan to inspect its progress on e-waste rectification.[7]

However, enforcement returned to business as usual for the remainder of the year. In October 2014, the local EPB, in response to a tip-off from local homeowners, cut off electricity to factories that had been caught illegally burning waste. The same day, 100 factory owners protested these measures outside the township government building. The local EPB quickly backtracked on its punishments and restored electricity to the polluters that day.[8]

In early 2015, Qingyuan restarted its crackdown. City authorities (including officials from environmental and law enforcement agencies) conducted a wave of audits and inspections in all local counties. In one county, the authorities determined that only 104 of the 967 factories inspected had proper permits; 412 were found to be "operating illegally" for failing to move to designated industrial parks.[9] Enforcement teams promptly ordered 1,295 factories to voluntarily evacuate their premises by a set deadline. Factories that had once been shielded from punishment were suddenly facing threats to have their electricity cut off, raw materials seized, and factory equipment destroyed.[10] In another county, local cadres and party members involved in the industry were asked to take the lead in stopping production and to refrain from renting out land to "illegal" factories.[11] The city shuttered a total of 2,358 factories in just a few months, which affected 29 village associations, 302 village groups, and approximately 20,000 workers. In July 2016, the province again sent a supervision team to Qingyuan to inspect its progress on e-waste rectification.[12]

At first glance, the Qingyuan city government's actions may seem like a determined effort to rapidly eliminate polluting industries. However, a closer look reveals a lack of logic in the timing and pattern of enforcement in the city: Why did its government shutter the recycling factories within a few months, instead of spacing the closures over 2012–15 to ease the economic shock? And why did they shutter factories in early 2014, then turn around and protect high-profile polluters from enforcement, only to close down these same factories a few months later?

4.2 EXISTING EXPLANATIONS

4.2.1 Blunt Force Regulation as a Deterrence Campaign

Blunt force regulation is sometimes portrayed as an extreme deterrence strategy. Known in China as "killing the chicken to scare the monkey," the state punishes violators in a sudden and highly visible manner to shock all other actors into changing their behavior.

This argument builds on a central tenet of deterrence theory: Actors are more likely to comply with rules when they face a higher risk of punishment. However, governments that lack the personnel and funds to sustain threats of punishment sometimes resort to an intense bout of extreme sanctions – otherwise known as a regulatory campaign. The hope is that a wave of high-profile sanctions against a few will shock the majority into compliance long after the immediate regulatory threat has faded. In other words, blunt force regulation represents the state's attempt to reestablish society's respect for its authority and rules, even when it lacks the resources to enforce them (Wedeman 2005; Zhan, Lo, and Tang 2014).

This argument was used to explain China's infamous "Strike Hard" (*yanda*) campaigns in the 1980s and 1990s, in which the state launched a flurry of prosecutions and executions to stamp out crime (Bakken 2005; Tanner 2000). It has since been extended to describe China's environmental enforcement campaigns: Local authorities ratchet up pollution inspections to scare firms out of their complacency, and central authorities throw their weight behind local authorities to strengthen the threat of future punishment (van Rooij 2009, 14–15).

When enforcement takes on this concentrated, shocking character, it is bound to affect polluters' behavior. Admonitory rhetoric from Beijing combined with sudden, coordinated action from normally rivalrous local enforcement agencies signals the state's determination to punish violations. Past studies have found that under these conditions, polluters do decide to respect the law and take compliance seriously (Liu et al. 2015; van Rooij 2002, 21; Shen and Ahlers 2019). In the case of Qingyuan, for example, I found that some factory owners had decided to upgrade their pollution abatement infrastructure after surviving the crackdown. They told me that the severity of the campaign finally convinced them that the government was serious about enforcing pollution standards.[13]

However, if local officials in Qingyuan were using blunt force regulation to deter current and future noncompliers, why did they pursue such indiscriminate, irreversible enforcement measures? Specifically, why did local authorities shut down nearly 900 compliant, cleaner, upgraded factories alongside roughly 400 noncompliers? Deterrence campaigns are supposed to target a handful of high-profile noncompliers to scare the remaining majority into compliance, not to scare a handful by closing down the majority – as we see in Qingyuan.

Scholars have suggested that indiscriminate enforcement can be an unfortunate byproduct of top-down campaigns. The state does not set out to punish compliant firms, or to disregard varying capacities to comply. However, when enforcement is carried out according to centrally determined targets and is concentrated into a short period, due process and proportionate sanctions inevitably fall by the wayside (Wang and Minzner 2015, 348; Tanner 1999, 174–5; van Rooij 2006, 71). Sometimes the monkeys get killed alongside the chicken.

However, this still does not explain why authorities in Qingyuan resorted to such indiscriminate *and* irreversible measures, including permanently closing factories. Why shut down factories if they could have achieved the same deterrent effect with less extreme measures – such as heavy fines, prosecutions, or temporary shutdowns?

Consider the actions of the Qingyuan government in an earlier enforcement campaign, In 2011, provincial officials ordered city officials to initiate a campaign to rectify factory pollution. In response, city officials launched a series of inspections and sanctioned firms that had failed to install pollution abatement infrastructure.[14] These actions only targeted noncompliers, and reflected the standard "arm's-length" regulatory approach, in which the state can sanction polluters for failing to meet established standards, but cannot forcibly stop their productive activity. Why, then, did local authorities choose to shut down and dismantle the vast majority of factories in 2014 and 2015 to deter future violators? Why not repeat their less intrusive enforcement measures, which deter violations without destroying an industry? The Qingyuan government's widespread factory closures suggest their overriding goal was to get rid of the entire industry, not to improve future compliance with the law.

4.2.2 Blunt Force Regulation as Industrial Policy

It may be that blunt force regulation is not about improving future compliance with the law. In the case of pollution policy, for example, scholars and the media often classify blunt force regulation as a form of industrial policy or economic restructuring, where the state intervenes in the economy to eliminate ailing industries.

This explanation aligns with recent Chinese government rhetoric, which often describes blunt force regulation as a program to upgrade the country's economy. Work reports released by the Ministry of Environmental Protection (MEP) assert that policies to control pollution, reduce overcapacity, and restructure industry all go hand in hand.[15] Key policy makers argue that as China's economy grows and moves towards more service-oriented sectors, the government can accelerate this inevitable economic transition by forcibly shutting down entire industries.[16] While such forcible closures go beyond conventional approaches to regulation (where the state can only control risks at an arm's length) they do reflect the practices of industrial policy, where governments intervene in the economy to redirect the outcomes of market activity.

Previous studies of blunt force pollution regulation show that the process entails an element of industrial restructuring. Local governments try to consolidate industry by moving them into industrial parks, or by forcibly eliminating some industries to accelerate the transition towards cleaner growth (Kostka and Hobbs 2012, 777–8). Local officials also shut down ailing sectors with overcapacity, stating that they would have dissipated "naturally" anyway (Wang 2018, 898).

Finally, blunt force regulation is portrayed as a form of urban planning. As cities expand into peri-urban areas and residential districts creep up to the borders of industrial zones, the government realizes that it has to relocate factories to protect citizens from industrial hazards. City governments therefore force factories to relocate to new industrial parks, knowing that dirty, low-end factories cannot afford the higher costs of operation in these parks.[17] In this way, the state mitigates industrial hazards while eliminating the worst sources of pollution.

From this perspective, blunt force regulation in Qingyuan took on an indiscriminate, irreversible character because local officials were trying to upgrade their economy. Rather than regulating polluters, they were taking preemptive measures to eradicate ailing, dirty companies that were unlikely to relocate, upgrade, or survive an economic slowdown.

However, at the beginning of the campaign, the city government openly announced that it was pursuing a policy of "closures first and relocations [into industrial parks] second."[18] This suggests that urban planning was not the main goal of the crackdown. Moreover, some of the companies I visited in Qingyuan did not fit the description of "dirty and ailing" or "contributing to overcapacity." These firms were profitable, had consistent customers, and had installed an up-to-date pollution abatement infrastructure in anticipation of the government's "war on pollution." These firms also relied largely on machine technology, rather than human labor, which put them at the more advanced end of the upgrading spectrum. If industrial upgrading was the city's main goal, why were these companies subjected to production bans for days or weeks at a time to deal with air quality problems?[19]

The experiences of these companies mirror reports from around the country of firms (both large and small) being forced to stop production, despite being profitable and even though they had recently upgraded

their infrastructure.[20] China has a long history of state-directed industrial upgrading to streamline a bloated economy, including programs to
"advance the big and let go of the small" (抓大放小) or "advance the
state and retreat the private sector" (国进民退). Yet what is striking
about blunt force pollution regulation is that enforcement measures
extend to companies that are driving economic growth, including large,
profitable companies that comply with regulations. For instance, as the
party secretary of Shijiazhuang city publicly stated just prior to destroying the city's cement industry:

> To prevent air pollution...in addition to resolutely eliminating those
> small, backwards industries that contribute little to employment and
> revenue, we must also eliminate those big industries and companies that
> conform to our industrial policy, but are contributing too much to
> pollution.[21]

The state's indifference to compliance has led to considerable frustration in the more upgraded sectors of an industry. As one chemical
industry insider complained to me during a blunt force campaign,
"Why are they punishing the good citizens alongside the bad?"[22]

Moreover, even if Qingyuan's campaign was about upgrading industry and restructuring the economy, why did enforcement have to be
conducted so suddenly, and in such a concentrated period? If city
officials launched a plan to clean up the e-waste industry in 2012,
why did they wait until 2014, and then close down the industry in
one go? Why not enforce punishment in a more consistent manner so
as to ease unemployment shocks and soften the transition for factory
owners?

Note that when Qingyuan announced its e-waste rectification plans
in 2012, it was in the midst of a luxury development boom. Real estate
developers were flocking to Qingyuan, opening up a new stream of
revenue from greener industries. This gave local officials strong incentives to initiate industrial upgrading and close down the dirty e-waste
industry. Yet the local government continued to protect polluting
industries during the height of this development boom in 2012–14.
They even angered the newly arrived middle-class residents (and risked
scaring off future real estate investments) by openly backtracking on
their promise to punish polluters.

This laissez-faire attitude to implementing policies and enforcing
regulation suggests that Qingyuan officials were not exclusively
motivated by industrial upgrading. What, then, prompted the city

government to suddenly turn against the e-waste industry after years of shielding them from punishing regulations?

4.2.3 Blunt Force Regulation as Political Signaling

It may be that Qingyuan's officials were not concerned about compliance or delivering policy outcomes. Rather, they may have undertaken blunt force regulation as a public relations campaign, to appease both the luxury property developers and their political superiors who had been grumbling about the waste industry's pollution.

Some scholars argue that lower-level officials (such as city and county officials) initiate blunt force regulation as their own form of political signaling: As year-end performance assessments loom and city officials seek promotions, they carry out costly, high-profile campaigns to demonstrate their loyalty to political superiors, but then return to business as usual once a crucial assessment period has passed (Wang 2013, 420–2; Wang 2018, 898). This theory could explain Qingyuan's reluctance to begin enforcement in 2012, followed by its sudden crackdown on polluters in 2014. Local officials used blunt force regulation to signal their loyalty to provincial officials, but reverted to old habits once a crucial period had passed.

However, if Qingyuan's city leaders only wanted a brief, high-profile show to signal loyalty to their superiors, why not use the less intrusive, more reversible enforcement measures they employed during the 2011 pollution rectification campaign, namely, intensified inspections and penalties? Why go to the extent of irreversibly destroying thousands of firms, leading to enduring losses to the city's revenue and employment? Indeed, studies of signaling or "performative governance" (Ding 2017) indicate that the state often engages in more superficial, reversible activities to demonstrate loyalty or assuage public concerns, rather than actually addressing pollution problems.

In sum, the events that took place in Qingyuan could be attributed to some degree of deterrence, industrial restructuring, and performative signaling. However, none of these theories fully explain the city's level of indiscriminate, irreversible enforcement. Nor can they fully account for why local officials were so unpredictable in their enforcement approach, first punishing firms indiscriminately, then reverting to their previous practice of weak enforcement and tolerating polluters. Why, then, did local authorities in Qingyuan implement such brutal, one-off enforcement against local industry?

4.3 BLUNT FORCE REGULATION TO DISCIPLINE THE BUREAUCRACY

Drawing on the evidence above, I argue that blunt force regulation is driven by the need to control *bureaucrats* and scare them into compliance. Faced with years of bureaucratic evasion, higher-level officials recognize that they can only produce meaningful policy outcomes if local officials are ordered – under immediate threat of punishment – to take sudden, irreversible actions against polluters.

In the case of Qingyuan, I argue that the abrupt, concentrated nature of enforcement – interspersed with periods of enforcement laxity – suggests that it was higher-level officials who tired of protracted non-compliance and ordered local authorities to eliminate these pollution sources quickly. The province had been under pressure from Beijing to implement a centrally funded e-waste rectification project since 2012. After years of watching local officials drag their feet, the province forced city officials to pursue indiscriminate closures in 2014 and again in 2015 because they knew enforcement through ordinary channels was unlikely.

I further propose that enforcement took on this one-shot character – in which local officials chose to shut down factories instead of just fining them – because closures make it easier for higher levels of government to verify that local officials have complied. Note that both Qingyuan and Shantou – the two cities the provincial government had selected for e-waste rectification – initiated sudden, blunt force closures of their e-waste industries. Both cities were visited by the same provincial vice governor shortly after these closures. Moreover, just before the second crackdown began in Qingyuan in early 2015, local authorities announced, "We are currently awaiting special funds from the central government to carry out clean-up measures. Once the funds arrive, we will be able to destroy this e-waste industry."[23] In March 2015, central officials also came to Guangdong Province to evaluate its performance on soil restoration and heavy metal pollution in former e-waste sites.[24]

Qingyuan is one of several cases I came across, where top-down orders prompted blunt force regulation. For example, in another district near Guangzhou city, a large textiles company had been receiving special subsidies, tax breaks, and protection from the local government for several years. Then one year, the company was suddenly forced to clean up its act. As in Qingyuan, reports suggested that county officials came under pressure from higher levels of government to address pollution problems in the textile industry, and no longer had the political leeway to protect even this big, powerful company (Huang 2013, 10–12).

In sum, I argue that variation in blunt force regulation across China can be explained by degrees of bureaucratic policy compliance: City officials who shirk or underimplement environmental policies are ordered to undertake more blunt force regulation than those who *do* punish polluters. As a result, we should expect to see more severe blunt force measures in localities with low levels of bureaucratic compliance.

I focus on principal–agent problems between provincial officials (the principal) and city officials (the agents) in China's environmental enforcement. City (and county) officials are responsible for implementing the majority of environmental policies, including monitoring and controlling polluters, while provincial officials are directly responsible for ensuring their compliance. Provincial officials increasingly struggle to obtain compliance in environmental policy implementation because city officials still gain more from favoring economic growth policies. For instance, Jiang (2018, 995) shows that while provincial and city officials' objectives are aligned on economic and development policies, this alignment falters in non-economic policy areas.

This is not to say that central officials are excluded from efforts to bring about local bureaucratic compliance. As explained in the earlier case study, while the province often decides how (and how much) cities implement blunt force regulation, the guiding blunt force policy (including forcibly reducing industrial production) often originates from the center and is supported by central funding; provincial officials act as intermediaries. Figure 4.1 illustrates how dynamics between higher-level officials (the principals) and local officials (the agents) change under blunt force regulation.

This argument – that higher-level officials (provincial and central government officials) use blunt force regulation to overcome policy noncompliance by local bureaucrats (city and county officials) – leads to the study's central hypothesis:

Hypothesis 1: Political leaders will order local (city) officials to carry out more intensive blunt force regulation in cities with low bureaucratic compliance on environmental policies, irrespective of pollution levels.

Rival hypotheses suggest that blunt force regulation is undertaken to address severe pollution and punish noncompliant industries.

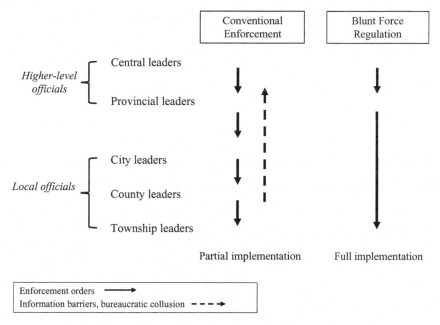

Figure 4.1 The logic of blunt force regulation

Bureaucratic compliance is less important, because the main goal is to punish polluting companies. This leads to the hypothesis:

Hypothesis 2: Political leaders will order local officials to carry out more intensive blunt force regulation in cities with high pollution levels.

Alternately, theories suggest that the provincial (and central) government uses blunt force regulation to reduce industrial over-capacity and consolidate industries into larger, more efficient facilities. From this perspective, pollution levels and bureaucratic compliance should have little bearing on blunt force regulation. Instead:

Hypothesis 3: Political leaders will order local officials to carry out more intensive blunt force regulation in cities with high levels of production in bloated industries (such as steel and coal).

Finally, blunt force regulation is depicted as a slightly accelerated process of economic upgrading that local officials initiate independently in wealthier areas, often as a means to signal loyalty. This leads to the hypothesis:

Hypothesis 4: Blunt force regulation will be more intensive in wealthier localities.

In the following section, I use original data on blunt force regulation to evaluate these competing hypotheses.

4.4   WHAT DRIVES BLUNT FORCE REGULATION?

4.4.1   Data

To evaluate the hypotheses, I collected data on blunt force regulation in each of China's 283 prefectural-level cities. I do not include the four province-level cities (直辖市) of Beijing, Tianjin, Shanghai, and Chongqing in this analysis because these cities report directly to the central government, so principal–agent problems are less acute. Given its ad hoc nature, statistics on blunt force regulation are not easy to find. The most aggressive blunt force interventions also tend to be directed at small or unregistered firms, so it is difficult to find a paper trail of how many firms have been targeted. In general, evidence of blunt force regulation tends to be anecdotal, appearing occasionally in media public interest stories.

Documents from the central Ministry of Industry and Information Technology (MIIT) contain more robust evidence. Since 2010, it has issued targets for forced reductions in industrial capacity in 18 industries chosen for their high levels of air and water pollution. (Chapter 5 details how these targets are assigned by different levels of government, and the policy process used to draw up these blunt force orders.) Each year from 2010–15, the MIIT published a list of firms in highly polluting industries across the country that would be forced to reduce their production output by specific amounts. Firms may be forced to reduce as little as 1,000 tons a year or as much as 6.1 million tons a year, but the combined impact on a region's industrial output can be significant. In Hebei Province, for example, these orders amounted to a 13% forced reduction in steel capacity in 2011, followed by a 35% forced reduction in cement capacity in 2012.[25]

Although billed as a measure to "eliminate outdated industrial capacity" (淘汰落后产能), work reports from the MEP – as well as interviews with national-, provincial-, and city-level environmental officials[26] – confirm that this was also a central policy designed to reduce pollution across the country. Beijing sets overall targets for production cuts, but provincial governments take the lead in dividing and assigning targets down to the city and county levels. Central government leaders do not give specific instructions on how provinces should carry out these capacity reduction orders, or command them to focus on noncompliant firms,[27] but they do require local governments to meet these predetermined targets by the end of the year. Provincial officials must also submit the final list of companies to be targeted for central ministries to review and approve. This process highlights how deeply the central government is involved in blunt force regulation.

To identify nationwide patterns of blunt force regulation, I compiled a list of all firms in the country that were targeted for forced production cuts during the height of these interventions (2010–15). I focus exclusively on the industries that contribute to air pollution. I identified the location of each firm to the city level, and then calculated the total number of firms and total tons of industrial capacity that were targeted for forcible reduction in each city.

Table 4.1 reports the descriptive statistics of these forced reductions from 2010–15. During this time, Beijing ordered 269 out of 283 prefecture-level cities to carry out forcible reductions in industrial capacity. The variation in forced reductions across the country is illustrated by the map in Figure 4.1. The 14 cities with zero production cuts tend to be either very wealthy and developed, such as Shenzhen, or small towns in remote areas, such as Karamay in Xinjiang. I now turn to a quantitative assessment of what predicts variation in the amount of blunt force regulation ordered by the central government (Figure 4.2).

4.4.2 Independent Variable

The main independent variable is the level of bureaucratic policy compliance. While *polluter* compliance can be measured by pollution levels, or how much a firm's polluting emissions exceed set standards, bureaucratic policy compliance is difficult to measure directly with pollution levels because local officials could be intensively monitoring and fining polluters, but unable to prevent uncooperative firms from violating emissions standards.

The Institute of Public and Environmental Affairs (a well-respected, independent nongovernmental organization in China) has developed a Pollution Information Transparency Index (PITI) that offers a more effective measure of *bureaucratic* policy compliance. This index calculates local officials' performance on enforcement activities that do not require

TABLE 4.1. Descriptive statistics of forced reductions in industrial output (Unit = 10,0000 tons)

Year	Mean	Median	Min	Max	Total Tons	Cities targeted
2010	61.34	19.25	0.36	1,393.00	16,783	189
2011	90.17	28.80	0.10	3,565.00	24,907	217
2012	125.00	46.80	0.20	1,837.00	34,686	215
2013	48.36	10.00	0.50	1,446.00	13,326	168
2014	70.36	2.70	0.20	2,740.00	20,013	156
2015	68.69	40.00	0.50	443.00	6,594	96
			Total		116,309	269

Source: Author dataset

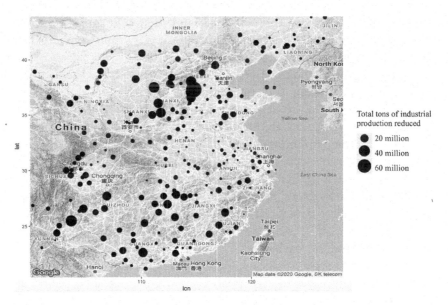

Figure 4.2 Variation in forced industrial reductions ordered by MIIT, by city, 2010–15.
Source: Author dataset

firm cooperation, such as 1) monitoring polluters, 2) disclosing emissions data, and 3) responding to public complaints – all of which reflect a bureaucrat's will to enforce policies (the Appendix contains details on PITI data). However, the index includes fewer than half of all Chinese cities (113 in total), and disproportionately contains wealthier cities.

To sidestep this problem of incomplete data, I use *Per Capita Revenue* to proxy for bureaucratic compliance with pollution policies, since previous research has found it is strongly associated with bureaucratic compliance on environmental policies (van der Kamp et al. 2017). Per capita revenue is measured as "own source revenue" (i.e., all taxes and fees collected and kept at the local level) scaled by a city's population. Revenue-rich cities tend to perform well on monitoring and punishing polluters, while revenue-poor cities do not. Additional evidence indicates that officials in low-revenue cities are more likely to become pollution havens, deliberately attracting investment from polluting industries to cover their revenue shortfalls (Ibid.).

Two mechanisms link per capita revenue to bureaucratic compliance with environmental policies. First, local governments that lack revenue are less likely to invest in pollution inspections and monitoring, since these are resource-intensive activities. Second, the amount of revenue raised from local industry is one of the most important criteria for determining a city leader's chances of promotion (Lü and Landry 2014). Thus city leaders who struggle to raise revenue will have strong incentives to put the brakes on environmental regulation in order to protect polluters' tax contributions – one of their main sources of revenue. In addition, they might increase efforts to attract "dirty FDI" (investment from polluting industries), knowing they cannot compete with wealthier cities for "clean FDI." Leaders in cities with large revenue streams can afford to sacrifice polluters' tax revenue, leading to better compliance records on environmental policies.

Indeed, quantitative tests (see Table 4.2) indicate that during 2010–15, per capita revenue was the strongest predictor of strong performance on the PITI score, representing good bureaucratic compliance on pollution policies. By contrast, the overall wealth of a city (measured as GDP per capita), pollution levels, and distance from Beijing are not associated with high levels of compliance. I therefore use *per capita revenue* to proxy for bureaucratic policy compliance. However, I include a control for *GDP per capita* to ensure that per capita revenue is not picking up on the effect of a city's overall wealth, since high levels of economic growth could be driving blunt force regulation.

4.4.3 Other Explanatory Variables

Media reports suggest that central governments use blunt force regulation to curb excessive pollution, and will therefore target the most

TABLE 4.2. Effect of per capita revenue on bureaucratic environmental compliance

	Pollution Transparency (PITI) Score (/100)		
	(1)	(2)	(3)
Revenue per capita	20.869***	12.745**	9.624***
	(4.116)	(6.297)	(1.395)
SO$_2$ air pollution level	1.935	1.791	−2.537
	(1.800)	(1.800)	(1.482)
GDP per capita		16.291*	
		(9.058)	
Distance (km) from Beijing			−0.789
			(2.161)
Observations	539	539	562
Number of cities	109	109	117
City fixed effects	✓	✓	✓
Lagged dependent variable included	✓	✓	✓
Adjusted R-squared	0.311	0.317	0.101

[a.]Robust standard errors are in parentheses. *p < 0.1; **p < 0.05; ***p < 0.01. The dependent variable is the score out of 100 on the Pollution Information Transparency Index (PITI).
[b.]All independent variables are logged.
[c.]Columns 1 and 2 show results for fixed effects models. Column 3 displays the results for random effects models.

polluted cities. To test this hypothesis, I use (logged) *sulfur dioxide (SO$_2$) levels* – the main industrial pollutant – to measure air pollution. I develop two measures for SO$_2$ levels, one using satellite[28] data (which is considered more reliable as it is unlikely to be doctored) and one using government-reported data (which is a more direct measure of polluting emissions on the ground, but may be less accurate than satellite data).

Other hypotheses predict that central governments employ blunt force regulation to curb industrial overcapacity. To measure overcapacity, I use the ratio of gross industrial output (in million RMB) to the number of industrial firms in a city (*gross industrial output/no. of industrial firms*), which captures the efficiency of a city's industry. Cities with a higher ratio are expected to have less overcapacity and will therefore be subjected to less blunt force regulation than their less-efficient counterparts. I also use *total steel output* (in million tons) to test the effect of industrial overcapacity. This is because steel companies are one of the main targets of blunt force regulation, and the most voluble rhetoric on curbing overcapacity (in both national and international media) focuses largely on the steel industry.

In addition to industrial output variables, I also include measures for total GDP from the services industry (*GDP services*) and revenue from the real estate industry (*real estate investment*). These variables test the theory that blunt force regulation is undertaken to accelerate the process of industrial upgrading, especially in cities with a growing GDP income from the services or real estate industries. The Appendix defines all variables and details their data sources and the main model specifications.

4.5 FINDINGS

I use a fixed effects model to assess the effect of bureaucratic compliance on blunt force regulation. Table 4.3 presents the results, which confirm the key prediction that blunt force regulation is associated with bureaucratic noncompliance. The coefficient for bureaucratic compliance (*revenue per capita*) is negative and significant in all models. In other words, cities with *lower* bureaucratic policy compliance are subjected to *more* blunt force regulation, even after controlling for pollution levels and economic and industrial variables.

These findings challenge the conventional wisdom in three ways. First, they show that blunt force regulation is not just about curbing excess pollution or scaring polluters into future compliance. Instead, the intensity of blunt force regulation depends on a city leader's history of enforcing environmental policies. Cities with low revenue levels – where local leaders have less will and fewer resources to enforce environmental policies – are more likely to be subjected to blunt force regulation by higher levels of government. Cities with higher revenue – where local leaders are more likely to comply with environmental policies – face less blunt force regulation. These results indicate that central and provincial governments *do* use blunt force regulation to overcome bureaucratic principal–agent problems in enforcement.

The second way in which the findings challenge the conventional wisdom is that the variables for industrial overcapacity (*Steel Output* and *Gross Industrial Output/No. of Industrial Firms*) are not significant. This suggests that blunt force regulation is not focused exclusively on

TABLE 4.3. Effect of bureaucratic noncompliance on blunt force regulation

	Blunt force regulation (Million tons reduced – logged)			
	(1)	(2)	(3)	(4)
Revenue per capita	−0.899** (0.430)	−0.948** (0.479)	−0.951** (0.478)	−0.948** (0.480)
SO$_2$ air pollution level (satellite)	−0.004 (0.202)	−0.023 (0.200)	−0.022 (0.201)	
SO$_2$ pollution emissions (government)				−0.133 (0.110)
GDP per capita		0.771 (0.987)	0.390 (0.919)	0.733 (0.975)
Gross industrial output/ no. of industrial firms		−0.545 (0.364)		−0.434 (0.370)
GDP services		−1.434 (1.414)	−1.354 (1.415)	−1.651 (1.431)
Real estate investment		0.160 (0.245)	0.196 (0.240)	0.159 (0.247)
Steel output			6.792 (4.251)	
Observations	1,396	1,391	1,391	1,376
Number of cities	282	282	282	282
City fixed effects	✓	✓	✓	✓
Province*Year fixed effects	✓	✓	✓	✓
Lagged dependent variable included	✓	✓	✓	✓
Adjusted R-squared	0.159	0.158	0.157	0.162

[a.]Robust standard errors are in parentheses. *p < 0.1; **p < 0.05; ***p < 0.01. The dependent variable is the (logged) annual total (in millions of tons) of industrial production that Beijing has ordered a city to reduce.
[b.]The dependent variable is measured for the years 2010–14, whereas the independent variables are measured for 2009–13.
[c.]All independent variables are logged.

industrial restructuring or eliminating inefficient industries. Indeed, the MEP's major role in implementing this policy suggests that blunt force regulation is targeted at environmental policy compliance – a finding confirmed in my interviews with senior government officials.

Third, the nonsignificant findings for *GDP per capita*, *GDP services*, and *GDP real estate investment* show that blunt force regulation is *not* more intense in areas that are wealthier or economically advanced. This suggests that blunt force regulation is not undertaken by local governments to accelerate industrial upgrading in wealthy cities that have tired of older, dirtier industries. Rather, revenue-poor, polluted cities – those with the fewest resources to withstand sudden unemployment or revenue losses – are bearing the brunt of forced reductions ordered by higher-level officials. This finding underscores how costly and painful blunt force regulation can be, and why cash-strapped local officials are unlikely to initiate this process independently.

4.6 SUMMARY

This chapter provides evidence to support the theory that blunt force regulation is motivated by a desire to exert bureaucratic control. Using data from China, I demonstrate how it is used to reassert leaders' control over the bureaucracy. I further reveal that the state only undertakes blunt force regulation as a last resort. Central leaders are wary of the cost of such measures, and even openly condemn one-size-fits-all enforcement to achieve certain policy goals. Local officials – especially in the cash-strapped cities most likely to be subjected to blunt force regulation – are reluctant to turn on polluters, which may well be the engine of their local economy. Nevertheless, after repeated policy implementation failures, higher-level officials find that the only way they can get the job done is through ruthless, one-size-fits-all enforcement.

But does blunt force regulation work? Under direct orders and scrutiny from high-level officials, do local officials truly find they have no choice but to concede? More broadly, does temporarily reducing bureaucratic discretion actually force bureaucrats to comply with central orders? Do orders to enact indiscriminate, one-shot sanctions against polluters result in changes in pollution outcomes? In short, does blunt force regulation reduce pollution?

In the following chapter, I assess these questions. Using remote sensing data on pollution and an original dataset on municipal enforcement measures, I compare the ability of blunt force regulation vs. conventional regulatory measures to reduce pollution. I find that blunt force regulation has become one of the most widespread and effective means for systematically reducing pollution in China's cities.

NOTES

1 Interview X11211219 with employee of chemical business, Shanghai (December 2019).
2 Interviews X2110815, X10080416, X7a190416a, X7a190416b, X7a190416c, X7a190416d with factory owners in Hebei and Guangdong provinces (2015–2016) and in Jiangsu Province (December 2019).
3 *China Environment News*, "Qudi feifa chaijie zhen you name nan?" [Can a crackdown on illegal e-waste truly be this hard?], December 12, 2014, http://news.cenews.com.cn/html/2014-12/12/content_21729.htm.
4 MEP 环发 [2012] 110 号, www.mee.gov.cn/gkml/hbb/bwj/201209/t2012 0910_235928.htm.
5 *China Environment News* 2014; 2015 Qingyuan Yearbook.
6 2014 Guangdong Yearbook, 190.
7 2015 Qingyuan Yearbook, 196.
8 *China Environment News* 2014.
9 Qingyuan City News [*Qingyuan Benshi Wen*], April 25, 2015 "Qingyuan: Wei zhili wuran dui wuzheng qiye qiangzhi duandian chaichu shengchan shebei" [Qingyuan suspends electricity and dismantles equipment of illegal enterprises to clean up pollution], http://qingyuan.benshixinwen.com/2015/qingyuanxinwen_0425/35009.html.
10 *The Southern Daily*, July 26, 2016, "Guangdong Qingyuan 40 nian dianzi chaijie ye zhuanxing" [Guangdong Qingyuan's 40-year-old e-waste industry is transformed], www.chinanews.com/sh/2016/07-26/7951598.shtml.
11 Longtang County enforcement official, as quoted in *The Southern Daily* 2016.
12 See *Qingyuan Daily News*, July 6, 2016, http://qy.southcn.com/content/2016-07/06/content_150827176.htm.
13 Interview X7a190416d with owner of a large waste processing factory, Qingyuan (April 2016).
14 2011 Qingyuan Yearbook, 148–49.
15 See 环境保护工作综述, 中国环境年鉴 2013年, 2014年, 2015年 ("Environmental protection work report," *China Environment Yearbook* for the years 2013, 2014 and 2015).
16 Speech by key policy makers to the China Coal Cap lobby group in Beijing, March 26, 2015.
17 Interview X7b200416 with industrial park manager in Guangdong Province (April 2016).
18 *Qingyuan City News* 2015.
19 Interviews X7a190416a, X7a190416b, X7a190416c, X7a190416d with factory owners, Qingyuan (April 2016).
20 Interview X2140515b with business consultant in Hebei Province (May 2015); Interview X5201015 with a factory owner from Dongguan city (April 2016). See also Reuters, "China says end to 'one size fits all' environmental policies," May 28, 2018, www.reuters.com/article/us-china-pollution/china-says-to- end-one-size-fits-all-environmental-pol-icies-idUSKCN1IT094; see also Hebei Steel Association (河北省冶金

行业协会), November 5, 2019, 关于报送钢铁企业对婷限产和环保相关问题意见的函.

21 Sun Ruibin, party secretary of Shijiazhuang, as quoted in *Economic Daily* (经济日报), "Farewell to the 'Cement Corridor'" (告别"水泥走廊"), December 17, 2014, www.ce.cn/xwzx/gnsz/gdxw/201412/17/t20141217_4138023.shtml.

22 Interview X11190619 with chemical industry insider, Shanghai (June 2019).

23 Longtang County official, quoted in *China Environment News* 2014.

24 2016 Guangdong Yearbook, 215.

25 This is the statistic for production cuts in 2012 for Hebei's cement industry. See the Appendix for full details on production cuts.

26 Interviews X3a240615a, X2110815a, X6210116, X1120516 in Hebei Province (summer 2015), Guangdong Province (January 2016), and Beijing (May 2016).

27 Interview X2140515a with provincial official at the National Reform and Development Commission (May 2015). See also State Council, October 6, 2013, www.gov.cn/zwgk/2013-10/15/content_2507143.htm.

28 Obtained from NASA's OMSO2e dataset (see the Appendix).

CHAPTER 5

THE IMPACT OF BLUNT FORCE REGULATION

On the morning of December 17, 2013, at a dusty industrial site on the outskirts of Shijiazhuang city in northern China, senior government dignitaries gathered for an official ceremony. Lining up under a banner, they delivered solemn speeches to the audience of gathered journalists and local villagers.

"In the face of unprecedented pressure to control air pollution, Shijiazhuang must part with their treasures and make the necessary sacrifice," announced the city's Party Secretary. "[We must] eliminate [e] those big industries and companies that conform to our industrial policy but are contributing too much to pollution," he implored. "Through sacrificing our short-term and local interests, we will bring about long-term gains for the public good."[1] Minutes after his speech, this "elimination" began. A button was pressed, dynamite exploded, and the audience (which included former factory employees) watched more than a dozen cement factories fall to the ground.

Two months later, dignitaries, journalists, and villagers congregated again to watch the obliteration of the Hengdaxin cement factory, another key employer and source of revenue for the county.[2] An official placard near the destruction site informed the audience that this was the "second-stage demolition of cement factories," and that participants had just witnessed the destruction of 18 cement factories and 377 storage facilities covering an area of 900 hectares.[3] Overall, this winter of demolitions reduced the city's cement producing capacity by 40%.[4] Both destruction ceremonies were widely reported in the national press, including a special evening broadcast on China's national CCTV station.[5]

Blunt force regulation is often perceived as a form of political theater in which local governments use a dramatic, highly publicized spectacle to convince a disgruntled public that it *is* serious about pollution and *is* turning away from unbridled economic growth. These events make headlines, demonstrate leadership resolve, and are designed to quell the public's too vocal discontent over degrading air quality. Why else would government officials hold a public ceremony to mark the permanent destruction of local industry?

But political theater is not designed to have a substantive impact on overall policy outcomes. Instead, the real business of environmental regulation is expected to take place through routine inspections, penalties, and punishments, all implemented by increasingly well-funded and well-staffed local environmental agencies.

This chapter demonstrates that blunt force regulation goes beyond political theater. The obliteration of Shijiazhuang's cement industry represents a more extreme version of a longstanding enforcement repertoire practiced throughout China, in which the state abruptly destroys factories. Some cases are covered by the media (most are not), but such events have been happening regularly throughout the past decade. These enforcement practices are spearheaded by high-level government planning, enlist the efforts of several government agencies, and are part of a concerted, multiyear strategy to address pollution.

In this chapter, I present evidence showing that Beijing's blunt force policy is working: it *is* being implemented by local officials, and it *is* reducing pollution levels throughout the country. Through quantitative tests I demonstrate that cities that have been ordered to carry out blunt force regulation are more likely to record reductions in air pollution levels. Blunt force regulation is also associated with a much greater impact on reducing air pollution than conventional enforcement measures. These findings challenge assumptions that blunt force regulation is mere political theater, with only a bit part in the nation's overall pollution control efforts.

5.1 POLITICAL THEATER OR POLICY IMPLEMENTATION?

Chinese leaders have a long history of using dramatic public performances to win legitimacy and acclaim, especially in the wake of a crisis. Anticorruption campaigns, for example, are widely seen as an attempt to regain public trust by exposing government corruption (Lorentzen and Lu 2018; Manion 2004). Similarly, local authorities resort to eye-catching but superficial enforcement tactics when they lack the resources (such as personnel and money) to improve enforcement on an urgent issue (Ding 2020). If they cannot implement policies through normal channels, officials settle on a short burst of activity to create the illusion of policy effectiveness (Tanner 2000).

Thus, when officials in Qingyuan raze a 50-year-old recycling industry to the ground, or when the press lines up to watch cement factories in Shijiazhuang dynamited to smithereens, many assume that this is just another piece of political theater. They believe that leaders use blunt force pollution regulation to ease public concerns over pollution, to demonstrate the government's commitment to reduce pollution regardless of the cost (Kostka and Hobbs 2012), or simply to remind the public of their power (Huang 2015).

Blunt force regulation has also been depicted as a form of signaling to political insiders. According to this interpretation, high-level politicians initiate costly, risky, resource-intensive campaigns to show their rivals and subordinates that they maintain full control over the governing apparatus, thereby dissuading internal challenges to their power (Mertha 2017). The more costly and difficult the task required, the more vivid the demonstration of power (Zhu, Zhang, and Liu 2017).

Because the underlying goal is performative, such campaigns must achieve a high level of media publicity. Cases involving more extreme, theatrical versions of blunt force regulation (such as dynamiting firms) are often accompanied by a high-profile media blitz, especially during the height of China's war on pollution.

However, during the National People's Congress in 2019, when journalists questioned the use of blunt force regulation during an economic downturn, leading politicians (including Premier Li Keqiang and Environment Minister Li Ganjie) quickly decried the use of one-size-fits-all measures.[6] "We will go after officials both for being slack as well as for imposing arbitrary measures," Li Ganjie told the conference. He also condemned the use of blanket production bans for "hurting the image of the party and the government, the legitimate rights of enterprises, and causing inconvenience to the public."[7]

If Beijing initiated blunt force regulation as a media campaign to win public approval, why would central government officials then publicly distance themselves from this implementation approach?

Political theater is also expected to have only a minimal impact on policy outcomes. The goal is to use a staged event to convince an audience that reforms have been undertaken, even if real reform efforts have been minimal. This is why it so often happens in contexts where governments lack the resources to implement policies. For instance, in a survey measuring public approval of local environmental governance, Ding (2017) shows that staged performances succeed in winning public approval, even when they fail to produce substantive changes in pollution levels.

However, the data on blunt force regulation (introduced in Chapter 4) shows that such measures have not been limited to a small number of highly publicized cases in a few hotspots across the country. The tactic has been applied in 269 of China's 287 cities during 2010–15 (see map in Chapter 4) and has affected nearly every major polluting industry. If blunt force regulation were mere political theater, why would the Chinese government insist on shutting down polluters across the country? Why undertake such an extensive restructuring of polluting industries when a few high-profile, well-publicized cases would be enough to win public approval?

In the following sections, I present evidence that, unlike political theater, blunt force regulation forms part of an established policy implementation process designed to reduce pollution through industrial cuts. I draw on evidence from interviews and government documents to show that blunt force regulation is a national pollution reduction policy initiated by Beijing and applied throughout the country – and that it is substantively improving environmental outcomes.

5.2 BLUNT FORCE POLICY IMPLEMENTATION IN CHINA

As with many policy directives in China, blunt force regulation begins with Beijing issuing national targets for forced reductions in industrial capacity. These targets represent specific quantitative goals that local governments must achieve. For instance, in 2013, China's State Council determined that by 2015, municipal and county governments would have to forcibly reduce industrial capacity in iron, steel, and cement industries by an additional 15 million, 15 million, and 100 million tons, respectively.[8]

Beijing sets province-level targets, taking into account their political and economic characteristics. Provincial leaders then begin negotiating with local governments (including municipal and county leaders) on which firms and industries will be targeted for forced reductions. The central government's political interests must also be considered when selecting which firms to target. The final list of firms' names must be sent to central ministries for review and approval,[9] which gives central officials the chance to protect firms with higher-level connections.[10] For instance, a top economic official in Hebei province said that he would have to wait for approval from central ministries on the list of selected firms before they could begin carrying out measures to reduce steel capacity to fulfill the province's assigned target of 60 million tons.[11] This may explain why (as I show in Chapter 7) so few of the most powerful, polluting firms in a city show up on these lists, even though production cuts in these firms would significantly reduce overall pollution levels. The Ministry of Industry and Information Technology (MIIT) then publishes the final list of targets. The number of firms targeted for blunt force measures each year range widely in the sample, from 1 to 132.

Allowing local officials to choose which firms to close may seem to violate the logic of blunt force regulation because it grants them discretion in enforcement. However, this discretion is constrained by Beijing's requirement that local officials meet its predetermined targets in specific industries by the end of the year. Officials may choose how much each firm bears the brunt of blunt force regulation, but they cannot choose to ease the overall burden imposed by Beijing, or extend the deadline for meeting such strict targets.

The list of firms drawn up by local officials and published by the MIIT does not represent the universe of firms targeted for blunt force measures. The State Council's guiding statement also encourages the reduction of capacity in "illegal" firms (i.e., those without proper land, business, or environmental permits). This instruction is directed at small and medium enterprises (SMEs), which seldom have the necessary permits, and become easy targets for government cleanup campaigns. This means that widespread closures of SMEs can occur in tandem with forced capacity reduction orders directed at firms on the approved list of targets. For instance, in 2010 the government of Ningbo city reported in its yearbook that it had eliminated 329,000 tons of industrial production and 62 factories, boasting that this "exceeded the orders sent down for eliminating production from the MIIT and provincial government."[12] Indeed MIIT records indicated that Ningbo city was only required to eliminate 178,000 tons of production that year. The measures directed at "illegal capacity" often constitute the most extreme version of blunt force regulation: entire districts of small firms, or entire industries run by SMEs, are wiped out in a short period of time.

While Beijing does not give specific instructions on how provinces should carry out these capacity reduction orders, the policy's guiding statement encourages them to reduce their production output by eliminating capacity in older, less advanced industrial sectors, preventing the construction of new projects, and targeting production in "illegal" sectors.[13] This guiding statement reads as if the policy is largely about industrial restructuring rather than pollution control. However, my interviews with central, provincial, and municipal officials indicate that pollution control is one of the policy's main goals. For instance, when I asked a provincial official how environmental enforcement has changed since 2015, he responded:

> Before, we were evaluated on specific measures, such as how well we performed on limiting steel and coal production levels...But now, a big part of the evaluation is based on how much air quality has improved, which means each city has more flexibility in planning how to meet environmental targets. For instance, if a city doesn't produce much steel, then they won't have to focus on meeting specific steel reduction targets.[14]

It is striking that, when discussing the implementation of environmental targets, this official spoke primarily about limiting steel and coal production, rather than about more typical regulatory actions, such as punishing pollution violations. This official was from a northern industrial province, so his preoccupation with industrial restructuring was to be expected. Yet, a provincial official from one of China's more developed, coastal provinces also focused on industrial restructuring, going so far as to state that:

> Right now, the most important measures [for reducing pollution] are the policies on industrial restructuring and eliminating industrial overcapacity. So far, we have tried to do this by moving polluting industries to remote areas where pollution will be less concentrated... or by closing down smaller firms and strengthening the bigger ones.[15]

A municipal EPA official even exclaimed:

> Of course those campaigns for forced reductions of industrial capacity are linked to efforts to reduce emissions! As you can see, the "outdated industries" targeted in forced reductions are often the most polluting industries.[16]

In sum, these interviews reveal that when local authorities close down factories, cut off electricity, or relocate companies, they are not simply restructuring local industry to reduce overcapacity. Nor are they deploying "quick fix" measures to meet emissions targets or address urgent pollution problems. In fact, they are applying the enforcement tools developed specifically for this policy to reduce pollution through industrial production cuts. Moreover, they are implementing a policy that Beijing handed down with specific, predetermined targets.

5.3 THE IMPACT OF BLUNT FORCE REGULATION

A second important dimension for assessing blunt force regulation is its impact on environmental outcomes. In Chapter 4, I demonstrate that higher-level leaders initiate blunt force regulation to force local bureaucrats to implement environmental policies. Historically less compliant localities therefore bear the brunt of this policy. The implementation process described above illustrates how Beijing issues these orders in an attempt to rectify previous enforcement failures. But do these orders work? Is pollution reduced? More broadly, and to answer the central question of this book, is blunt force regulation effective at overcoming bureaucratic noncompliance?

5.3.1 Research Design and Data

To determine whether blunt force regulation reduces air pollution, I examine the factors that explain changes in levels of industrial air pollution across China's 283[17] prefecture-level cities. Analysis of satellite data on sulfur dioxide (SO2) levels shows that air pollution decreased considerably during this period. Figure 5.1 records the fluctuating aggregate SO2 levels (in Dobson Units, DUs) of all 283 cities from 2009 to 2015. Figure 5.2 displays the aggregate percentage change in SO2 levels for all these cities from 2009 to 2015. In both figures, the bars illustrate variable levels from 2009 to 2012, followed by a steady decrease (10–20%) from 2012 onwards.

Figure 5.3 breaks down this data to depict the distribution of percentage changes in pollution levels across the 283 cities from 2010 to 2015. This histogram helps visualize national variation, and shows that the vast majority of cities in China reduced their pollution during this period by an average of 25.2%. Moreover, the right skew of this distribution means that the median city reduced at a higher rate

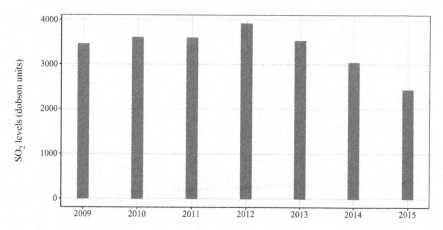

Figure 5.1 Industrial pollution levels (SO$_2$) in urban China – national aggregate, 2009–15.
Data Source: OMSO2e NASA SO$_2$ data

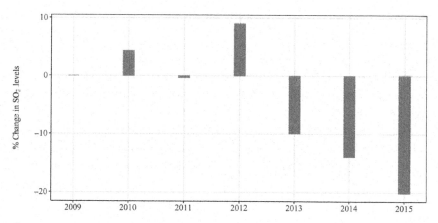

Figure 5.2 Year-on-year percent change in pollution levels (SO$_2$) in urban China – national aggregate, 2009–15.
Data Source: OMSO2e NASA SO$_2$ data

(28.6%), and some cities reduced by up to 80%. However, a few outlier cities increased their pollution levels.

To what extent can these overall reductions in industrial pollution be attributed to blunt force regulation? Using my original dataset (introduced in Chapter 4), which documents blunt force enforcement

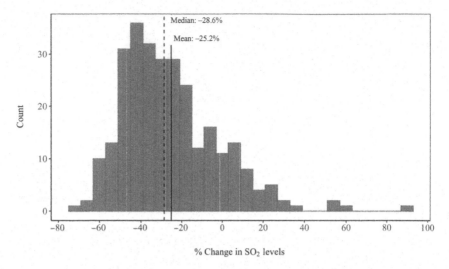

Figure 5.3 Distribution of percent change in SO_2 levels for all Chinese cities, 2010–15. *Data Source:* OMSO2e NASA SO_2 data

measures during 2010–15, I run a fixed effects model to assess whether blunt force regulation is associated with changes in air pollution during this period. I control for conventional enforcement measures, as well as key economic, geographic, and political variables that might also effect changes in levels of industrial air pollution.

The goal of this analysis is not to explain variation in pollution reduction across China, but to establish that blunt force regulation is being implemented beyond a few high-profile cases, and that it is affecting air pollution levels.

5.3.2 Dependent Variable

The dependent variable is the absolute level of industrial pollution in each of China's prefecture-level cities between 2010 and 2015. I focus on SO_2 levels for each city, because SO_2 is a common measure of industrial air pollution. To overcome the limitations of Chinese government pollution data – which tends to be incomplete or falsified (Ghanem et al. 2014) – I use satellite measures of ground-level SO_2 from NASA's OMSO2e dataset[18] to calculate SO_2 levels (measured in DUs; see the data appendix for details). Using satellite data and SO_2 atmospheric levels to measure SO_2 industrial emissions raises some concerns, since these estimates are sensitive to extreme weather patterns, severe cloud cover, snow coverage, and larger solar zenith angles. The OMSO2e dataset corrects for some of these issues.

To address these concerns and to minimize measurement error, I use Fioletov et al.'s (2011) method of calculating changes in SO_2 from the OMSO2e dataset, which includes averaging emissions over 3 years of data, and only for the summer months of May–September. This method can accurately detect changes in point source SO_2 emissions (Fioletov et al. 2011, 3). To develop accurate annual measures, I calculate 3-year moving averages for all years in the study period. For instance, for the year 2010, SO_2 levels would be calculated as:

$$(SO2\ Levels\ 2009 + SO2\ Levels\ 2010 + SO2\ Levels\ 2011)/3$$

The SO_2 levels measured using satellite data may also include industrial emissions blown in from neighboring cities. I therefore control for changes in SO_2 levels in all neighboring cities less than 100km away, since satellite analysis reveals that pollution blown in is only a concern for cities within 100km of each other (Fioletov et al. 2011, 2). The measure of neighbors' emissions is weighted inversely by distance, because a city's overall SO_2 levels are more likely to increase the closer a neighboring city is.

5.3.3 Explanatory and Control Variables
The main explanatory variable is the intensity of blunt force regulation. To calculate this variable I use the dataset – described earlier and in Chapter 4 – that documents the intensity of "reduce capacity" orders in all Chinese cities.[19] To produce this dataset, I collected the MIIT's list of all Chinese firms that were targeted for forced production cuts due to air pollution in 2010–15 – the height of these interventions. I then identified which city each firm was located in and calculated the total number of firms and total tons of industrial capacity that were targeted for forcible reduction in each city in each year. Figure 5.4 displays the distribution of total blunt force regulation carried out by each city during this period. For the following tests, I measure blunt force regulation as the total production output (in tons) that polluting companies were ordered to forcibly reduce each year, aggregated at the city level.

To limit omitted variable bias from parallel efforts to reduce pollution through conventional regulation, I control for two forms of conventional regulation: 1) pollution fees (排污费) and administrative

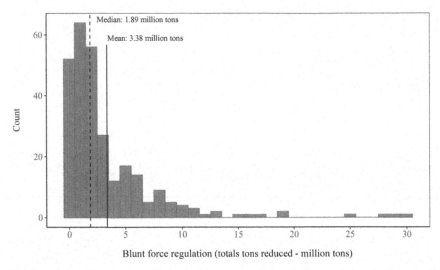

Figure 5.4 Distribution of blunt force regulation (millions of tons reduced) for all cities, 2010–15.
Data Source: Author dataset

fines (罚款) issued by city-level governments and 2) pollution inspections, which include the total number of inspections (检查) and monitoring visits (监察) conducted by city-level governments. Local Environmental Protection Bureaus regularly undertake both types of enforcement measures throughout the year. Unlike blunt force regulation, they are not ad hoc, but written into the rules of environmental regulation. This data was collected and hand-coded from city yearbooks (城市年检), which record descriptive data on enforcement in the "environmental protection" section.

In addition to administrative enforcement measures, I also control for a broader measure of a local government's efforts to comply with conventional environmental regulation, captured as each municipal's government score on the Pollution Information Transparency Index (PITI) index. This score, developed by a well-respected, independent nongovernmental organization (NGO), is calculated based on each city government's performance on 1) complying with daily emissions standards, 2) monitoring polluters, 3) disclosing data on emissions levels, and 4) responding to public petitions related to pollution. It represents a more objective measure of city officials' efforts to reduce pollution through conventional, rules-based methods because official performance is assessed by an independent expert body. However, this score is only assessed for 120 cities, fewer than half of the country's prefecture-level cities.

Finally, I include a set of controls for factors that may be associated with changes in SO2 emissions, such as city-level electricity consumption (in kilowatt hours), which take into account changes in the coal-fired energy sector during this period. While power plants were not included on the list of firms ordered to reduce capacity, they are by far the biggest contributors of SO_2 industrial emissions in any locality and can emit up to 2.5 times more SO_2 than the steel, cement, chemical, and petroleum industries combined. This is based on 2005 figures, though the ratio may have changed somewhat in the past few years (Nielson and Ho 2013, Chapter 2). Moreover, the bulk of China's electricity was generated by coal-fired power plants at this time (Liu et al. 2015). Thus, the electricity consumption variable will proxy for any changes in coal consumption in the energy sector during this period.

I also control for changes in GDP. In recent years, China's GDP growth rates have started to decline, so this measure controls for any reductions in industrial output (and related reductions in SO_2 industrial emissions) that can be attributed to general market slowdowns. GDP and electricity consumption data is drawn from the National Bureau of Statistics. The appendix defines all variables, their data sources, and the main model specifications.

5.3.4 Model Specifications

I use a fixed effects model to assess how blunt force regulation affected SO_2 air pollution levels. This model uses city-level fixed effects to control for time-invariant geographical features that make it harder to reduce pollution (such as basins, elevation, and climate) as well as distance from Beijing, since nearby cities face much greater pressure to monitor their air quality. The model also controls for the city's overall industrial profile, since cities with a heavy industrial base will generate more pollution than those with a service-based industry. I also include a dummy variable for year to account for common shocks to all cities.

Industrial (SO_2) pollution levels (the dependent variable) are measured for the years 2010–15, whereas the pollution enforcement variables (blunt force regulation and the three measures of conventional regulation) as well as the control variables are measured for the years 2009–14. The Appendix details how I assess the impact of the conventional regulatory measures and blunt force regulation differently because they reduce pollution in different ways. I lag the independent variables because my case studies, interviews, and news reports indicate that blunt force measures are typically carried out in the fall and winter months in anticipation of heavy winter pollution. However, SO_2 levels (the dependent variable) are only measured for pollution levels in the summer months of May to September. Thus, the impact of each year's blunt force measures will only be reflected in the following year's pollution levels. The same logic applies to the conventional enforcement variables: pollution inspections, pollution fines, and pollution transparency are expected to take time to affect factories' behavior, and therefore pollution levels. Control variables are also lagged (2009–14), but the variable "Neighbor SO_2 levels" is measured for the years 2010–15 as the effect on a city's pollution levels will be immediate.

5.4 FINDINGS

Table 5.1 presents the results of the fixed effects model assessing the impact of blunt force regulation on changes in pollution levels. The results show a statistically significant, negative correlation between blunt force regulation and air pollution across all models. This indicates that orders to forcibly reduce industrial capacity *are* associated with decreases in air pollution across China's cities. In other words, blunt force regulation does change environmental outcomes. This finding is robust, even after controlling for conventional regulatory measures and geographic and economic variables. It is also robust to changes in model specifications, including adding controls (such as changes in a city's overall industrial output and population)[20] and dropping controls.

Model 3 in Table 5.1 (the main model with all controls) indicates that every million tons of blunt force regulation imposed is associated with a decrease in SO_2 levels of 0.250 DUs, holding all other variables constant at their means. This means that for the average city (where about 4 million tons would have been reduced between 2010 and 2015), this would equate to about a 1 DU reduction in SO2. The unit of measurement makes these results difficult to interpret, but further analysis reveals that this average city would experience about a 2% drop in SO2 levels as a result of this level of blunt force regulation (with estimates based on a model including all controls). This effect may also be underestimated, because the models measure the reduction in pollution indicated by satellite data. This is a much noisier measure

TABLE 5.1. Effect of enforcement measures on air pollution levels

	SO$_2$ levels			
	(1)	(2)	(3)	(4)
Blunt force regulation	−0.233***	−0.226***	−0.250***	−0.257*
	(0.065)	(0.064)	(0.065)	(0.133)
Pollution inspections			−0.004	
			(0.009)	
Pollution fines			−0.004	
			(0.005)	
Pollution transparency score				−0.022
				(0.019)
Neighbor SO$_2$ levels		1.464***	1.434 ***	1.721***
		(0.233)	(0.250)	(0.265)
Electricity consumption		0.200***	0.211***	0.115*
		(0.061)	(0.065)	(0.060)
GDP		−0.5845 *	−0.557	0.239
		(0.342)	(0.347)	(0.417)
Observations	1,410	1,384	1,209	548
Number of cities	282	281	271	116
City fixed effects	✓	✓	✓	✓
Year fixed effects	✓	✓	✓	✓
Adjusted R-squared	0.25	0.35	0.34	0.43

Note: The table reports the results of fixed effects models. Robust standard errors are in parentheses. Significance: *p < 0.1; **p < 0.05; ***p < 0.01. The dependent variable is the absolute change (reduction or increase) in SO$_2$ levels between 2012 and 2015.

of emissions because the connection between reduced SO$_2$ *emissions* at the factory level and reduced SO$_2$ *levels* in the air can be affected by wind, geographic features, and weather patterns. While these models indirectly control for wind and weather variables, the fact that the bare minimum of officially recorded blunt force measures register a discernable impact on SO$_2$ levels indicates that blunt force regulation is affecting city-level SO$_2$ emissions.

One other way to put these findings into context is to come back to the case of Shijiazhuang mentioned in the introduction of this chapter. The 35 large cement factories that were destroyed[21] eliminated 40% of the city's cement-producing capacity. According to government data, this contributed to a 14% drop in the city's overall industrial pollution levels between 2013 and 2014, though satellite data suggest the actual figure may be as high as 30%.

Models 3 and 4 in Table 5.1 illustrate negative correlations between all three conventional enforcement measures and air pollution levels, though none of these variables is statistically significant. This indicates that pollution inspections, penalties, and pollution transparency measures, when implemented, are *not* associated with reduced levels of pollution. This suggests that administrative approaches are not as effective as blunt force regulation. This finding about inspections is consistent with my own findings that the inspections campaign had short-lived effects (van der Kamp 2021), while the finding on pollution transparency is consistent with recent results showing that government transparency leads to greater information sharing but has no impact on pollution levels (Seligsohn et al. 2018).

The variables presented in Table 5.1 are measured on very different scales, which makes it difficult to compare their relative impacts on air pollution reduction. In Figures 5.5 and 5.6, I present the same results with standardized variables. I rescale the variables to have a mean of 0 and a standard deviation of 1, which makes it possible to compare the effect sizes of predictors on the outcome variables.

The results in indicate that blunt force regulation has a much greater impact on reducing SO2 emissions than other enforcement measures. A 1-standard-deviation increase in blunt force intensity leads to a 0.16-standard-deviation decrease in pollution levels, approximately 32 times the effect of inspections, and 7 times the effect of pollution penalties. (Appendix Table A5.1 reports the full results of the models using standardized variables, with robust standard errors.) The effect of blunt force regulation may also be underestimated in these models, because this measure does not include (undocumented) forced closures of small firms. This type of intervention has the greatest long-term impact on pollution levels, but may not always be carried out in tandem with the officially recorded blunt force measures documented here.

These models also show that neighboring cities' emissions have a substantial effect on a city's pollution level. A 1-standard-deviation increase in pollution blown in from a city less than 100km away is associated with a 0.646-standard-deviation increase in pollution levels – almost four times the impact of blunt force regulation. This result is to be expected: Given that SO2 levels in the air are sensitive to wind, cities

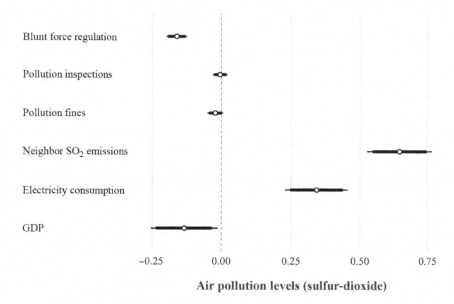

Figure 5.5 Effect of inspections and fines on SO₂ levels (with standardized variables)
Note: The figure displays the results of an ordinary least squares (OLS) regression with city and year fixed effects. The plot shows the effects of standardized variables. The dependent variable is SO₂ levels for the years 2010–15. Each circle indicates a point estimate. The thin horizontal bars represent the 95% confidence intervals, and the thick bars the 90% confidence intervals.

with high-polluting neighbors will experience increases in their own pollution levels, while those with low-polluting neighbors can expect improvements. This is why the majority of Beijing's efforts to improve the city's air quality are directed at neighboring cities in Hebei Province.

These strong results for pollution from neighboring cities suggest another reason why this model may underestimate the overall impact of blunt force regulation. A city that has significantly reduced end-of-pipe emissions through blunt force regulation may nevertheless experience only minimal changes in pollution levels because of a highly polluting neighbor upwind. Thus, Chinese cities, especially those that are closely clustered together, must coordinate regional pollution reduction measures.

5.5 IMPLICATIONS

The results reported here illustrate that blunt force regulation does affect environmental outcomes across the country. This supports the

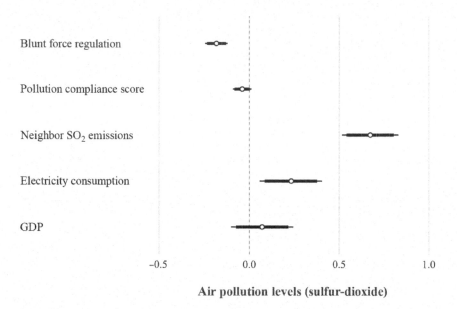

Figure 5.6 Effect of pollution compliance score on SO_2 levels (with standardized variables)
Note: The figure shows the results of an OLS regression with city and year fixed effects. The plot shows the effects of standardized variables. The dependent variable is SO_2 levels for the years 2010–15. Each circle indicates a point estimate. The thin horizontal bars represent the 95% confidence intervals, and the thick bars the 90% confidence intervals

argument that blunt force regulation is more than just political theater, and that Beijing's use of blunt force measures to overcome bureaucratic noncompliance is improving implementation on the ground. The leadership's strategy to force cadres to follow environmental orders is working.

Yet this strategy still involves an element of political theater. When Beijing forces local officials around the country to shutter industry, it is also a display of strength and control. After all, a leader who can make local officials close down factories across the country certainly appears difficult to challenge or unseat in the future (Minzner 2015; Zhou 2017; Zhu, Zhang, and Liu 2017). Local officials might also participate in this political theater to advance their own careers. When Beijing sets tough targets for implementation, some ambitious officials rise to the challenge by trying to outperform their counterparts. For instance, the short window that local officials are given to implement targets sometimes drives them to implement blunt force regulation even more ruthlessly, not focusing on compliance but on where cuts can be achieved most expediently. Reports from Hebei, for example, show that provincial officials exceeded the targets set by Beijing, even closing down companies that were not on the agreed list.[22] However, the findings from this chapter show that implementation outcomes are the main driving force behind blunt force regulation; political theater is a sideshow.

The results also demonstrate that blunt force regulation is more effective than conventional regulation, which suggests it may not face the same degree of bureaucratic shirking as conventional measures. When Beijing orders local officials to forcibly reduce industrial production through ad hoc closures, air quality is more likely to improve than when local officials apply standard administrative sanctions against firms.

This result has important implications for regulating in weak institutional environments. In much of the developing world, states with limited fiscal and administrative capacity struggle to enforce pollution regulation. To date, theories have focused on bottom-up solutions to this problem, which involve political leaders leveraging civil society's surveillance power and activism to put pressure on noncompliers (Amengual 2016; Greenstone and Hanna 2014; van Rooij, Stern, and Fürst 2016). Chapter 6 discusses these theories in more depth.

The problem is that this approach asks a lot of civil society (Blackman 2009; Chng 2012; Grabosky 2013; Konisky 2009). Not only must they participate in monitoring violators; they must also be ready to protest, file lawsuits, and sustain a credible threat against powerful local companies and local authorities. What if a state lacks an informed and active civil society? Or what if competing interests neutralize the power of civil society? Will citizens truly police polluters if they depend on these same companies for jobs? Will they care that much about the environment if the economy is plunged into a depression? For every environment-loving activist, there will be many more citizens who have become resigned to pollution (Lora-Wainwright 2021).

The evidence presented in this chapter suggests that China is advancing a top-down regulatory solution to combat this trend, which requires little support from the courts, and little participation from grassroots groups. It appears to be working: Pollution is declining. By resorting to short-term, ad hoc measures, China appears to be developing a viable model for pollution regulation in weak institutional environments.

However, these findings create two puzzles. First, the results show that conventional regulation, while less effective than blunt force regulation, is still being carried out. This suggests that Beijing is still investing in conventional regulation alongside blunt force regulation, and that cadres are occasionally using these measures to curtail pollution. While I focus here on the 2010–15 period, qualitative evidence illustrates that the government continued to apply blunt force measures throughout 2015–20. If conventional regulation shows signs of working, why does the state continue to revert to blunt force regulation, especially when it undermines the norms of compliance that make conventional regulation effective?

In the second puzzle, if blunt force regulation is effectively reducing pollution, this means local officials around the country are taking actions that are highly detrimental to the local economy and their own revenue streams. This contradicts what the literature has been predicting and proving for decades – that cadres systematically dismiss policies that hurt growth, and prioritize revenue collection above all. Why, then, are cadres conceding to these blunt force orders from Beijing? Why are they agreeing to damage their local economies?

In the following two chapters, I address these questions. Chapter 6 explains why China continues to apply such a contradictory, counterproductive approach to regulating pollution, while Chapter 7 describes why revenue-hungry cadres concede to blunt force regulation.

NOTES

1 *Economic Daily* (经济日报), "Farewell to the 'Cement Corridor'" (告别"水泥走廊"), December 17, 2014, www.ce.cn/xwzx/gnsz/gdxw/201412/17/t20141217_4138023.shtml.

2 *China Enterprise News* (中国企业报), "The pain of smog reduction in Shijiazhuang" (石家庄治霾阵痛), March 8, 2018, http://finance.sina.com.cn/roll/20140308/050118445006.shtml.

3 *China Comment* (半月谈网), "Hebei suppresses production capacity: smashing the people's rice bowl for the 'black hats'" (河北压制产能:为了乌纱帽砸别人饭碗?), June 6, 2014, www.cssn.cn/jjx_bg/201406/t20140606_1200233.shtml.

4 *China Enterprise News* 2018.

5 CCTV, "Economy Time" (中央电视台《经济半小时》), "Report from the frontlines of reform: the aftermath of demolishing cement factories" (来自改革一线的报道:水 泥厂爆破之后), April 13, 2016, http://tv.cctv.com/2016/04/13/VIDEVLZLeyoYiLIDWFpQgDKz160413.shtml.

6 *Caixin*, 李干杰解读重污染天气成因 回应"一刀切"等问题, March 11, 2019, http://topics.caixin.com/2019-03-11/101391008.html; *Caixing Global*,

"China won't push 'one-size-fits-all' production cuts in upcoming smog season, ministry says," August 21, 2019, www.caixinglobal.com/2019-08-21/china-wont-push-one-size-fits-all-production-cuts-in-upcoming-smog-season-ministry-says-101453249.html.

7   *South China Morning Post,* "Chinese pollution curbs must consider needs of businesses, says environment minister," October 29, 2018, www.scmp.com/print/news/china/politics/article/2170568/chinese-pollution-curbs-must-consider-needs-businesses-says.

8   These amounts were in addition to the forced reductions in capacity that were already imposed in preceding years. See State Council, "Guiding opinion on overcapacity" (国务院关于化解产能严重过剩矛盾的指导意见), October 6, 2013, www.gov.cn/zwgk/2013-10/15/content_2507143.htm.

9   Interview X2140515a with provincial-level NRDC official, Hebei Province, May 2015

10 *China Comment* 2014; *China Enterprise News* 2014

11 Interview X2140515a with provincial-level NRDC official, Hebei Province, May 2015

12 See City Yearbook of Ningbo 2010 (宁波 2010 年 城市年鉴), which states, "全年共淘汰产能...超过国家工业和信息化部和省政府下达的淘汰任务."

13 *Ibid.*

14 Interview X2110815a with provincial EPB official, Hebei Province (August 2015).

15 Interview X4090116a with provincial EPB official, Province X (January 2016).

16 Interview X6210116 with city-level EPB official, Guangdong Province (January 2016).

17 This includes all prefectural cities, but does not include the four province-level cities (直辖市) of Beijing, Tianjin, Shanghai, and Chongqing.

18 https://disc.gsfc.nasa.gov/datasets/OMSO2e_003/summary?keywords=omi%20so2.

19 Raw data obtained from the MIIT.

20 These variables are not included in the main model, because data is missing in several cities where significant blunt force regulation took place.

21 CCTV 2016.

22 *Economic Daily* 2014.

CHAPTER 6

WHAT ARE THE ALTERNATIVES?

On August 3, 1996, the State Council (China's highest ruling body) announced that 15 categories of small polluting enterprises – or the "Fifteen Smalls" (十五小) – would have to be closed by September 30, 1996.[1] Within 2 months, local governments had shuttered 60,000 small polluting enterprises across China. Only two provinces (Guizhou and Yunnan) were granted an extension, on account of being so poor that they would not be able to survive a sudden shock to their industrial base.

The State Council had already banned production in the Fifteen Smalls back in 1984 (van Rooij 2002, 20). What ensued was 12 years of foot dragging, complaints of inadequate resources, bickering between government departments, followed by a sudden, violent, and highly coordinated shutdown in 1996 (van Rooij 2002, 18–19).

In 2015, nearly 20 years later, I sat in the ascetic offices of a county environmental enforcement team in Hebei province. The team leader – an intelligent, thoughtful man – sat before me, rapidly reciting facts and figures about Hebei's past and future environmental challenges. He had just attended a government-organized training conference and was eager to share his newly acquired knowledge on the province's strategy for its war on pollution.

"But what role does your team play in addressing these challenges?" I asked.

"Our focus is on cleaning up the Fifteen Smalls," he responded, the same Fifteen Smalls that the government had banned back in 1984.

He then explained how cash shortages and inter-agency coordination problems had made it very difficult to regulate these small polluters.

Scholars of China's environmental politics are sometimes struck by a sense of déjà vu. Why does the state ban industries, only to get caught up in banning them again? Why do they launch campaigns to destroy industries, only to find the same campaign roll around a few years later? And why does nothing seem to stick? Why, a mere few years after a nationwide blunt force campaign, was steel production rebounding and pollution on the rise,[2] even in the midst of major economic disruptions (Almond et al. 2021)? In short, why has blunt force regulation become such a regular fixture in China's enforcement repertoire?

Evidence from earlier chapters suggests that the state repeatedly uses blunt force regulation because it is effective in overcoming bureaucratic noncompliance; the only way the state can make sure Hebei County's officers clean up the Fifteen Smalls is to order them to close them all down. And the only way to make sure they are all closed is to narrow the window of enforcement, making it easier for higher-level officials to verify compliance with short-term enforcement targets.

But is blunt force regulation the only solution to bureaucratic non-compliance? Is a more measured response possible? In this chapter I assess the alternatives to blunt force regulation. I show that there is a potential alternative in the form of bottom-up enforcement – also known as "informal" (Blackman 2009, "pluralistic" (van Rooij, Stern and Furst 2016), or "community-driven" regulation (O'Rourke 2004). This is an approach to regulation that engages the supervisory powers of non-state actors (such as NGOs, activists, consumers, and market actors), using pressure from civil society to supplement the state's inadequate enforcement powers. Moreover, it is an approach that the central government has been building towards for decades.

Yet the leadership shows a persistent ambivalence to bottom-up enforcement. On the one hand the central government promotes it, advancing multiple channels for citizen reporting, which China's environmentally aware population does make use of. On the other hand, the state also constrains participation from civil society. They limit media reporting, discourage public activism, and narrow the options for legal recourse, curbing the utility of bottom-up activism. What explains the leadership's ambivalence?

Through a "most likely" case of bottom-up enforcement, I show that this ambivalence is tied to the regime's insistence on preserving political discretion. Leaders engage with citizens when it is in their interests, but then dismiss citizens' contributions when it comes into conflict with other state interests.

Some argue that prioritizing political discretion is an indelible feature of Chinese governance, and a hallmark of their "adaptive governance" model (Heilmann and Perry, 2011a). The regime prefers to maintain discretion because it allows them to stay flexible, respond to crisis, and protect special interests. In other words, it allows them to govern loosely by the rules. Viewed through this lens, blunt force regulation is a deliberate fixture of Chinese governance. Despite the risks of corruption or the tendency towards short-term solutions, leaders find that addressing problems through ad hoc, extralegal campaigns is still the most preferable way to govern.

In this chapter, I show that the regime's ambivalence to bottom-up enforcement also stems from an authoritarian dilemma: Regime leaders want the information-gathering powers offered by citizen engagement. They want the threat of protest to scare local officials into action. But they also want to direct and control these powers of civil society, leveraging them when they coincide with leaders' interests, but constraining them when they threaten important political allegiances. Moreover, as I show in this case, citizens are not unaware of the state's discretionary response to their claims. They can spot sudden changes in local authorities' behavior and do suspect that political interests no longer align with their case. This may provoke protestors to escalate confrontation or to give up the hope of bottom-up enforcement. Thus, this case suggests that the Chinese leadership may find it difficult to maintain the political discretion that undergirds adaptive governance while also building up the surveillance powers of civil society. This may be why it persists with the suboptimal solution of blunt force regulation, despite recognizing the value of bottom-up enforcement.

6.1 BOTTOM-UP ENFORCEMENT: AN ALTERNATIVE TO BLUNT FORCE REGULATION

China is not alone in its environmental enforcement problems. Across the world, leaders struggle to recognize when bureaucrats are shirking orders or which polluters should be targeted for punishment. However, instead of defaulting to blunt force regulation, several governments recognize the power of using civil society groups to monitor polluters.

This bottom-up approach can be more efficient, especially when governments lack the resources to obtain accurate, on-the-ground information. This is because citizens, who are at the frontlines of policy implementation, will always have more information than central leaders on the everyday performance of local bureaucrats, especially in large states with complex bureaucracies (Bardhan and Mookherjee 2006; Faguet 2012, 2014; Weingast 2014). Thus, citizens can act as "fire alarms" (McCubbins and Schwartz 1984) alerting interested authorities to major instances of noncompliance or providing information on compliance when government monitoring falls short (Chng 2012; Hochstetler 2013).

Moreover, when the state lacks the authority to challenge powerful firms, they can sometimes leverage the disruptive power of NGOs or citizen activists to put direct pressure on polluters, thereby supplementing the state's enforcement power (Bell and Narain 2005; Dubash and Morgan 2013; Kagan et al. 2003; Gunningham et al. 2004). In Vietnam, for instance, central officials turned to local communities who, through their ability to recruit NGO and media support, were able to force powerful state-owned factories to invest in pollution abatement technology (O'Rourke 2004, 59–68, 215). Similarly, in Indonesia, the government encouraged citizens to report complaints or file lawsuits against noncompliers, using the threat of citizen-driven disruption to deter persistent violators (García et al. 2007; Pargal and Wheeler 1996). In other words, when formal mechanisms for regulatory inspections and sanctions fall short, governments rely on citizen activists to create an added layer of accountability.

Bottom-up enforcement can be adversarial and chaotic; civil society actors tend to raise the alert or punish violations arbitrarily, focusing on visible, tangible, or superficial issues – such as smells, or fear of unspecified "radiation" – at the expense of more serious but invisible risks (Auyero and Swistun 2009, 109–18; Gunningham et al. 2004, 318). However, bottom-up activism can also evolve into a more stable cooperation between the local state and civil society, leading to more consistent regulation. For instance, Amengual (2013, 2016) documents a case from Argentina where agro-businesses, tiring of an uncertain regulatory environment, decided to open up their operations to close scrutiny by regulators in exchange for technical support and advice. In return, regulators agreed to protect businesses from adversarial lawsuits and tolerate some degree of noncompliance, so long as businesses made a consistent effort to improve their infrastructure.

Participation from civil society is the lynchpin in this process, because without continued scrutiny from activist groups, state-business partnerships can quickly descend into old patterns of corruption and cronyism. However, if the regulators, companies, and civil society actors all play their roles with equal parts persistence and forbearance, this "co-produced," bottom-up enforcement can engender long-term improvements in enforcement outcomes (Amengual 2016, 8).

Bottom-up enforcement has three advantages over blunt force regulation. First, enforcement occurs within the law. Governments drive polluters and bureaucrats into compliance by getting civil society to hold them accountable to written rules, not by overriding regulatory norms. Thus, while this process does not require a strong state or strong institutions to be effective, it can slowly build towards stronger enforcement institutions.

Second, bottom-up enforcement is less costly overall. It reduces demands on the state's administrative capacity by outsourcing the cost of monitoring regulators and polluters to society (McCubbins and Schwartz 1984; Weingast 1984). It also mitigates the cost on the economy because it works through conventional regulation, encouraging regulators to internalize norms and getting polluters to self-regulate instead of shutting them down completely (Braithwaite 2006; Gunningham et al. 2004; Vogel 2005).

Third, bottom-up enforcement builds what Mann (1984, 6) calls "collective power" – that is, the power of groups to solve coordination problems and deliver collective benefits. Frequent engagement between citizens and local officials – of the type produced by bottom-up enforcement – helps to build this collective power, because it develops pathways for problem solving and a greater sense of accountability. In a study of cities in the global south, for example, Heller (2017) shows that in cities with a fragmented society, where businesses, lobbyists, and community groups distrust and act against each other, attempts to improve infrastructure and urban planning fail, even if central leaders are wholly committed to improving outcomes. In contrast, in societies where citizens have become accustomed to negotiating directly with city officials, cities are able to solve environmental and urban governance problems, despite a legacy of weak administrative and enforcement capacity.

In sum, like blunt force regulation, bottom-up enforcement enables governments to overcome bureaucratic noncompliance and improve regulatory outcomes. However, unlike blunt force regulation, bottom-up approaches are institution building, and are more likely to guarantee sustainable results at lower cost to society and to the economy.

To be sure, bottom-up enforcement also asks a lot from civil society (as I explain in Chapter 5). Sometimes local communities do not have the knowledge, will, or energy to act as fire alarms for pro-environment politicians. Yet the persistence of environmental protest in China, even in adversarial circumstances (Johnson et al. 2018; Li 2019; Lora-Wainwright et al. 2012), suggests that there is an energy for bottom-up enforcement to be harnessed in China.

6.2 BOTTOM-UP ENFORCEMENT IN CHINA

As an authoritarian state, China is not an obvious candidate for bottom-up enforcement. Autocracies are wary of direct public engagement because information sharing by citizens, if uncensored, could lead to a widespread recognition of collective complaints, while frequent protests could transform into broader collective action – both threatening scenarios for single-party states.

However, in addition to its cost-saving and institution-building advantages, bottom-up enforcement offers two unique advantages to autocracies. First, it solves some basic information problems. In autocracies, censorship and constraints on political freedoms limit leaders' access to accurate, on-the-ground knowledge, making it harder for them to know where pockets of noncompliance are emerging (Huang 2018; Manion 2016; Magaloni 2006; Wallace 2016). In contrast, citizens have abundant information on local misdeeds, but without a free press or frequent elections, they lack channels to share this information with central rulers. Corrupt local bureaucrats take advantage of these information barriers, leading to a phenomenon known as "local protectionism" in China (Edin 2003; Hillman 2010; Ong 2012b).

Bottom-up enforcement breaks through these barriers. By openly sanctioning citizen participation, and by providing citizens with channels to share their knowledge upwards, leaders find ways to access information normally buried from sight (Chen 2012; Lorentzen 2014; King, Pan, and Roberts 2013).

Second, bottom-up surveillance adds a layer of unpredictability to enforcement. Typically, conventional regulation follows predictable patterns, and is enacted through fixed relationships. Local polluters know which agencies are responsible for enforcement and when inspectors will visit – which makes it easier for them to bribe bureaucrats or game the system to evade sanctions. This adds to the problem of credible punishment in autocracies.

In contrast, bottom-up enforcement is a lot more unpredictable because it is not timed according to the state's preferences, nor limited to certain issue areas (Dasgupta 2000; Gunningham et al. 2004, 325; McCubbins and Schwartz 1984, 172; Silbey 1984). Polluters never know when citizens will protest, or when protests will escalate and reach the attention of higher levels (Snow et al. 2006; Blecher 2002; Holzner 2004; Michelson 2007; van Rooij 2010). When citizens have been galvanized into outright confrontation, it is also a lot harder to silence them through bribes or payments (O'Brien and Li 2006; Michelson 2008; Cai 2010). This unpredictability creates stronger incentives for bureaucrats to self-police and for polluters to self-regulate.

The central government recognizes the unique advantages of bottom-up enforcement. In the past decade, Beijing has increasingly opened channels for direct citizen reporting through social media (Wang, Paul, and Dredze 2015), digital environmental monitoring (Schlæger and Zhou 2019), environmental hotlines, traditional letters, and office visits (Wang 2018), and even protests (Chen 2012; Li 2019). Citizens are also encouraged to participate in deliberative forums, such as forums discussing environmental permits for new industrial projects. In theory, these forums allow citizens to express views autonomously, providing the government a barometer on true public opinion (He and Warren 2011).

These channels are more than just mere window dressing. Studies show that citizen participation is genuine, and their input does influence government decision-making (Meng et al. 2017; Mertha 2009; Teets 2014) or prompt changes in policy implementation (Distelhorst and Hou 2017). The government has also begun to share information downward with citizens through its transparency and open government initiatives (OGI). Citizens are called on to use this information to identify noncompliant actors (Seligsohn, Liu, and Zhang 2018; Tan 2014), or seek out third parties to enforce regulation against violators (Wang 2018).

And yet, the state continues to show ambivalence to bottom-up enforcement (Kostka and Mol 2013; Stern 2013; van Rooij et al. 2016). On the one hand, citizens *do* use these channels to expose noncompliant polluters and local officials *do* take advantage of these measures (Hesengerth and Lu 2019; Johnson 2016; Wang 2016). For instance, as one municipal environmental official explained to me, companies in his city have found that they need to address their "public relations" problems and make sure "local residents approve before they can expand their factories." He argued, "This is why even those small, poor polluting firms might be willing to invest money in pollution reduction! They are scared of local residents protesting."[3]

On the other hand, the leadership frequently interferes in these measures, rolling back reforms just as citizen participation begins to gain ground (Minzner 2015). Citizens who use these channels find that they stumble into hidden roadblocks, where valid lawsuits are summarily dismissed, and pollution complaints are acknowledged but then disappear within the black box of bureaucratic decision-making.[4]

From where does this ambivalence come? How does it affect the prospects for bottom-up environmental enforcement in China? To examine possible consequences of this ambivalence, I turn to a place I will call "District X," where I watched a case of bottom-up enforcement unfold. This case was distinctive because it involved a high degree of cooperation between state and civil society. Moreover, both sides eschewed adversarial confrontation, with both protestors and government officials exhibiting the persistence and restraint that makes co-produced, bottom-up enforcement successful. In the following sections, I piece together the reactions of residents, protest leaders, and government officials as the protest unfolded. Through exposing the views of different stakeholders, I examine how the state's insistence on maintaining political discretion alters the mechanisms that give civil society its enforcement power.

6.3 BOTTOM-UP ENFORCEMENT AND THE CASE OF DISTRICT X

Pollution protests in District X began in late 2015, when homeowners from a suburban district on the outskirts of a wealthy Chinese city noticed a noxious smell permeating their residential complex at night. They suspected a group of factories – located adjacent to the complex – as the source of the smell and organized an online community of 1,000 homeowners to put pressure on local officials to clean up this smell. In the ensuing weeks, they sent 500 complaints to the district-level Environmental Protection Bureau (EPB) and hung multistory banners from their balconies with slogans like "protest illegal pollution!" or "sly companies polluting secretly!" These efforts won the attention of the local media, with both print and television media broadcasting stories on the homeowner's fight against polluters.

In many respects, this is a case where bottom-up enforcement should have been a success (also known as a "most likely" case). In recent years, luxury developments had sprung up around District X, attracting a young and upwardly mobile middle class. The success of these developments, and the rapid transformation of the district into a pleasant suburban neighborhood, had displaced the district government's dependence on local industries for revenue. This made them more accommodating towards environmental protection measures. District X was also located in a satellite district of a large city, where the city government had shown a clear commitment to environmental protection, and where environmental agencies were well resourced and supported by local law enforcement agencies.

The protestors themselves – which included lawyers, professionals, and university professors – were also unusually well connected, and able to draw on their expertise and elite networks to advance their cause: For instance, one protestor who inspected factories for a living was able to use his skills to test local factory emissions. Protestors also included a number of academics, who used their connections to arrange dialogue sessions with provincial officials.

Finally, the attitude of protestors and local officials made this an ideal case for cooperative enforcement between state and civil society. Rather than acting in an adversarial manner through street protests, citizens were willing to engage local officials to find peaceful administrative solutions to their concerns. Meanwhile, local officials were sympathetic to the protestors' cause, and were themselves frustrated with local polluters. As one district official I interviewed told me:

> I've gone to the homeowners' residences; I've experienced the smell they are describing. The problem does exist... The homeowners are unhappy because the problem has not been completely fixed, and we can understand why they feel that way.[5]

Initially, both state and civil society approached the case with a highly cooperative attitude. District environmental officials launched a flurry of inspections against local polluters, surprising factories with sudden emissions testing. They even invited a group of homeowners along on their nighttime inspections to demonstrate the steps that were being taken. When interviewed in early 2016, a number of homeowners agreed that as a result of these actions, "the pollution has improved."[6] One homeowner said that if she called the EPB late at night, the chemical smell would stop almost immediately after her call. As a result, she believed the district EPB officials "did care a lot about the homeowners, and were doing everything they could to fix the problem."[7] As the district EPB official told me "The factories are aware of homeowners complaints so they don't dare to pollute so much anymore."[8]

However, while the district EPB was relatively successful at regulating small firms in response to pollution protests, they openly admitted that they could do nothing to address the pollution caused by larger firms. In an inspection report submitted to homeowners in December 2015, district officials concluded that the "irritating chemical smell" was caused by a local chemical factory, but the "coal smoke smell" was from "outside sources," namely, large factories from industrial districts in the city across the river. In fact, the report concluded that the pollution experienced in District X was caused primarily by "outside sources."[9]

Homeowners had long suspected that industrial site A – a major industrial site across the river – was responsible for the strong coal smoke smell, because these factories began operating at around the time that homeowners started noticing this smell.[10] After receiving the district's inspection report in December, homeowners considered directing complaints to the EPBs responsible for industrial site A. However, the district EPB refused to provide any further information on whether industrial site A was involved in the case. Nor did they provide any updates on what was being done to address "outside sources" other than "continued inspections." Without this evidence, homeowners were unable to push their case further through formal channels.

Around this time, a number of homeowners decided to use their elite connections to organize a dialogue session with provincial environmental officials. During the meeting, one protest leader, frustrated at the failure of formal complaint channels, asked the provincial EPB official for some "tips or tricks on how to proceed with this case against outside sources of pollution, because we don't want to resort to open unrest." He further pressed the provincial official, demanding to know why the district EPB would not share evidence on polluting firms when the law required them to do so. The provincial EPB official responded, "To be honest, if you've taken all these actions, gotten the city EPB to spend all these person hours on inspections, and they still won't share the information, then it is likely that government leaders have some bigger economic interests involved."[11]

Note that throughout this process, homeowners acted with restraint. They focused their campaign on gathering evidence and using formal, administrative channels to put pressure on polluters. They refrained from open unrest, choosing instead to file petitions, seek dialogue, and assist regulators in gathering evidence so that they would have a strong case against polluters. Only the banners hung from apartments signaled a latent threat; homeowners told me that they did this to alert potential homebuyers to the pollution problems, hoping that this threat to real estate sales might corner developers into putting pressure on local officials. Yet they were also willing to take down the banners when asked by the local government. In sum, each of these actions signaled a commitment to cooperate with officials, not to challenge them in a way that could threaten their position.

But as homeowners encountered more and more roadblocks, cooperation began to break down. In response to stonewalling from the district EPB, the homeowners' unity against the state began to erode. One group believed that the EPB truly was continuing to pursue the case against industrial site A. The other group started to suspect that the EPB was deliberately misleading them. For instance, one homeowner (who had been in close dialogue with district officials throughout the event) argued that the EPB's actions had been mere window dressing, resulting in superficial changes that would not last in the long term. He said:

> It is easy for the EPB to take strong action now because they are treating it like a case of accidental pollution, an unexpected occurrence, so they can concentrate all their resources into punishing a few small firms. In reality this pollution is caused by many firms, maybe hundreds of firms. If we stop protesting now, would the EPB decide to force three hundred firms to stop polluting or to change their equipment just because a new law says so? I don't think so![12]

Some homeowners agreed that if the situation didn't improve, they would "go for a walk" (a euphemism in China for street protests). One protest leader even said:

> Our case is not being resolved because there is no social unrest. Leaders only care if there is social unrest, that's what we learned from meeting with them. Right now, we're using a lawful approach and if things improve, we'll proceed in a cooperative manner. But if things don't improve, we might consider more extreme measures.[13]

6.4   DISCRETION AND BOTTOM-UP ENFORCEMENT

How did a "most likely" case of bottom-up enforcement unravel so quickly? Why was the initial high level of cooperation not able to bring about enforcement measures against the large firms suspected of causing a coal smoke smell? And why did highly cooperative state-society relations suddenly descend into distrust and threats of street protest?

One interpretation is that China's notoriously fragmented bureaucracy made it difficult for the district EPB to investigate pollution from industrial site A, even when under pressure from local residents. Scholars have documented how overlapping responsibilities between different government bureaus and different levels of government can turn a simple enforcement issue into an extended, intractable bureaucratic process (Lieberthal and Lampton 1992; Mertha 2005; Ran and Han 2014). Moreover, local regulatory authorities (such as the local EPB) need approval from city leaders or higher-level authorities before they can force factories to stop production. However, as described in more detail in Chapter 3, city leaders are often pulled in two directions, finding that they also need to please the powerful business owners that are responsible for pollution violations.

However, in the case of District X, the district EPB official told me that the local police were assisting them in their investigation, which helped them overcome jurisdictional or enforcement limitations when investigating and sanctioning polluters. Note also that protestors were able to reach out to and address provincial officials directly, speaking not just to environmental officials but also representatives from the powerful discipline inspection committee (纪委) and national land and resources agency (国土资源). This indicates that there *was* a degree of interagency cooperation in response to the issue. Finally, by agreeing to engage in a dialogue session with homeowners, provincial officials provided a tacit public recognition of the problem, which should have made it easier for district officials to do their job. District officials could no longer complain that they didn't have approval from higher levels, because higher levels knew of the case. These details suggest that bureaucratic fragmentation was not an overwhelming obstacle to sanctioning polluters in District X.

Indeed, the actions of District X's EPB officials have a hint of the "performative governance" that Ding (2020) documents from her first-hand insights on how city or county EPBs respond to citizen complaints. In cases of performative governance, local regulators will engage in busy work, designed to assure protestors that they are responding. This might take the form of inviting homeowners along on nighttime inspections or holding dialogue sessions with protest leaders – just as we see in the case of District X. Ding argues that when local agencies have low substantive capacity but are dealing with a high visibility issue (such as pollution protests), they will engage in a flurry of busy work to distract citizens from the fact that local regulators cannot – or will not – take substantive actions against polluters (such as shutting down a factory).

Consider also the revealing exchange, where a provincial official suggested that the District EPB was stonewalling because "there are higher-level interests involved." His words suggest that when regulators fail to punish large polluters, it is not simply a matter of fragmented authority, or weak control over polluting firms. In fact, it may be a deliberate decision by local authorities to collude with or protect certain firms. In the case of District X, for example, city and provincial regulators were aware of the pollution problems. Not only did the district EPB report the case to them, but citizen activists also informed provincial officials directly of this case.

If city or provincial officials had truly intended to take action against the large firms responsible, they could have drawn on public pressure from homeowners to coerce the firms into compliance. Alternately, if industrial site A was acting within the law, the state could have allowed homeowners to pursue their case against industrial site A through formal channels, using administrative procedures, backed by conclusive evidence, to demonstrate why the homeowners' case did not hold water. My interviews suggest that a more transparent process could have appeased some of the more radical homeowners in the group. Instead, government agencies chose to withhold information from activists, denying them the scientific evidence and legal means to put pressure on large firms, and refusing to explain why the case was not allowed to go further.

However, regulators did respond to the homeowners' complaints against small local firms. Moreover, in the following year (nearly two years after the protests started) they did prosecute cases against these factories. This suggests that higher-level decision-makers will take advantage of grassroots pressure to police smaller polluters where fewer political interests are at stake. However, higher-level officials (at the province and above) also have a strong interest in limiting the impact of citizen activism to frontline regulators, such as the district EPB.

For higher-level officials, confining the impact of bottom-up pressure to frontline regulators has two advantages. First, regulatory action in response to citizen pressure will be limited to small firms that are unlikely to involve "bigger economic interests." This is because frontline regulators seldom have the administrative authority to punish larger firms (Leng 2020). Second, regulators can buy time and possibly force protestors into frustrated inaction under the guise of coordinating with higher-level environmental agencies, even while refusing to let protestors engage directly with responsible agencies (Auyero and Swistun 2009; Lora-Wainwright et al. 2012; Lora-Wainwright 2021).

In sum, the state's approach to bottom-up enforcement in District X demonstrates a logic of selective enforcement: They take advantage of the information citizens provide when it is in the state's interests, or when the impact is small, but control or suppress that power when the impact is threatening or large. This pattern suggests that the state likes to maintain discretion over how and how far public input will be used in the enforcement process. Moreover, it is this insistence on selective enforcement – based on the political or economic value of a firm – that causes cooperation between state and civil society to unravel.

6.5 WHY SELECTIVE ENFORCEMENT BACKFIRES

Why does selective enforcement cause cooperation to unravel? Recall the two reasons why China turns to bottom-up enforcement: First, it provides channels for citizens to break local information barriers, easing authoritarian information problems. Second, it adds a layer of unpredictability to enforcement, scaring polluters into a minimal level of compliance. However, the state's insistence on maintaining discretionary powers ends up curbing both these functions of citizen-led enforcement.

Consider again the events that unfolded in District X. In the beginning, local regulators solicited, even welcomed, the information that homeowners shared on small, local polluters and supported their efforts to monitor polluter behavior. But once homeowners' actions targeted higher-level firms, the state obstructed their efforts, preventing them from pursuing further action through the courts or the formal complaints system. In effect, the state reduced participation to a mere transmission belt, where citizens provide information but play no part in how this information is used. This led to frustration amongst protestors.

Frustrated protestors tend to respond in two ways: They either acquiesce, or they escalate (Michelson 2008). Acquiescence is problematic for the regime because they lose the citizens who are willing to act as fire alarms, exacerbating the leadership's information-gathering problems. But escalation is also problematic because it threatens to spill over into other issues areas, or to garner support from other sectors of society. Moreover, as Li (2019, 18–19) has argued, local authorities' incompetent handling of protestors can be the trigger for a sudden escalation from cooperative to antagonistic protest events. Escalation is not just a function of protestors' individual preferences.

Second, citizen activists can be leveraged as a powerful enforcement tool because their actions are unpredictable, and therefore less easily preempted by noncompliant polluters and bureaucrats. However, when the state uses their discretion to stonewall activists, they send a signal to polluters that the written rules of regulation do not apply. Even if polluters are clearly violating standards, or facing open challenges from society, so long as they can find higher-level officials to protect them, they can evade enforcement measures. In other words, discretionary enforcement undermines the credible threat of monitoring and punishment from society.

In the case of District X, for example, by protecting industrial site A from homeowners' further scrutiny, the state signaled to large polluters that they could evade enforcement pressure, even if the homeowners escalated their investigations. In the following Chapter 7, I show this happens on a broader scale in China; the state disproportionately protects politically connected firms from blunt force regulation, even if these firms are major polluters. This is supported by wider scholarly evidence of higher environmental noncompliance among large or politically connected firms (Eaton and Kostka 2017; Karplus et al. 2020; Lorentzen et al. 2014).

Of course, citizens retain their threat of protest, even if the state truncates their formal enforcement powers, and protests always create a high level of unpredictability. In the case of District X, homeowners stated openly to provincial officials that they might still resort to street demonstration to push higher-level officials to investigate industrial site A. However, once the situation escalated to the point of protests, homeowners (who had, until then, been united in their action) began to turn on each other. The regime's record of silencing street protest raised the costs of public unrest, dissuading the less-risk-taking actors.

The problematic dynamics of bottom-up enforcement in District X can be seen on a broader scale in the outcome of China's 2016–2017 central pollution inspections campaign. This campaign – where thousands of central inspectors were sent to every province and city in China to investigate and punish pollution violations – was designed, once and for all, to scare polluters into respecting China's war on pollution. To strengthen the threat of discovery, Beijing encouraged citizens to phone in suspected pollution violations to local hotlines. Central inspectors would then use this information to guide their inspections and assess where public concerns were most acute. It was, in effect, a nationwide experiment in bottom-up enforcement. Moreover, because it was undertaken in a campaign style where each region had to meet specific enforcement targets, officials had strong reason to respond quickly to citizen input and demonstrate their enforcement successes to Beijing.

Yet, as I show in a related study (see van der Kamp 2021), the pollution inspections campaign had no discernable impact on air pollution levels. Twenty-five thousand enterprises were fined a total of 1.24 billion RMB, 16,500 officials were disciplined, and 1,400 people were prosecuted.[14] However, there was no statistically significant change in pollution levels,[15] even 6 months after the campaign (Karplus and Wu 2019).

A closer look at the mechanics of this campaign reveals that yet again, citizen input was engaged in a highly supervised manner. Citizens could phone in violators at will and could check public documents to see the status of their complaints, but the regime controlled the agenda, timing, and scope of participation. Follow-ups on complaints were confined to the bureaucratic apparatus, and the officials tasked with rectifying enforcement failures were part of the very same local government bureaucracies that had allowed these problems to fester in the first place.[16]

In short, these cases suggest that the regime's emphasis on preserving discretionary powers, and its insistence on controlling citizen input, ends up taking away citizens' power of unpredictability, weakening the threat of citizen action. It also erodes trust between citizens and the state, undermining channels for bottom-up information sharing in the future.

The regime's ambivalence towards bottom-up enforcement raises some important questions: Why is it so important to preserve political discretion, even when it undermines key policy goals – such as using the public to gain more information? More broadly, why do leaders curtail the very aspects of bottom-up enforcement that could solve their information and enforcement problems?

6.6   THE AUTHORITARIAN DILEMMA

For autocracies, bottom-up enforcement improves information flows, but it also introduces new risks. To break the local information barrier, leaders need citizens to raise the alert publicly – through the media, protests, or online forums – otherwise local officials can censor, hide, or distort complaints to prevent exposure (Lorentzen 2014; Truex 2014; Wallace 2016). However, once citizens are allowed to share information publicly, the risk of collective action increases. Complaints can expose shared grievances, prompting citizens to recognize that local problems and local scapegoats stem from *central* government policies (O'Brien and Li 2006). Alternately, citizens may use information sharing to connect and coordinate across the country, raising the risk of protests (King, Pan, and Roberts 2013). Large-scale collective action is more threatening to authoritarian leaders because – unlike their democratic counterparts – they cannot use elections or leadership turnover to appease public demands for government accountability (Huntington 1991; Nathan 2003; Haber 2006; Gandhi and Przeworksi 2006).

Second, unlike blunt force regulation, bottom-up enforcement operates through the conventional regulatory system – where citizens hold polluters and bureaucrats accountable to written rules. For this to be effective, citizens must see that rules are enforced, and that the state will punish noncompliers, otherwise channels for upward information sharing begin to seem like a farce.

However authoritarian leaders are wary of clarifying or adhering closely to written rules, because this will limit their discretionary powers. As O'Brien and Li (2006) show in the case of rural tax reform in the 1990s, central leaders would avoid spelling out laws or making specific policy commitments, because citizens could point to the gaps between what the laws promise and what is actually implemented to hold leaders accountable. Likewise, in the case of pollution regulation now, if leaders accept that citizens can use written rules to sue violators or subject government agencies to administrative action, they must also accept that all violators – including political cronies or powerful polluters – are held accountable to these rules.

China's leaders may tolerate holding polluters accountable to the law, as we see in their determination to pass stricter environmental laws and enforcement measures. However, given the collusion that we see in pollution regulation in China, exposing polluters to the law also means exposing party cadres to the law, and to bottom-up accountability. And Chinese leaders are wary of instituting bottom-up accountability mechanisms for cadres within the bureaucracy, because this constrains their bandwidth for protecting allies or pursuing a more flexible approach to policy implementation (Birney 2014; Cai 2014; Heilmann and Perry 2011b).

This retreat from rule of law and this tendency towards more discretionary top-down control has been amplified in the Xi Jinping era, as the regime moves to centralize enforcement powers. Consider, for instance, the central government's approach to the much-vaunted public interest litigation clause in its new environmental law. In 2017, one brave NGO decided to test the limits of the public interest litigation by filing a case against a local EPB in Yunnan Province. It accused the EPB of negligence in implementing environmental impact assessments, filing a lawsuit to that effect.[17] Their suit was rejected, and shortly after, Beijing introduced an amendment to the environmental law, clarifying that civil society actors would not be allowed to target environmental violations by government departments.[18] Only people's procuratorates (a state organ for legal supervision) were allowed to file lawsuits against administrative bodies.

The regime's retreat from bottom-up enforcement can also be seen in the passing of a new NGO law in 2018 which effectively eliminated foreign NGOs in China,[19] or with its crackdown rights protections lawyers and woman's rights activists.[20] A similar ambivalence is reflected in the governments' stance towards NGOs (Teets 2014), the media (Repnikova 2017; Stockmann 2013), protestors (Lorentzen 2014), and the legal system (Hendley 2015); the state offers judicial fairness in the commercial sphere, but maintains judicial discretion in the political realm to protect state officials from direct scrutiny (Hendley 2015; Hurst 2016; Wang 2015; Stern 2017).

In other words, in authoritarian contexts, bottom-up enforcement – and the institutions that support it – can act as a double-edged sword. Leaders gain information on the inner working of their government, but also risk undermining the regime's legitimacy, and their own room to maneuver. This makes them reluctant to govern according to written rules.

Note that blunt force regulation operates by an entirely different logic, of governing loosely by the rules, or sometimes even governing *outside* the rules through extralegal measures. This logic stems from an approach to bureaucratic governance in China – known as "adaptive governance" (Heilmann and Perry 2011a) – which extends back to the imperial times. Adaptive governance is characterized by a lack of clear rules or formal dictates to direct state action. Instead, leaders issue nebulous orders to bureaucrats and implement policies on an ad hoc basis, depending on the priorities of the times (Strauss 2006, 2009; Mei and Pearson 2014). Absent the need to live up to written rules and contracted obligations, the state can adapt quickly to new challenges and respond flexibly in times of crises – hence the name adaptive governance (Heilmann and Melton 2013, 34–5; Strauss 2009, 1178). Past examples of adaptive governance include the Chinese Communist Party's use of mass campaigns, such as efforts to alleviate agricultural or environmental disasters (Shapiro 2001). Leaders ratchet up revolutionary appeals to mobilize subjects and state officials to engage in one brief but transformative policy implementation effort. Governing loosely by the rules also maximizes the regime's opportunities to exercise political discretion.

Of course, prioritizing discretion has its drawbacks. Discretion enables higher levels of corruption (Birney 2014), while ad hoc solutions to policy problems can lead to severe unintended consequences (Wang and Minzner 2015, 347–8) – as we see in the case of blunt force pollution regulation. However, adaptive governance offers one key advantage: it provides the leadership with a method for delivering important policy outcomes while still evading constraints on their decision-making powers. In fact, some scholars argue that China's leaders are so determined to maintain their political discretion and enforcement flexibility that they embrace the trade-offs; they will govern without clear rules, even if it undermines the mandate of local cadres, weakening bureaucrats' implementation power (Chan and Fan 2021; Mattingly 2020; Zhi and Pearson 2017, 411) or causing clumsy policy implementation (Zhou 2017).

Indeed, Li (2019) goes so far as to argue that popular contention will only be tolerated in China so long as both sides "play by the informal rules." Both authorities and protestors can recognize the legitimacy of each other's claims, but protestors must accept the primacy of political discretion and concede to resolving conflict through back channels. Informal engagement ensures that authorities can maintain the upper hand, using their discretion to address issues on a case-by-case basis without ever conceding to hard institutional constraints on their power. In contrast, when protestors push for more institutionalized responses to claims (such as through the courts), relations with the state quickly sour. This is because these formal challenges force author-ities to either concede the illegitimacy of their actions or resort to repressive measures in order to prevent further challenges to their discretionary powers.

If adaptive governance has become the regime's dominant govern-ance paradigm, then blunt force regulation will be here to stay, despite its suboptimal nature, and despite its failure to overcome bureaucratic noncompliance in the long term. It is not that bottom-up enforcement fails to offer a viable solution. It is that the authoritarian leadership's priorities also force them to truncate the powers of civil society actors, taking the wind out of their sails.

6.7 THE FUTURE OF BOTTOM-UP ENFORCEMENT

The state's ambivalence to citizen activism does not mean that the space for public engagement is closed, nor that effective courts and bottom-up surveillance mechanisms are precluded in China. Over decades, wily and experienced citizen activists have learned to exploit divisions within the state to advance broader social interests, even when it is not in the immediate interest of the government (Distlehorst 2017; O'Brien and Li 2006). In some issue areas, these "policy entrepreneurs" can bring about unexpected reversals in govern-ment policymaking (Mertha 2009).

Social movement scholars argue that activism is at its most powerful when it is ad hoc and unpredictable, operating outside the controlled forums that the states provide (Kuran 1991; O'Donnell et al. 1986; Tarrow 2011). We see this knowledge reflected in the actions of China's grassroots activists. Civil society actors are learning to sidestep the state and use market forces to confront polluters directly. For instance, NGOs target brand-sensitive companies, using information disclosed by the central government to shame these companies into cleaning up production (Haddad 2015).

Even in the case of District X, where homeowners made an effort to cooperate, to not ruffle feathers, and to act through the state-provided forums, they still knew how to wield their disruptive power. They used their elite connections to broker direct dialogue with provincial officials, circumventing the disclaimers of local officials. They even confronted higher-level officials directly with the threat of protest. In fact, so unusual was this kind of direct, higher-level negotiation that District X's EPB leader exclaimed, on hearing of this meeting from a homeowner, "But you have gone farther than I ever will!"[21]

My interviews revealed that these actions did throw local regulators off their guard, forcing them to act more aggressively against smaller polluters. As the district official told me: "We know the homeowners are not content, and think the situation hasn't been fixed. This is what gives us so much pressure."[22] The district EPB official also admitted that most of his actions to obtain proof and punish firms – including nighttime inspections and visiting more than fifty firms – was to show higher-level officials that they had done everything they could to address protestors complaints. This suggests that the local EPB's enforcement actions were more than mere performative governance. It also suggests that, unlike in some cases where protestors might be distracted by superficial responses from local officials, these protestors were not so easily hoodwinked or distracted; they could see the difference between performative appeasement and substantive change.

Indeed, this case received considerable attention when the central inspections team came to investigate the city during the 2016–2017 central pollution inspections campaign. Inspectors from Beijing went to visit the local factories in the county that were suspected of causing pollution, and several cases were submitted for formal investigation, including one case for criminal investigation by the police. In their report documents, central inspectors noted that channels for inter-jurisdictional cooperation would be needed to resolve the issue of the noxious smell coming from across the river. This seemed to provoke some response from the EPB responsible for industrial site A across the river. By the spring of 2017, District X's EPB reported that their colleagues across the river had identified the source of the nightly smell, naming two factories. These factories were ordered to install new waste processing infrastructure to reduce the noxious smell. Media reports from later in the year noted that some residents, when interviewed on the issue of pollution, agreed that the smell had gotten better that year. This ties in with patterns seen in cases around China where a pollution issue that drags on for years is suddenly resolved in response to a combination of media coverage and central scrutiny (Tilt 2007, 929).

However, the power of disruption alone is not enough to sustain enforcement outcomes. In addition to disruption, protestors also need to build strong, cohesive communities that can attract outside allies (such as NGOs, the media, or sympathetic officials) and that can sustain bottom-up pressure against violators. Otherwise, citizens will struggle to counteract the collusion that allows polluters to go unpunished and fail to move beyond a mere information-gathering function to generate actual pressure for policy enforcement (O'Rourke 2004, 59–68). In the case of District X for instance, by 2021 (4 years after the central inspectors pushed for a resolution) local news reports filtered through of renewed talks between the provincial EPB and district residents to resolve the issue of cross-river pollution problems. Meanwhile, the government issued documents pledging to strengthen cross-jurisdictional information sharing on cross-river pollution issues that were continuing to irritate the residents of District X. This suggests that the regulatory responses and success of the spring of 2017 may have been short-lived.[23]

It remains to be seen, given the trade-offs the regime faces when using bottom-up enforcement, whether public engagement in environmental regulation will continue to evolve in such a contested manner. Can citizens create strong, cohesive enforcement communities if they are only allowed to share information sporadically, and in closely watched channels? Can they build up a watchdog role, seek higher-level allies, or scare bureaucrats into compliance when officials imbue enforcement with discretionary powers, cutting off attempts to act on evidence? And can state-provided channels for grassroots input move beyond a mere transmission belt function if leaders insist on maintaining discretionary powers, and using them to curtail bottom-up enforcement?

It also remains to be seen how political leaders, who have a lot at stake in China's pollution problems, will navigate their ambivalence towards public engagement, and the institutional solutions that can build collective power. As the rulers of a single-party state, China's leaders enjoy highly centralized authority, which enables them to skirt or override public attempts to seek formal accountability. It also allows them to protect important party members or allies from exposure. Will rulers with such absolute powers choose to make themselves and their allies accountable to social scrutiny, especially if they have been effective at governing without rules in the past? Will groups in society continue to distrust the regime's regulatory powers, and exacerbate regulatory uncertainty by confronting it? Or might the regime reverse its recent policies, reopen the space for public engagement and allow state–society interactions to evolve into a more lasting collective power?

6.8 CONCLUSION

Are there alternatives to blunt force regulation? Taking into account China's problems with bureaucratic control, is there a way to credibly threaten noncompliant bureaucrats and polluters without having to shut down entire sectors of the economy?

In this chapter, I argue that bottom-up enforcement could provide a viable alternative, particularly for environments where enforcement institutions are underdeveloped. When bureaucrats refrain from regulating through the law, the state can use citizens to sound the alarm, as they demonstrated on a vast scale in the central pollution inspections campaign of 2016–2017. Moreover, bottom-up enforcement is a solution that works within the rules. It buttresses the enforcement powers of conventional regulation, instead of undermining these powers through ad hoc, extralegal measures – which is the core problem of blunt force regulation.

Clearly, the Chinese leadership recognizes the advantages of bottom-up enforcement and has made a concerted effort to create the channels that could make it work. And yet, as I show through the case of District X, their wariness of specifying rules that could one day constrain their own authority, or of empowering civil society actors that could one day hold them accountable, has led to a persistent ambiguity towards bottom-up enforcement: Environmental laws are introduced and strengthened and enforcement agencies are empowered and funded, only to be subverted by highly politicized and selective enforcement. Meanwhile citizen activists work towards building co-produced enforcement with the local state, only to be stonewalled as their efforts gain ground. As a result, bottom-up solutions languish, pushing the regime back to costly, counterproductive, blunt force solutions.

Proponents of China's adaptive mode of governance may argue that the regime is willing to tolerate such costly solutions if it allows rules to stay fluid, and the regime adaptive. Moreover, the state's considerable leverage over businesses and labor – the two strongest potential opponents of blunt force regulation – facilitates the implementation of such a costly, coercive solution to ongoing pollution.

However, in the following chapter, I show that coercion is not a cost-free exercise, and the state only gets away with blunt force solutions by degrees. Through case studies of on-the-ground implementation of blunt force regulation, I show how entire industries are forcibly shuttered, but then business owners vote with their feet by investing in other provinces or countries. Powerful companies agree to shut down, but only after exhaustive diplomacy, negotiations, and promises for future concessions. Workers acquiesce but only because the worst damage is done to the most powerless groups in society. Moreover, empowered workers do protest, or demand compensation. And as the case of District X shows, citizens are aware of their disruptive powers and – despite the regime's threat of coercion – are willing to use them. Together, these social forces amplify the political risks of persistent blunt force regulation.

In sum, this chapter demonstrates that there are viable, workable alternatives to blunt force regulation – alternatives that the Chinese government believes in and invests in because it is less costly. But the authoritarian regime's combination of strengths (its coercive power) and weaknesses (its fear of independent constraints on the state powers) drives it back to blunt force regulation again and again.

NOTES

1 State Council, *Decision of the State Council on Several Issues Concerning Environmental Protection*, 1996, http://english.mee.gov.cn/Resources/Policies/policies/Frameworkp1/200710/t20071017_111494.shtml.
2 *China Dialogue*, "Is China returning to old, polluting habits?" December 26, 2018, https://chinadialogue.net/en/pollution/10995-2-18-is-china-returning-to-old-polluting-habits/.
3 Interview X6210116 with city-level environmental official (January 2016).
4 Interview X1110515 with environmental activist (May 2015). Interviews X1150115, X1100415b, X1100415c, X1100415d with environmental lawyers (July 2012, January 2015, April 2015).
5 Interview X4a270116b with district EPB official (January 2016).
6 Interviews X4a170116a, X4a170116b, X4a170116c with homeowners (January 2016).
7 Ibid.
8 Interview X4a270116b with district EPB official (January 2016).
9 District X Government, *Report on Outside Sources of Bad Smelling Pollution in District X*, December 2015.
10 *Environmental Governance in District X*. (Report produced by homeowners to present to district officials).
11 Interview X4090116a with provincial EPB official, Province X, January 2016.

12 Interviews X4a140116d, X4a170116a, X4a170116b, X4a170116c with homeowners (January 2016).

13 Ibid.

14 Data from Ministry of Environmental Protection public records.

15 The study uses a matching function to assess the impact of pollution inspections on changes in pollution levels.

16 *China Economic Weekly*, "The formidable power of the central pollution inspections: covering all 31 provinces in two years," November 7, 2017.

17 *China Dialogue*, "Yunnan chemical factory becomes testing ground for citizen lawsuits," August 23, 2017, https://chinadialogue.net/en/pollution/9983-yunnan-chemical-factory-becomes-testing-ground-for-citizen-lawsuits/.

18 Article 25 of China's modified Administrative Procedure Law.

19 *South China Morning Post*, "Why foreign NGOs are struggling with new Chinese law," June 13, 2017, www.scmp.com/news/china/policies-politics/article/2097923/why-foreign-ngos-are-struggling-new-chinese-law.

20 *New York Times*, "China targeting rights lawyers in a crackdown," July 22, 2015, www.nytimes.com/2015/07/23/world/asia/china-crackdown-human-rights-lawyers.html; Reuters, "Chinese police detain five women's rights activists," March 12, 2015, www.reuters.com/article/us-china-rights/chinese-police-detain-five-womens-rights-activists-idUSKBN0M819K2015031 2?feedType=RSS&feedName=worldNews.

21 Interview with homeowner (January 2016).

22 Interviews X4a270116a, X4a270116b with district EPB official (January 2016).

23 Details on the pollution inspection outcomes and later developments in District X were obtained from a combination of provincial, city, and county government documents as well as city and county news reports. Source details have been withheld to protect the anonymity of key stakeholders in this case.

CHAPTER 7

MANAGING THE RISKS

In the summer of 2015, I visited a stretch of highway that had once formed China's "cement corridor." Located in the northern industrial province of Hebei, the factories clustered in Pingshan and Luquan counties had been major producers of Hebei's cement industry for more than 50 years. Yet within a few short years, this once bustling industry was reduced from hundreds of factories to just two.

Once upon a time, these counties formed a prosperous industrial center, home to a plethora of large cement companies and smaller cement factories. Abutting the limestone quarries of the Taixing hills, these companies thrived on their proximity to raw materials, and to the once booming city of Shijiazhuang – the provincial capital of Hebei Province. Cement production brought prosperity and growth to the area, and revenue intake was so high that Pingshan and Luquan were frequently on Hebei's list of top-performing counties. By the early 2000s, however, the residents of Shijiazhuang were blaming the cement factories for the city's terrible air pollution.

The cement corridor's decline began in 2007, when approximately 90 small factories were forced to close in a first stage of restructuring. A second wave of closures took place in 2011 2012 (this wave targeted all factories operating cement mills of less than 3m in diameter). In 2013, as part of its Air Pollution Prevention and Action Plan,[1] Beijing ordered the entire province of Hebei to reduce cement production by 61 million tons. Provincial officials determined that one-eighth of this reduction (approximately 7.5 million tons) would come from Luquan and Pingshan.[2] This culminated in the dramatic "destruction ceremonies" – described in the opening of Chapter 5 – where the remaining large, profitable, technologically advanced cement companies were obliterated within months.

The closure of these 35 large firms cost the economy a total of 1.8 billion RMB, led to a 300 million RMB loss in government revenue (about a 50% drop),[3] and reduced output value by 6.1 billion RMB.[4] Yi'an township, the administrative center of Luquan and Pingshan counties, lost 90% of its local revenue,[5] and 3,780 workers were laid off. The broader economic repercussions led to the loss of an estimated 28,000 jobs; few of these workers received compensation. Local workers returned to their home villages, hoping to find seasonal work. They ventured out to the local employment center each day hoping to land a part-time job, but the options were limited.[6] Younger and more educated workers had already left the county, seeking employment elsewhere.[7]

Yet, despite the complaints and lamentations voiced by workers and factory owners, the overall sense of acquiescence is striking. Thousands of people experienced a sudden reversal of fortunes, powerful factory bosses struggled to recoup lost assets, and a once prosperous county was plunged into decline – all at the hands of the state. But then these groups simply moved onto the next job, the next investment, and the next cycle of political targets.

Luquan's acquiescence to its demise creates the perception that, for a state with such strong coercive powers, blunt force regulation is a cost-free exercise. Other countries shy away from forcible methods of pollution control due to fears of causing social instability or a backlash from the business class. But China's leaders know they can command its bureaucracy to implement scorched earth tactics, that companies will concede to these tactics, and that these efforts will yield immediate results. Put simply, the state uses blunt force regulation because it can get away with it.

However, in this chapter, I show that blunt force regulation is *not* cost free. Drawing on evidence from local news reports and my own case studies, I show that workers do protest, businesses do push back, and local bureaucrats do publicly criticize the short-term nature of these solutions. In response, the state uses two strategies to preempt dissent and protect itself from the more serious political risks. First, higher-level officials use their discretionary powers to exempt politically valuable firms and groups of workers from the most extreme blunt force measures (such as closures). Second, local officials give connected firms preferential access to funds and compensation (disbursed by the center) to ease the cost of shutdowns or stop production orders.

In sum, the state does not prioritize pollution reduction or economic efficiency when deciding how to pursue blunt force regulation. It instead applies the most politically expedient solutions, which focus on minimizing pushback from business and labor. This approach is hardly surprising. Given the conflicting pressures on local officials to fulfill Beijing's demands while containing local discontent – and local officials' tendency to be treated as scapegoats for systemic problems (O'Brien and Li 2006, 36; Stern 2010, 89) – it is rational for local officials to do their utmost to limit the political risks of reducing pollution. Yet these pressures lead to a highly unjust process in which the businesses that contribute the least to overall pollution levels may be the first to be punished, and individual workers with the fewest protections are often the first to be sacrificed.

7.1 THE POLITICAL RISKS OF BLUNT FORCE REGULATION

The news media often portrays China as a state that can respond quickly in a crisis, using its centralized authority to amass resources and apply solutions with dizzying efficiency. Who can forget China's response to capacity shortages in the early months of the COVID-19 crisis, when the government built a hospital in Wuhan in a matter of days?[8]

Yet, viewed from the ground up, these processes are not always so seamless. As I encountered case after case of blunt force regulation in my fieldwork, I discovered that there are at least four types of friction behind the scenes.

First, workers *do* protest. In Tangshan, a city where two-thirds of Hebei's forced reduction in steel capacity took place, a labor rights nongovernmental organization reported a sudden spike in labor protests around the time that steel plants were closed in 2014.[9] While these protests were not widely reported in the media, I later confirmed they took place in interviews with local authorities.[10]

Second, businesses do push back against the state's draconian measures, by refusing to accept impossible timelines or meager compensation offers. For instance, following a deadly explosion in the Chenjiagang Chemical Industry Park in March 2019,[11] the Jiangsu provincial government released a plan on April 1, 2019, detailing exactly how it planned to clean up the chemical industry. The document stated that chemical plants would be cut from 4,000 to 2,000 by the end of 2020, and then reduced to just 1,000 plants by the end of 2022.[12] The chemical industry reacted with anger, objecting to the arbitrary targets and unnecessary closures imposed on their industry. In response, on April 27, the provincial government released a new plan that erased all mention of targets for closures.[13]

In a third type of friction, there have been dissenting voices from within the government: local authorities have expressed their wariness over unrest or public distrust. In 2008, for example, during an earlier case of blunt force regulation in Guangdong Province, an industry expert openly criticized the regime for its lack of transparency. He argued that "the government should never resort to direct administrative methods to close down companies without clear principles or guidelines... otherwise it becomes hard for companies to trust the government."[14] Six years later, a provincial official in Hebei echoed this sentiment. Amid the destruction of the construction industry in Luquan, he noted, "If we rely only on administrative orders to drive forward forced reductions, or if we act with too much haste, demolishing factories simply because we have said we will do so, then we run a high risk of causing unrest."[15]

Finally, the quantitative analysis in Chapter 4 concluded that blunt force regulation tends to be concentrated in revenue-poor polluted cities. In other words, businesses are destroyed and workers laid off in the cities that are *least* able to afford it.

How does the state confront the risk of protest from workers and businesses when it has few resources to appease dissent? What strategies do local officials use to mitigate the potential damage to their careers, especially when they have no choice but to enforce these targets?

In the following section, I outline the strategies the state uses to reduce the political risks of blunt force regulation. I highlight the state's differing treatment of large, politically valuable state-owned enterprises (SOEs) versus less powerful, private companies. I show that all companies can be swept up in indiscriminate production bans that take place in the winter, or during sudden campaigns. However, large firms are more likely to be spared more costly, drastic blunt force measures like long-term closures; smaller, private, and politically less valuable companies bear the brunt of these costs. When large firms do become targets of indiscriminate closures, local officials engage in "cooperative regulation" (Scholz 1984a): They wheedle, negotiate, and pay powerful companies to bring them around to extreme enforcement measures. In sum, the state mitigates the riskiest aspects of blunt force regulation by protecting those higher up in the economy and in society's political hierarchy.

These strategies smack of discretion, which seems at odds with a key characteristic of blunt force regulation – its indiscriminate, one-size-fits-all nature. However, case studies in this and other chapters show that the choice to discriminate between large and small firms happens at the higher, decision-making levels of the state, at the central and provincial levels. This is in line with the logic of blunt force regulation: Higher levels of government issue one-size-fits-all enforcement targets after using information shortcuts and political discretion to decide which categories of firms will be protected from these targets.

Lower-level officials (municipal and county officials) also exercise discretion, but only over *how* they implement these targets in such a short period of time. Central and provincial leaders will still force them to achieve specific capacity reduction targets that require them to make an economic sacrifice. However, local officials can decide how they will negotiate with firms or disburse special compensation funds to achieve these short-term targets. They often choose to enforce targets quickly and forcibly, applying the state's full coercive power to get companies to comply. Yet the following cases reveal that local officials are also capable of a cooperative enforcement approach – where they use deferential, even obsequious, measures to convince large, state-owned firms to shut down by set deadlines.

This evidence of cooperative regulation reveals that there are political risks to blunt force regulation, and that the state cannot strong-arm all actors in compliance. However, the fact that local officials only use this softer approach on a select few companies illustrates that there is a hierarchy to how the state mitigates the costs of blunt force regulation, and that successful implementation is not seamless, but the result of a fractious, negotiated process.

7.2   MITIGATING THE POLITICAL RISKS

7.2.1   Labor
The Chinese state's control over labor is renowned. Despite representing one of the largest workforces in the world, Chinese workers are forbidden from developing independent labor organizations that can defend their interests (Friedman 2014; Fu 2017; Gallagher 2006). Strikes occur, but

leaders are often jailed (Chan and Ngai 2009). Workers are forced to file complaints against management individually, and formal challenges through the courts are often funneled to informal appeasement or arbitration channels (Su and He 2010, 164–9, 173–6). Formal constraints aside, the regime has also shown an uncanny ability to use divide-and-rule tactics to demobilize workers. For example, workers in SOEs are granted different rights from informal, migrant workers, which makes it harder for workers to identify their shared grievances or join forces in the face of mass layoffs (Lee 2007, 72, 84, 106).

However, while the Chinese state is experienced in preventing and neutralizing labor unrest, it is not complacent about the risk, especially during extraordinary measures like blunt force regulation. This became clear to me during an interview with a provincial-level official from the National Reform and Development Commission (NRDC – one of China's most powerful government agencies). When asked how the government planned to manage the social costs of the province's blunt force campaign, he volunteered that private firms had been the main targets of government efforts to clean up the local cement industry, whereas SOEs were more likely to be protected.[16]

There is nothing new about the state taking extra steps to protect SOEs. Prior studies suggest they tend to be protected from the costliest government reforms because of their political connections, size, and ability to influence policy (Lorentzen et al. 2014, 185; He and Pan 2013, 50; Kennedy 2009). SOEs are also given preferential access to credit, which means the government has a direct stake in their success (Pearson 2011; Tsai 2015). In this case, however, the NRDC official clarified that the state targeted private firms for closure because their workers are less likely to protest in response to layoffs.

Private firms tend to employ temporary, migrant workers who are unlikely to receive compensation or social insurance payments. If they are laid off, these workers simply move away, or seek jobs in other industries or other locations. Workers from SOEs or very large firms are offered formal employment contracts, which entitles them to compensation and unemployment benefits. As a result, SOEs tend to attract younger, more educated workers who are more competitive on the job market. In Shijiazhuang's Luquan County, for example, SOEs were able to hire workers with a high school diploma because they offered insurance and benefits, while Luquan's privately owned cement companies were only able to attract less educated villagers or migrant workers, because they could only offer a basic salary (Yang 2015).

When mass layoffs occur, SOE workers also pose a greater risk to the local government because the state is contractually obliged to pay them social insurance. If local officials cannot afford these payouts, they risk provoking collective protests from this educated group of workers. This is exactly what happened in the era of SOE restructuring in the northeast, when mass layoffs escalated into mass protests in the 1990s (Lee 2007).

During the interview, the NRDC official posited that Hebei Province's deep restructuring of polluting industries was unlikely to cause the same dislocations as the mass layoffs in the 1990s, because the state would not have to provide the same level of social security payouts. The majority of workers from the cement corridor who lost their jobs were transient, informally employed, and expected to move to other cities and provinces to find new jobs.[17] His predictions have so far proven correct: Aside from occasional reports of strikes in Tangshan Province (where 40 million of Hebei's 60 million tons of reduced steel production took place),[18] Hebei seems to have evaded the threat of mass unrest, despite major shutdowns over the last few years.

This differentiated treatment of workers in state-owned versus private companies is evident in the case of Shijiazhuang's Luquan County, introduced in the beginning of this chapter. While the government provided clear rules for compensating factory owners, they placed the burden on factory owners to compensate their workers.[19] Only one of the 35 companies destroyed between 2013 and 2014 was an SOE – Dingxin Cement. This company spent 2 million RMB of the 45 million RMB in compensatory funds it received to pay off its workers. Each worker was given a sum based on how long they had worked at the company, and an additional 10,000 RMB bonus (approximately 5 months' salary for line workers) in severance pay.[20]

The rest of the closed factories were privately owned and employed workers on temporary contracts, so the majority of laid-off workers were unable to claim formal compensation. Several workers had come from neighboring villages, and simply returned home to look for seasonal work in the construction industry, or domestic services. Otherwise, they went to other provinces to seek work elsewhere. In addition to the factory workers who lost their jobs, the restaurants and shops that had once served this bustling cement industry also had to close, exacerbating the unemployment woes. "It's really hard to find work now, especially when there is so much competition for jobs" a local villager and former factory employee said. "Before we could earn up to

2,000 [RMB] a month; now it's probably 1,000."[21] In 2014 the county government promised to hold a job fair to help resettle workers, but by the end of 2015 several villagers were still unemployed.

A similar level of acquiescence can be detected in the case of Qingyuan (covered in Chapter 4) after the state closed down the recycling industry. Several of the factory owners were migrants themselves, merely renting the premises from local residents who had left the business long before.[22] Following the crackdown, many workers simply returned to local villages to await new opportunities, and the factory owners moved to other provinces to set up new ventures.[23]

The silent retreat of workers in Qingyuan and Shijiazhuang may seem surprising. Yet these mass layoffs are part of a broader trend in China. Workers employed by small, privately owned factories tend to be migrant workers, and are accustomed to frequent turnover in their employment. This usually happens en masse after the spring festival, especially in southern China, when workers decide to seek new jobs after the break, and factory owners must replace their ranks of workers.[24] An employer from Guangdong Province told me that workers might also be laid off after a couple years and forced to seek new jobs because their constant exposure to chemicals has made them "too sick" or "unemployable."[25]

This practice of frequent turnover in the labor force explains why local officials are ready to risk mass layoffs through blunt force measures: they do not expect resistance from the transient, informally employed migrant workers they target with shutdowns. However, businesses are much less likely to acquiesce, because capital has more clout in the political hierarchy. Moreover, the state relies on private businesses and investors to increase its revenue targets (Ang 2016; Dickson 2008; Lardy 2014). How, then, does the state mitigate the political risks of angering businesses and alienating potential investors?

7.2.2 Businesses
In my interviews, I discovered that in addition to targeting private firms, the state also concentrates the most severe blunt force measures on small and medium-sized enterprises (SMEs), which are much less likely to push back against forceful government measures than large firms. Previous research has found that large firms, regardless of their sector or ownership structure, are more likely to subvert restrictive measures or successfully lobby for regulation that advances their interests (Kennedy 2009; Deng and Kennedy 2010, 106–7).

This is because large firms are better connected and can use these high-level contacts to protect themselves from regulatory sanctions (Deng and Kennedy 2010; 106–13; Huang 2013, 12–14; Leutert and Eaton 2021, 209; Wang 2015). Given their higher profit margins, large firms also contribute more to local government revenue. This makes local officials reluctant to meddle in their operations. Lorentzen et al. (2014) find that, holding pollution levels constant, bureaucrats in China are less likely to expose and punish polluters when the local economy revolves around one large, dominant firm rather than many small firms. In short, for a state seeking to protect revenue streams and preserve business interests, it is more expedient to sacrifice many small firms to reduce pollution than it is to sanction one large firm.

Like central officials, local officials also have an interest in targeting small firms, because they are less likely to have a direct, personal stake in them. While local officials may secretly own majority shares in local companies or demand kickbacks from firms (Bernstein and Lü 2000; Ong 2012b, 196; Tsai 2011, 148–9), they tend to focus on large, more profitable businesses since the payoffs of corruption are higher. Local officials might also seek to protect firms that have been awarded special government grants or investments, because their chances for promotion are partly based on the performance of these investments. However, these grants also tend to go to large, established firms (Huang 2013, 7–10).[26]

This difference in the political cost of closing small versus large firms is reflected in the vastly different tactics and language that local officials used in Qingyuan – where shutdowns were largely directed at small firms – versus in Luquan (Shijiazhuang) – where much larger firms were forced to close.

In Qingyuan, local officials implemented their enforcement targets aggressively, shuttering factories, cutting off electricity, and destroying factory equipment in a few months. Examples of similar tactics against small firms appear throughout the book, in the cases from Linyi, Foshan, Handan, and Anhui.

In Shijiazhuang, as in Qingyuan, the local state was also given an extreme mandate: to reduce the city's cement-producing capacity by 40% in just one year. However, unlike Qingyuan, these forced demolitions included large, powerful, well-connected companies (including SOEs), which were more likely to push back against blunt force measures. Thus, in contrast to Qingyuan, the local officials in Luquan employed much more deferential tactics, which focused on getting companies to independently agree to close down.

Over the course of 2013, local officials in Luquan began a campaign to win over factory owners, offering them multiple incentives to take the lead in shuttering their factories: for every 10,000 tons of reduced production, owners would receive 170,000 RMB. An additional 10,000 to 50,000 RMB would be provided as compensation for the destruction of warehouses.[27] To formalize this process, factory owners were asked to sign a "demolition agreement." Owners who agreed to close down before February 17, 2014, would receive an additional 1 million RMB in compensation.

Firms in Luquan and Pingshan initially resisted these measures, just as in Qingyuan. Factories were being asked to close even though they were still profitable, and had orders lined up for the next year.[28] Other factories had recently made major investments to upgrade their infrastructure. For instance, 5 years previously the SOE (Dingxin Cement) had acquired three new factories for 300 million RMB, and the government was asking it to voluntarily close down in return for only 45 million in compensation. The owner, Mr. Feng, initially refused to accede to the government demands, explaining, "The loss is just too great."[29] Several other factories quickly followed suit, claiming, "Dingxin is an SOE! If they won't shut down, we won't either."[30]

Instead of ignoring or silencing them, local officials shifted to a more obsequious approach in three respects. First, they visited every single factory to explain the compensation process, to solicit feedback on reinvestment in new industries, and to listen to factory owners' complaints. One local official even recounted visiting a factory owner's mother in hospital to pay his respects – all part of the process of persuasion.[31] Local officials also decided to lean on their closest connections in the industry; those who had formerly been protected by government connections were now being asked to close down first. The government asked Dingxin Cement to take the lead in signing the demolishment contracts on the basis that it had a "social responsibility" to do so as an SOE. After Mr. Feng eventually conceded, the other factories fell into line.[32]

In a second shift in approach, local officials openly acknowledged the unfairness of these forced closures throughout the process, and openly sympathized with factory owners about the difficulties they faced. A county official in charge of the Bureau of Information and Industry (经信局) noted that "Luquan's cement industry has gone from 166 factories to just two. Most of these factories were profitable, so you can only imagine how hard it was to close them down."[33] Recall also the "demolition ceremonies" arranged during this period, as described in the opening of Chapter 5, which applauded firms for their "sacrifice" – a stark contrast to the firms in Qingyuan that were berated for their "noncompliance."[34]

Third, in the aftermath of these demolitions, the local government continued to provide support to the owners of large factories, encouraging them to reinvest in new, cleaner industries so they could rebuild the local economy. They sent a select group of factory owners on ten separate "business tours" (考察项目) around China to develop new investment ideas and acquire contacts in different industries.[35] Compensation funds in hand, former cement company bosses began to consider how to convert their factory sites into new money-making ventures. Old cement factories were repurposed into workshops for stainless steel products and various food and agricultural manufacturing projects.[36] An Zhongpin, a factory owner who had worked in the cement industry for 20 years, decided to reinvest in a walnut processing facility on the site of his factory. When he suddenly ran out of investment funds, the district government provided a further 3 million RMB in compensation to help cover his start-up costs. Reports suggest that a significant portion of the funding for new investments came from one-off central transfers.[37]

In many respects, the state's approach to closing cement factories in Luquan reflects the cooperative approaches to regulation mentioned in Chapter 2 – where regulators increase compliance through building trust rather than through aggressive threats. The events in Luquan therefore illustrate that the state is capable of these methods. However, these methods require considerable effort and resources. Local officials must provide compensation funds, continue to support business owners after closures, and invest time in building relationships.

7.2.3 Is This Just Industrial Restructuring?

In China, there is nothing new about this strategy of "grasping the big and letting go of the small [firms]" (抓大放小). For decades, the state has used the same approach to restructure industry. Moreover, if the goal is to streamline industry, protecting large firms makes sense, because it allows the state to concentrate production and competition in the largest, most efficient entities. According to this logic, reducing pollution is not the main goal, but a useful byproduct of these closures.[38]

However, in the industries targeted for blunt force regulation, "letting go of the small" does not always streamline competition or consolidate production, because small and large firms compete in different markets. SME owners who I interviewed mentioned that they produced entirely different products or represented entirely different nodes in the supply chain than large factories. For instance, in the waste recycling industry, small firms may be producing plastic pellets from recycled plastics, while large firms are using these pellets to create higher-end goods. Neither firm is competing with each other.[39] Thus, eliminating small firms does not consolidate market competition; it simply eliminates one sector of the industry and destroys one part of the local economy.

Moreover, in the industries targeted with blunt force regulation, disproportionately closing down private firms could hamper future innovation and economic growth. The Chinese government favors SOEs and large successful firms with access to subsidized credit (around 85% of the loans offered by state-owned commercial banks go to SOEs) and preferential access to worker compensation funds (Tsai 2015, 7). This treatment gives SOEs greater guarantees against market failure, but also reduces their incentives to innovate (Tsai 2015).

Smaller private firms, with their low profit margins and risky business environments face greater pressure to innovate to survive (Chen 2014; Huang 2008, Ong 2012a). For instance, I interviewed a representative of a large conglomerate that had become an industry leader in cutting-edge recycling techniques. This firm had received many major government innovation awards and was frequently held up as an example to visiting foreign dignitaries. However, this representative admitted that most of its cutting-edge technology – including techniques to recycle scrap cars and produce high-end recycled plastic – had come from acquiring smaller companies in the business.[40]

To be sure, industrial restructuring is a component of China's blunt force regulation. However, in the industries targeted for such measures, the state's approach to closing down firms seems better designed to protect political interests than to upgrade the economy or clean up the environment. This suggests that politics is an equally important component in deciding how the state undertakes blunt force regulation.

7.3   ASSESSING THE STATE'S STRATEGY

To determine how widespread the strategy of targeting informal workers and privately owned firms to contain the political costs of blunt force regulation is, I collected data on the ownership characteristics of firms targeted for blunt force measures. Based on my analysis of the list of firms forced to reduce production between 2010 and 2015, I present three pieces of evidence which suggest that smaller, privately owned firms *are* disproportionately targeted over large firms and SOEs.

7.3.1 Targeting Small Firms

First, I examine the characteristics of the firms targeted for blunt force measures between 2010 and 2015, starting with the list of "key monitored enterprises" (重点监控企业), produced each year by the Ministry of Environment Protection (MEP). Each city is required to draw up this list of key enterprises that account for 65% of its total industrial emissions based on data from the previous year.[41] These lists must include *all* coal-fired power plants (the biggest producer of industrial pollution by far) as well as all large firms in cement, crude oil processing, coking, ferrous and nonferrous metal smelting, and plate glass industries. Thus the final list of key monitored enterprises can account for much more than 65% of the emissions in each city.

To assess the extent to which small polluting firms were targeted by blunt force regulation, I compared this list of key monitored enterprises from 2010–2015 to the list of firms forced to reduce their production during the same period, which comes from the data (used in Chapters 4 and 5) on the number of blunt force orders issued against firms. I find that in more than half of Chinese cities (149 out of 283), no key monitored enterprises were targeted for forced reductions even though blunt force regulation occurred in 269 cities. In the remaining 134 cities where at least one key monitored enterprise was targeted, they make up only 8.5% of all enterprises targeted in these 134 cities (Figure 7.1).

Since the companies on this list of key monitored enterprises tend to be very large, closing just one would reduce roughly the same amount of industrial emissions as shutting down multiple small companies. It therefore makes sense that more small companies should be targeted for closure. Small companies also tend to have less advanced abatement technology, so it is likely that per unit of production they pollute far more than large companies. Therefore a fair comparison should focus on the *quantity* of forcible reductions in large versus small firms in each city. I develop a measure, "proportion of blunt force reductions undertaken by key monitored enterprises," to assess the relative contribution

143

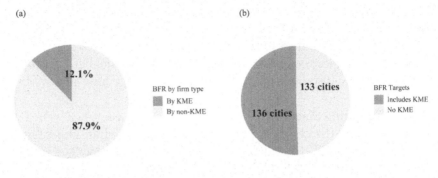

Proportion of total blunt force regulation undertaken (in tons) by key monitored enterprises (KME)

Proportion of cities in which at least one key monitored enterprise (KME) was targeted with blunt force regulation

Figure 7.1 Proportion of large firms targeted in blunt force regulation nationwide, 2010–15.
Source: Author graphic, data from author and MEP

of key monitored enterprises to each city's forced industrial reductions. This is measured as a ratio:

$$\frac{\text{Total forced reduction in industrial output by key monitored enterprises in a city (tons)}}{\text{Total forced reduction in industrial output by all enterprises in a city (tons)}}$$

My analysis indicates that of the total 1.163 billion tons of production that was forcibly reduced under blunt force policies nationwide, only 141 million (approximately 12%) was undertaken by key monitored enterprises (Figure 7.1).

I then break down this measure to the city level, calculating what proportion of blunt force regulation was undertaken by key monitored enterprises in each city. I find that in the 134 cities where key monitored enterprises were targeted, on average those large polluting firms were only ordered to reduce 25% of the total amount of industrial output that was eventually cut. Moreover, the median percent reduction by key monitored enterprises was only 19%, even though these enterprises collectively produce more than 65% of local emissions.

Figure 7.2 depicts the distribution of the proportion of blunt force regulation undertaken by key monitored enterprises in the 134 cities where they were targeted. The right skew in this histogram indicates that key monitored enterprises were targeted with blunt force

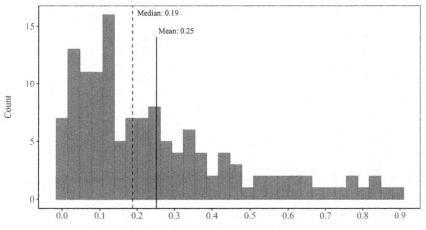

Figure 7.2 Proportion of blunt force regulation undertaken by large firms at the city level.
Data Source: Author dataset

regulation far less than smaller polluting companies, even though they produced the most pollution. These statistics, combined with the fact that more than half of Chinese cities did not target any key monitored enterprises, suggest that large polluting firms are generally spared from blunt force measures.

7.3.2 Protecting SOEs

In this section I examine whether the number of SOEs subjected to blunt force regulation between 2010 and 2015 was proportionate to the number of SOEs among China's polluting industries. Again, I return to the list of key monitored enterprises, which lists the largest polluting companies in a city, which is where we are most likely to identify SOEs that were subjected to blunt force regulation (at least, the large, central, or provincially regulated SOEs where political relations and worker protections are more likely to be enforced) (Karplus et al. 2020).

In the previous section I demonstrated that of the thousands of companies targeted with blunt force regulation in China, only 362 were key monitored enterprises – indicating a disproportionate focus on SMEs. In the next step of the analysis, I calculate that approximately

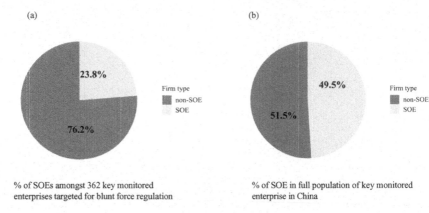

(a)

% of SOEs amongst 362 key monitored
enterprises targeted for blunt force regulation

(b)

% of SOE in full population of key monitored
enterprise in China

Figure 7.3 Statistics on disproportionate targeting of non-SOEs in blunt
force regulation.
Source: Author graphic, data from author and MEP

23% of these 362 enterprises were SOEs, compared to 50% from the
full list of China's key monitored enterprises for 2010–2015 (not
including industries such as the power sector, which were excluded
from forced reductions). In other words, compared to the proportion of
SOEs in the total population of large, polluting enterprises in China, a
much lower proportion of the large, polluting companies targeted for
blunt force measures were SOEs. These findings are illustrated in
Figure 7.3.

For a more fine-grained analysis of favoritism towards SOEs,
I select two cities where we are most likely to find SOEs on the list
of targeted firms. I first identified two provinces in which SOEs
produce a high proportion of the total industrial output: In
Shaanxi Province, SOEs produced approximately 60% of total industrial output in 2015,[42] and in Shanxi Province they produced
roughly 50% of total industrial output that year. I then selected
the city in each province that had the most firms targeted – Yulin
in Shaanxi Province, and Lüliang in Shanxi Province. I then identified the ownership structure of every firm that was ordered to
reduce production in these two cities, which I used to calculate
the total amount of blunt force regulation undertaken by SOEs.
Figure 7.4 illustrates the findings of this analysis.

In Lüliang, where SOEs produced 51% of total industrial output
(Figure 7.4a, SOEs carried out only 3% of the total tons reduced

1. Lüliang, Shanxi Province

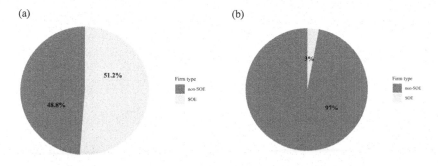

2. Yulin, Shaanxi Province

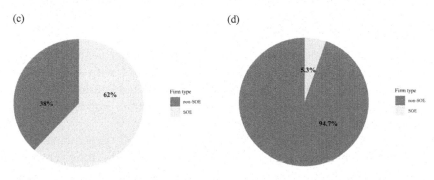

Measure 1: Proportion of total industrial output from SOEs

Measure 2: Proportion of total blunt force regulation performed by SOEs

Figure 7.4 Proportion of blunt force regulation carried out by SOEs in Lüliang and Yulin, 2010–15.
Source: Author graphic, data from author dataset and National Bureau of Statistics

under blunt force regulation (Figure 7.4b). Only one of its six key monitored enterprises was an SOE. In Yulin, where SOEs produced 61% of total industrial output (Figure 7.4c), SOEs carried out only 5.3% of the total tons reduced under blunt force regulation (Figure 7.4d). The only key monitored enterprise targeted in Yulin was a private company (see Table 7.1). This adds to the evidence suggesting that SOEs were disproportionately protected from blunt force measures.

TABLE 7.1. Statistics on SOE output and blunt force regulation in Lüliang and Yulin

Measure	Lüliang (Shanxi province)	Yulin (Shaanxi province)
Proportion of total industrial output from SOEs	51%	62%
Total number of firms targeted	102	61
Number of key monitored enterprises targeted	6	1
Number of key monitored enterprises targeted that are SOEs	1	0

7.4 IMPLICATIONS

This analysis provides strong suggestive evidence that SMEs as well as private companies are disproportionately targeted with blunt force regulation. The most politically connected or valuable firms are either spared blunt force measures or are targeted far less in proportion to the amount of pollution they produce.

Protecting large, connected firms may be politically expedient, but it aggravates the problems of regulating pollution in the long term. By protecting firms with the strongest political connections from blunt force closures, the state incentivizes firms to invest in better connections instead of better pollution compliance to survive the frequent regulatory culls.

A study of 1,000 industrial firms in 12 Chinese cities showed that small and medium SOEs – which have stronger political connections than their private counterparts – are less likely to invest in emissions abatement technologies than private or foreign-owned firms (Li and Chan 2016). Large SOEs are more likely than small SOEs to comply with pollution regulation because they are more closely regulated by the government. Yet even among central SOEs – the most tightly regulated category of firms in China – pollution noncompliance is rife. A recent study by Eaton and Kostka (2017) shows that they are the source of a large number of serious pollution incidents: six firms are responsible for more than 60% of violations by central SOEs. The authors argue that central SOEs get away with these major transgressions because limited capacity prevents effective oversight, but also because higher-level officials protect them. This finding echoes the provincial-level official's pronouncement in Chapter 6 that big polluters can evade punishments because "high-level interests are involved."

Firms that invest in pollution abatement but then face arbitrary closure may struggle to survive because they are not well connected or politically valuable. Most firms in China are connected to the state on some level because the state prevents them from acting collectively. Entrepreneurs find it more effective to advance their interests by building personal ties with state officials (Hou 2019; Tsai 2011) and joining the Party. However, the strength of these connections varies depending on how valuable firms are to the state (Kennedy 2009).

Throughout the war on pollution, stories emerged of provincial governments forcibly closing or relocating companies without offering any warning or compensation to the targeted companies. In Anhui Province in 2015,[43] 24 factory owners were so enraged by the province's arbitrary sanctions that they sued the provincial government for damages (described in Chapter 2). The provincial court eventually ruled in favor of these companies and ordered the provincial government to compensate them, an outcome deemed "inconceivable" by a prominent legal academic, who never thought a Chinese court would rule against a provincial government.[44] However, the firms struggled to obtain the court-ordered compensation from the government. Past studies have shown that courts are more likely to favor politically well-connected firms (Ang and Jia 2014), or those that are major revenue contributors (Wang 2016). Firms without strong state connections find it difficult to defend their interests, even when government actions are clearly illegal.

Thus by choosing to protect firms based on their size and political connections, the state signals that connections are more valuable than compliance. This strategy mitigates the short-term threat of political and social instability – especially from more powerful actors in society – but exacerbates the problem of continued disrespect for pollution standards. In other words, politicized blunt force closures may prove to be self-defeating.

Some may retort that the ends justify the means: the state doesn't care about reducing pollution or restructuring the economy efficiently, as long as it achieves its intended goals. Right now, the goal is to achieve these policy outcomes quickly, and without aggravating political risks – which means targeting politically and economically weak actors. The Chinese state is willing to pay this price to clean up the air.

However, in the case of blunt force regulation, it has become increasingly clear that the state is no longer able to focus its interventions exclusively on small firms. Cases throughout this book illustrate that when blunt force regulation takes the form of permanent factory closures, it does not stop at closing small factories. With each new phase, the targets are expanded until even large firms are forced to close. This occurred in Luquan, where the small companies were closed first, and the large closed later – the only difference was that large firms were offered some compensation and that local officials made the effort to negotiate with them.

The favoritism shown to large firms and SOEs only applies to more extreme blunt force targets, such as the complete destruction of firms. When blunt force regulation entails temporary, "stop production" orders, the measures are applied universally to companies big and small, private and state owned, compliant and noncompliant. Such orders are less politically risky because the impact on employment and the cost to firms is more manageable. Firm owners told me that they refrain from firing workers during this period, because it would be too expensive to hire and retrain them when they are allowed to restart operations. Instead, they furlough workers and use the production lull to make necessary upgrades in infrastructure, or for stocktaking.[45]

However, as large firms are increasingly targeted with closures or stop production orders, they may become more vociferous and public in their resentment, making blunt force regulation more politically risky. While businesses in China do depend on cultivating the right political connections to get ahead, the relationship between large firms and government officials can go both ways. Government officials often use SOE positions as patronage, rewarding supporters with appointments to key posts (Pei 2009, 108; Leutert 2018). SOE executives have also been known to use SOE resources to promote political cliques and protect their interests.[46]

This interdependent relationship between state and big business may explain why, in the winter of 2019, the Hebei Steel Industry association dared to write a public letter (意见涵) to the MEP decrying the sector's treatment as guinea pigs of ad hoc policy implementation. The clearest expression of their frustrations was buried halfway through the statement:

The MEP should take responsibility for finding an appropriate approach to restructuring polluting industries... it should develop the industrial art of pollution control, instead of treating all us companies like experimental sites as they test out different approaches and policies.[47]

The letter cited the case of steel companies that, following strict new standards from the MEP, had installed netting to prevent the wind from blowing coal dust from outdoor stockpiles. A month later, state authorities told them the netting was inadequate, and they would now have to build a complete enclosure. The Steel Association also pointed out that stop production orders directed at factories with tall furnaces (高炉) would *increase* pollution levels, because it took less energy to maintain a constantly burning furnace at a low level than to raise the temperatures from zero each time. Finally, they explained that industrial accidents were most likely to occur while starting and stopping furnaces, due to sudden changes in pressure. The letter cited the case of an industrial explosion in a steel enterprise in Tangshan and the reported case of an accident at Wuhan Xinhua Steel Company (兴华钢铁) in which seven people died.

These vociferous condemnations from big business may explain why Li Ganjie, head of the MEP, openly denounced blunt force regulation in a press conference in the fall of 2019. He called for a more transparent, rules-based approach to fixing pollution.[48] This speech suggests that the government felt the need to placate powerful businesses to ease the political risks of their stop production orders. This deference to business echoes the behavior of local officials in Luquan, who pursued a much more conciliatory approach once forced closures began to affect the powerful SOEs in their jurisdiction.

In sum, while there is nothing new about protecting SOEs or large firms, the state's choice to apply this strategy to environmental enforcement reveals two observations. First, there *are* political risks to blunt force regulation, which the state tries to mitigate by protecting the most politically valuable (if not economically viable) companies and classes of workers. Second, by pursuing these scorched earth enforcement strategies, the state exacerbates the long-term inefficiencies of blunt force regulation, eroding the fledgling norms of compliance that could transform pollution regulation in China.

7.5 PROTECTING BUREAUCRATIC RELATIONS

The analysis explains why the strategy of protecting large firms and SOEs ends up easing the risk of social unrest and anger from the business community. However, it does not tell us why local officials agree to close down so many factories in a short period of time, especially when their economies are already ailing. While small firms contribute less to local government revenue, suddenly closing hundreds of them – as in Qingyuan – can destroy local growth statistics and increase instability. In more extreme cases where even large firms must be targeted, blunt force measures can lead to irrecoverable losses in revenue. Given that revenue and growth rates are so essential to local officials' performance record and promotion prospects, why are they so ready to sacrifice these performance goals? Why do they accede to blunt force regulation?

One opinion is that local officials have no choice but to comply. The Chinese leadership may lack a system to monitor bureaucrats, but it still has immense coercive capacity. Moreover, with no viable challenger to the ruling party, central rulers' grip on power is uncontested; thus pleasing higher-level officials is the *sine qua non* of political advancement for local officials (Pei 2017). Ordinarily, the information problems of authoritarian regimes protect local officials who shirk their everyday duties (Hillman 2010; Zhou 2010). However, when all-powerful leaders suddenly subject local officials to direct scrutiny, or when they initiate extraordinary, one-off enforcement actions (such as blunt force regulation), local officials suddenly find they have no room to maneuver.

The center's use of sudden campaigns is designed to exhibit the full force of the leadership's coercive capacity. These campaigns are intended to scare local bureaucrats, "knock[ing] them psychologically off balance" (Mertha 2017) and forcing them to become hyper-vigilant to the center's signals and demands (Zhu, Zhang, and Liu 2017; Stern and O'Brien 2012; Huang 2015; Thornton 2009). Even corrupt local officials will do an about face, disregarding local needs and turning on their business cronies to implement drastic policies to demonstrate to Beijing that they are loyal and worthy of reward – or at the very least, deserve to keep their positions. These studies suggest that local officials are effectively brow beaten into accepting costly blunt force measures.

Yet leaders have long-term horizons, especially authoritarian leaders like Xi Jinping who have abolished term limits. If they trample all over their agents today, they may have none left to do their bidding tomorrow. Moreover, authoritarian leaders, who lack the legitimacy of a public vote, need the loyalty of the party rank and file to stay in power. By subjecting bureaucrats to constant uncertainty, leaders risk alienating their power base (Brownlee 2007; Lust-Okar 2005; Magaloni 2008). For instance, bureaucrats have deserted their posts in the aftermath of the anticorruption campaign because they are unable to handle the pervasive uncertainty.[49] They are also avoiding experimenting with policies or taking risks due to fears of unexpected retribution (Hasmath et al. 2019). Thus central leaders need to take measures to make blunt force regulation more palatable to local officials.

My case studies suggest that the center achieves this through fiscal handouts. Blunt force campaigns are usually accompanied by a sudden injection of fiscal resources, either from Beijing or from higher levels of government. Instead of forcing cash-strapped counties to sacrifice revenue by closing down firms, the central government will transfer special funds to offset the costs of carrying out these closures. In Qingyuan, for instance, officials openly stated that they had to wait for special funds from the provincial government to arrive before they could begin punishing polluting enterprises. In Shijiazhuang, special funds from the city and central accounts were transferred to Luquan and Pingshan counties to cover compensation costs.[50] Beijing has even developed a special fund to assist Hebei Province through its difficult transitional period during the war on pollution. According to reports from Hebei's government finance department, of the 7.02 billion RMB the province spent on air pollution control in 2014, 6.22 billion was paid by central government funds (Wong and Karplus 2017, 14).

In my own interviews in Hebei Province, local regulators confirmed that Beijing had provided subsidies to compensate factories that had been closed, and to support ad hoc programs such as eliminating highly polluting "yellow label cars."[51] Thus, while local officials might ordinarily face a difficult choice between collecting sufficient revenue to cover ad hoc expenditures and punishing the polluters that provide this revenue, under blunt force regulation, one-off fiscal transfers help ease this trade-off.

Of course, these fiscal transfers are unlikely to be sustained in the long term. Once the center's attention has waned, special earmarked pollution funds will be diverted to other priority projects in health or social welfare. However, local officials may be willing to sacrifice revenue from polluting firms when there is the potential for new cleaner industries to replace the polluting industries. For example, in Qingyuan, the government destroyed its 40-year-old waste recycling industry in anticipation of a boom in the local real estate and tourism industries.

My interviews with local officials further reveal that in a perverse way, blunt force regulation, while costly for the local economy, can actually ease bureaucratic relations. In normal circumstances, when local officials attempt to address pollution problems by singling out major violators for punishment, they risk implicating their colleagues or stirring up tensions between different departments. As one provincial Environmental Protection Bureau (EPB) official explained:

> Suppose a firm is caught polluting, then we have to go and investigate who in our administration [the EPA] ignored the regulations or who didn't know how to enforce the regulations. That's the problem with trying to punish non-compliant firms individually, you have to find who's responsible in your own ranks; you have to go chase after local cadres below you, or question your superiors, or sometimes you just end up sacrificing your own brothers. Who is willing to do that? Who is willing to enforce the law when you punish your own people?[52]

By contrast, blunt force regulation carries no punitive measures for bureaucrats. When pollution is controlled through one-size-fits-all sanctions, there is a much lower risk of implicating colleagues for bureaucratic malfeasance. Nor is there any risk of threatening higher-level interests, because the list of firms targeted for sanctions must be pre-approved by provincial (and sometimes even central) government officials (see Chapter 4 for details). As this provincial EPB official continued:

> When you apply a unilateral enforcement policy [where all companies in one category are punished], it doesn't matter what happened before or who is responsible. Firms are punished because they didn't meet a standard. You don't have to find out who failed at monitoring them.[53]

Compare this with the complaints of another provincial EPB official who was being forced to investigate firms for excessive pollution:

> Suppose a factory secretly emits polluted water at night. Once pollution hits the water, it also becomes the responsibility of the water bureau (水利部). So now we have to chase down the water bureau and get their cooperation for inspecting the water and cleaning up the pollution. It is such a headache! In my eyes, once the pollution hits the water, it should be the water bureau's responsibility. The EPB should only be responsible for checking if factories have installed the correct equipment.[54]

In ordinary circumstances, blame for "who failed at monitoring [polluting factories]" or "who is responsible [for cleaning up pollution]" is one of the biggest sources of inter- and intradepart-mental conflict. This reflects a notorious feature of China's bureau-cracies – their fragmented authority (Lieberthal and Lampton 1992; Jahiel 1998; Mertha 2005, 2009). Given the unclear delegation of authority and frequent squabbling over who is responsible for which tasks, often no one takes responsibility, and policies are not imple-mented. Alternately, different agencies may issue contradictory orders, leading to immense frustration among regulated entities – as illustrated by the Hebei Steel Association's angry feedback to the government.[55]

However, blunt force regulation absolves local officials of the need to find or attribute blame. This may explain why rivalrous agencies come together with an unprecedented level of coordination when implementing such measures. In Qingyuan and Luquan, blunt force campaigns were carried out jointly by the environmental agencies, the bureau of industry and development, the electricity bureau, and law enforcement officers. There are also examples of 18 previously bickering agencies coming together to "rectify" pollution (van Rooij 2002, 20); situations in which the EPB, security bureau, electricity bureau, and bureau of land and resources sign formal cooperation contracts to guarantee immediate support once the campaign begins;[56] and instances of state-owned power companies agreeing to cut off electricity to whichever district or company the EPB commands.[57]

In sum, local officials implement blunt force orders because they are under direct scrutiny from immensely powerful central or provincial leaders and have no choice. But they also accede because it gives them a brief window to carry out implementation orders without implicating each other or exposing the depth of their collusion with local businesses.

7.6 CONCLUSION

This chapter demonstrates that local officials have conceded to Beijing's demands to reduce pollution overnight by deploying a range of discretionary, extralegal tactics against polluters: they disproportio-nately target small firms, reserving the most irreversible sanctions for the least powerful companies; they also disproportionately target non-state-owned companies, and firms that do not offer their workers social insurance. By applying these measures, local officials evade responsibility for past bureaucratic misdeeds, and force polluting firms to shoulder the blame for China's urgent environmental problems.

None of these tactics represents the most efficient way to deal with present or future pollution. The closure of hundreds of small firms does not always produce the intended effect on pollution levels, because their contribution to overall pollution may be small in the first place. We see this in Luquan, where clever plans to "close the small and advance the big cement factories" ultimately did not solve local pollution problems; eventually, even the big firms had to be closed to achieve a noticeable impact on air quality. In previous chapters, regulators complained that small firms – the main targets of blunt force regulation – are the hardest to police in the long term, because they can easily set up shop elsewhere or begin again from scratch. In Qingyuan, for example, it took the government three rounds of small firm closures to completely destroy the recycling industry in 2015. Even in the aftermath of the closures, local officials had to take extra measures to prevent new factories from springing up: over a period of several months, the county government deployed six roaming inspection teams of 150 officers to prevent raw materials from being secretly transported into the area.[58] Such efforts to police and destroy small firms end up draining local resources.

The closure of large firms in Luquan seems to have been more enduring. After all, it is difficult to revive production in a large company when explosives have destroyed all of the infrastructure and equipment. The closure of large firms therefore ensures more lasting reductions in pollution levels. However, the data suggests that these large firms are rarely targeted, and even when they are forced to close, the less efficient class of these firms (SOEs) is more likely to be spared. This only exacerbates the long-term economic costs of pollution reduction. Yet local officials are willing to accept these costs because they receive fiscal resources from higher-level governments; because they anticipate an influx of revenue from cleaner, modern industries; and because one-off enforcement campaigns allow them to implement policy while shirking accountability for past misdeeds. Thus, what may seem like uncompromising enforcement from the outside turns out to be business as usual on the ground.[59]

In sum, the state gets away with blunt force regulation, and achieves acquiescence in society, but only by engaging in some major trade-offs. This type of regulation is therefore not an effortless, cost-free exercise of coercive power.

NOTES

1 State Council, "Notice on State Council air pollution prevention and action plan" 《国务院关于印发大气污染防治行动计划的通知，国发〔2013〕37号》, September 10, 2013.

2 *China Comment* (半月谈网), "Hebei supresses production capacity: smashing the people's rice bowl for the 'black hats'" (河北压制产能：为了乌纱帽砸别人饭碗?), June 6, 2014, www.cssn.cn/jjx/jjx_bg/201406/t20140606_1200233.shtml; 中国企业报 2014.

3 *China Enterprise News* (中国企业报), March 8, 2014; *Economic Daily* (经济日报), "Farewell to the 'Cement Corridor'" (告别"水泥走廊), December 17, 2014, www.ce.cn/xwzx/gnsz/gdxw/201412/17/t20141217_4138023.shtml.

4 *China Enterprise News* 中国企业报 2014.

5 *Economic Daily* 2014.

6 L. Yang, *Analysis of the Impact of Firm Closures on the Livelihood of the Local Informal Workforce* (企业关停对当地临时就业人员的生计影响研究), 2015.

7 Yang 2015.

8 Amy Qin, "China pledged to build a new hospital in 10 days. It's close," *New York Times*, February 3, 2020, www.nytimes.com/2020/02/03/world/asia/coronavirus-wuhan-hospital.html.

9 See China Labour Bulletin reports; *Straits Times*, "Steel city to still city," April 19, 2016, www.straitstimes.com/asia/east-asia/qianan-from-steel-city-to- still-city.

10 Interview X2140515a with provincial economic official (May 2015); Interview X2230815 with local academic (September 2015).

11 Austin Ramzy and Javier Hernandez, "Explosion at China chemical plant kills 64; employees detained," *New York Times*, March 22, 2019.

12 《江苏省化工行业整治提升方案 （征求意见稿）2019》, 江苏省委省政府.

13 《江苏省化工产业安全环保整治提升方案》（苏办〔2019〕96号），江苏省委省政府.

14 Expert on national policy quoted in Xinhua net (新华网), "Can closures bring about economic transformation?" (关停能否带来转型?佛山整治传统陶瓷业引发震撼), May 7, 2008, http://news.xinhuanet.com/energy/2008-05/07/content_8121660.htm.

15 Zhang Guisheng, the Hebei provincial EPB measuring team head, quoted in *China Comment* 2014.

16 Interview X2140515a with provincial-level NRDC official, Hebei Province (May 2015).

17 Interview X2140515a with local academic researching the topic, Hebei Province (May 2015).

18 *China Comment* 2014.

19 *Ibid*.

20 *Economic Daily* 2014; *China Enterprise News* 中国企业报 2014.

21 *Ibid*., 11.

22 *The Southern Daily*, July 26, 2016, "Guangdong Qingyuan 40 nian dianzi chaijie ye zhuanxing" [Guangdong Qingyuan's 40 year old e-waste industry is transformed], www.chinanews.com/sh/2016/07-26/7951598.shtml.

23 Interview X4050316 with Guangdong-based entrepreneur (March 2016), Interview X4120316 with industry expert (March 2016), interview X10050416 with industry consultant, Guangdong Province (April 2016).

24 Interview X10080416 with owner of factory based in Guangdong (April 2015).

25 Interview X7190416a with owner of factory in Qingyuan (April 2015).

26 Interview X9160316a with factory vice-boss, Jiangsu Province (March 2016); Interview X5201015 with factory management, Guangdong Province (October 2015).

27 *Ibid.*

28 CCTV, "Economy Time" (中央电视台《经济半小时》), "Report from the frontlines of reform: the aftermath of demolishing cement factories (来自改革一线的报道：水泥厂爆破之后)," April 13, 2016, http://tv.cctv.com/2016/04/13/VIDEVLZLeyoYiLIDWFpQgDKz160413.shtml.

29 *Ibid.*

30 *China Enterprise News* 中国企业报 2014; *Economic Daily* 2014.

31 CCTV 2016.

32 *Economic Daily* 2014.

33 *Ibid.*

34 Sun Ruibin, Party Secretary of Shijiazhuang, as quoted in *Economic Daily* 2014.

35 *Ibid.*

36 *Ibid.*

37 See Yang 2015.

38 Speech by key policymakers to the China Coal Cap lobby group in Beijing, March 26, 2015.

39 Interviews X9160316a and X9160316b with the managers of a plastics recycling firm, Jiangsu Province (March 2015).

40 *Ibid.*

41 Interview X6210116 with a city-level environmental official in Guangdong province. For details, see 《2012 年国家重点监控企业筛选原则和方法》*2012 Selection Criteria and Method for Key Monitored Enterprises*.

42 This calculation is based on CEIC data on each city's gross industrial output. See www.ceicdata.com

43 *Qianjiang Evening News*, "Anhui firecrackers companies win sue provincial government and win case" (安徽花炮企业状告省政府胜诉), April 24, 2015, http://qjwb.zjol.com.cn/html/2015-04/24/content_3027030.htm?div=-1.

44 Interview X1010715 with prominent legal academic, Beijing (July 2015).

45 Interview X10170120 with former factory manager, Hong Kong (January 2020); Interview X2140515a with local academic researching the topic, Hebei Province (May 2015).

46 *South China Morning Post*, 13 July 2015 "China's state-owned enterprises slammed for 'entrapping' officials into corruption." www.scmp.com/news/china/policies-politics/article/1838514/chinas-state-owned-enterprises-slammed-entrapping.

47 《关于报送钢铁企业 对限产和环保相关问题意见的涵》, 河北省冶金行业协会》, November 5, 2019.

48 See Caixin,李干杰解读重污染天气成因 回应"一刀切"等问题, March 11, 2019, http://topics.caixin.com/2019-03-11/101391008.html.

49 See Bloomberg News, "Disillusioned bureaucrats are fleeing China's ministries," March 12, 2019.

50 See *China Enterprise News* 中国企业报 2014; Yang 2015.

51 Interview X3a240615ba with county-level regulator, Hebei Province (June 2015).

52 Interview X4090116a with provincial environmental official, Province X, (January 2016).

53 *Ibid.*

54 Interview X2110815a with provincial environmental official, Hebei Province (August 2015).

55 《关于报送钢铁企业 对限产和环保相关问题意见的涵》, 河北省冶金行业协会》, November 5, 2019.

56 *Hebei Legal News* (河北法制网), "Wei county cracks down on 78 heavily polluting small recycling companies," August 26, 2014, (魏县取缔七十八家再生重污染小企业), http://news.hbfzb.com/2014/benwangyuanchuang_0826/62953.html.

57 魏县取缔七十八家再生重污染小企业, August 26, 2014, http://news.hbfzb.com/2014/benwangyuanchuang_0826/62953.html.

58 *The Southern Daily* 2016.

59 Similar processes can be observed in China's land reform policies, which are implemented in a way that benefits powerful political actors at the expense of more marginalized groups (Rithmire 2013, 2017).

CHAPTER 8

COMPARATIVE IMPLICATIONS

The preceding chapters have focused on understanding the rationale of blunt force regulation using the case of China. In this chapter, I examine the study's comparative implications. What broader lessons can be drawn from China's experience of blunt force regulation? Is this approach unique to China or can it be found in other contexts?

I first discuss how the persistence of blunt force regulation forces us to rethink our notions of state capacity and what powerful authoritarian states can achieve. I review how, despite scoring high on two key dimensions of state capacity – that is, coercive powers (where leaders can act without formal public consultation) and resource capabilities (where leaders have abundant revenue and personnel to carry out their goals) – the Chinese state is still unable to enforce longstanding pollution regulations. Political leaders can force bureaucrats to shutter firms, but they cannot make them regulate consistently. This paradox reveals that for all its coercive powers, China is lacking in a key dimension of state capacity – enforcement effectiveness. Moreover, the long shadow of blunt force regulation in China shows that coercion can only temporarily make up for this lack of infrastructural power.

Second, I explore whether strong coercive powers are necessary for initiating blunt force regulation. China's scorched earth approach to pollution control is often seen as a uniquely authoritarian solution. Yet I examine cases from the Philippines, India, and the UK to demonstrate that blunt force regulation is a widespread phenomenon that occurs in both democratic and authoritarian states, and in both developed and developing countries. However, its character may be shaped by a state's level of coercive capacity and resource capabilities.

8.1 RETHINKING STATE CAPACITY

China is often considered to be a state with high coercive capacity because of its "despotic" powers. Despotic power represents "the range of actions that the state elite is empowered to make without consultation with civil society groups" (Mann 2008, 355). Such power is often associated with strong, centralized authoritarian regimes because their ruling elites are insulated from direct accountability to citizens. Consider, for instance, how easily Chinese President Xi Jinping abolished presidential term limits just 6 years into his rule, paving the way for him to become "president for life."[1] In democracies, leaders require formal approval from the electorate for such drastic institutional reforms, especially ones that vastly expand presidential powers. But in China, Xi only required approval from a 'rubber stamp' parliament, which delivered a near-unanimous vote in his favor.

The Chinese state is also thought to have considerable coercive powers because of its "resource capabilities"[2] – that is, "the resources that a leader can command to pursue a goal" (Goldstone 2006, 265). Fiscal power (including the overall revenue a society generates) is a crucial measure of resource capabilities because it captures the *potential* resources leaders could deploy to further their goals (Gallo 1991; Goodwin 2001). Resource capabilities are also measured by the density and competence of a country's bureaucracy and military (Evans and Rauch 1999; Shue 1988; Tilly 1992; Yashar 2018) as well as the technology and equipment at the bureaucracy's disposal (Brinks, Levitsky, and Murillo 2019, 10, 20; Mann 2008, 3550). Due to its vast bureaucracy and highly centralized fiscal system (which concentrates the nation's revenue, fiscal authority, and spending power in central offices) China also scores high on this measure of state capacity (Wang and Herd 2013; Wu and Wang 2013).

Yet China falls short in one last crucial dimension of state capacity the "weight" (Soifer 2008, 239) or "reach" (Shue 1988) of the state. This dimension captures the "relationship between the central state and its radiating institutions" and "the effects... of the state on societal power networks" (Soifer 2008, 235). In other words, it measures whether rulers *can* achieve their intended goals using existing state resources, and whether they *do* successfully shape the lives of subjects, even in faraway regions. Another way to think of this dimension is a state's *enforcement* effectiveness (Brinks, Levitsky, and Murillo (2019, 38) – the key variable of interest in this book.

This dimension of state capacity – the weight of the state – recognizes that a state's ability to produce intended outcomes is not directly related to the amount of resources it has. Rather, achieving goals or implementing policies is a *relational* process (Brinks, Levitsky, and Murillo 2019, 22; Amengual and Dargent 2020; Centeno et al. 2017) in which changing levels of acquiescence within the population will alter ruling elites' ability to control society. In other words, a leader's success in implementing policies also depends on the reactions and power of the groups being acted upon (Migdal 2001).

Thus, a state may have abundant resources that are effectively deployed to get citizens to pay their taxes every year (as we see in many advanced industrialized democracies). Alternatively, ruling elites might find that, despite presiding over a vast, sophisticated bureaucracy, they still have to battle with defensive local bureaucrats or powerful wealthy citizens to extract the money owed to them on paper. In the case of taxation, the weight of the state marks the difference between how much revenue is *available* for a state to raise, and how much it is *actually* able to raise at a given point in time, given the balance of oppositional forces in society. More broadly, a high-capacity state emerges, not merely when ruling elites can boast of high coercive and resource capabilities, but when they can also use these powers to get subjects do to as they are instructed, despite potential opposition from society (Lieberman 2003; Amengual and Dargent 2020).

The case of environmental enforcement in China highlights why it is problematic to omit this final dimension of state capacity. Clearly, the Chinese state has significant despotic powers. In the sphere of environmental governance, state officials can cut off electricity without consulting factories, or order industries to stop production with minimal justification. The state also has immense resource capabilities. The frequency of campaign-style governance reflects not just the sheer quantity of resources at the state's disposal, but also the regime's skill in activating its latent resource capabilities. Central leaders can instantly compel tens of thousands of bureaucrats to engage in record-breaking efforts to inspect and punish polluters across the country. They can funnel vast amounts of money to send inspection teams to investigate pollution violations in every province, as occurred during the 2016–2017 inspection campaigns. And yet, as I show throughout this book, despite these exhaustive efforts, the state struggles to achieve its goal – to get polluters to comply with existing environmental regulations.

The Chinese state approximates this outcome through forced industry shutdowns and production stoppages. It draws on its strengths (high despotic power and high resource capabilities) to carry out this cruder approach to controlling pollution. But blunt force regulation also increases the risk of social or economic instability. And as scholars of state capacity argue, unintended consequences are usually a sign of weak institutions (Brinks, Levitsky, Murillo 2019) and weak state capacity (Yashar 2018). In short, coercive capacity can only temporarily compensate for low enforcement effectiveness.

The China case also illustrates why it is problematic to assume that state capacity applies uniformly to all policy spheres. China's reputation for high state capacity stems from the regime's success in delivering rapid economic growth while maintaining political stability. Unlike other reforming rulers, China's leaders managed to avoid the ever-present risk of regime collapse or regime change during transformative economic reforms (Gallagher 2002). Scholars have partly attributed this success to the reach of the Communist Party and its robust party infrastructure – which allowed leaders to grant local officials high discretionary powers without fearing indiscipline or upheaval from below (Heilmann 2009; Perry 2007; Shirk 1993). Only a handful of developing countries in the region exhibit this level of bureaucratic discipline (Slater 2010).

However, this book shows that while China has proven it is very good at producing its intended effects in economic growth, it has not been able to extend that effectiveness to the sphere of environmental policy implementation. For all its strong party infrastructure, enforcement effectiveness may change from place to place or issue to issue depending on what is at stake for local officials and society. Thus China faces the same challenge as other developing countries where "states that are good at promoting one valued good, say, economic growth, may not be good at facilitating another valued good, say inclusive development" (Centeno et al. 2017, 13).

In sum, by identifying shared challenges between China and weak-capacity states, this book makes a case for including China in the emerging literature on regulation in the Global South. Further, it shows how blunt force regulation is but one in a series of strategies – such as "forbearance" (Holland 2017) and "co-produced enforcement"

163

(Amengual 2016) – that these states have developed to overcome persistent institutional weakness.

Yet, by pointing out China's weakness in enforcement effectiveness, and identifying how it draws on two dimensions of state capacity (despotic power and resource capabilities) to overcome this weakness, this study raises two further sets of questions. First, are despotic powers a necessary precondition for blunt force regulation? Would a state be able to shutter entire industries or push through draconian measures if ruling elites had to contend with formal constraints on arbitrary action? In other words, is blunt force regulation an exclusively authoritarian strategy? Second, states that are weak in enforcement effectiveness typically also lack resource capabilities. However, China represents an unusual combination of strong resource capability and weak enforcement effectiveness. Does this mean that blunt force regulation is unique to China? I explore these questions in the following sections.

8.2 IS BLUNT FORCE REGULATION UNIQUE TO CHINA?

Blunt force regulation is not unique to China. It occurs in democracies and autocracies, in developed and less-developed countries, and in high-capacity and low-capacity states. Given this ubiquity, what is its relation to authoritarianism or resource capabilities? How might the three dimensions of state capacity (despotic power, resource capabilities, and weight of the state (or enforcement effectiveness)) alter the character of blunt force regulation? And if blunt force regulation occurs in high-capacity states, is it really a sign of weak state capacity?

In this section, I look at three cases of blunt force regulation from around the world to offer preliminary answers to these questions. I choose these cases for their variation on two key dimensions of state capacity: the state's 1) despotic power and 2) resource capabilities. I first examine the Philippines, which has high despotic power but fewer resources than China. The second case is India, which has low resource capabilities but less despotic power (it is a more stable, strongly institutionalized democracy). Finally, I investigate a case from the UK – a quintessential high-capacity state – to examine why blunt force regulation might still occur in contexts where institutions are strong and enforcement power is well established. Figure 8.1 illustrates how each of these countries map onto different combinations of state capacity.

Resource capabilities

	Low	High
Low	India	United Kingdom
High	Philippines	China

Despotic power

Figure 8.1 Four cases of blunt force regulation, classified by national governments' resource capabilities and despotic power

In all three cases, blunt force regulation occurred after higher-level authorities identified an urgent noncompliance problem and lower-level officials repeatedly failed in their attempts at enforcement. While ruling elites achieved their intended goals in all three countries, (clean up pollution, close down factories, control a pandemic), they varied in the scale, length, and effectiveness of blunt force regulation. These variations offer insights into how the character of blunt force regulation may change according to a state's resource and coercive capacity.

8.2.1 The Philippines: Blunt Force Regulation in Boracay

The Philippines is often considered a low-capacity state (Slater 2010, 8). Central to this characterization is the state's low resource capabilities. With a weak party infrastructure, and a per capita GDP that is half of China's, the state has limited fiscal and administrative resources to implement policies. The weight of the state in the Philippines is also low, given the central government's limited enforcement powers. State authority is fragmented, and central rulers find it difficult to penetrate and implement policy in local strongholds (Slater 2010; Kuhonta 2011).

While the Philippines is formally a constitutional democracy, central leaders exhibit a high degree of despotic power. According to Thompson (2021, 128), increasing military involvement in democratic institutions and growing restrictions on civil liberties in recent years have transformed it into "illiberal democracy" in which "the only robust institutional constraint on [the president] appears to be the military."

This characterization has grown stronger under President Rodrigo Duterte, who at the time of writing has been in power since 2016.

He has used his powers to muzzle the press, launch a war on drugs, and shut down Boracay, a world-famous tourist destination – one of the country's best-known examples of blunt force regulation.

On February 9, 2018, Duterte announced in a public forum that Boracay had become a "cesspool" as a result of untreated sewage from the tourism industry. He gave the environment secretary 6 months to resolve the issue, claiming that the problem risked destroying the local tourism industry. "There will be a time that no foreigner will go there," Duterte vividly predicted, "because...when he goes back to the plane to where he belongs, he will be full of shit going back and forth to the restroom."[3]

Boracay – an idyllic island just off the town of Malay in Aklan Province – is a jewel of the Philippines' tourist industry. The beach resort attracts around 2 million tourists per year, bringing in 1 billion USD in revenue to the region and employing 36,000 local residents.[4] Yet in recent years, the proliferation of new seaside businesses and resorts has stretched regulatory resources, allowing pollution problems to fester.[5]

Duterte's proclamation spurred Malay's local officials into action. From February to April, they worked with representatives from the central Department of Environmental and Natural Resources (DENR) to investigate businesses and compile a detailed list of violations. Prominent violators were ordered to suspend operations until they had rectified their problems.[6] During this time, the environment secretary oscillated between threats to shut down Boracay to revamp the island's sewage infrastructure[7] and proposals to keep it open but limit tourist numbers.[8]

In early April, the central government suddenly announced it would be imposing a 6-month closure of Boracay starting on April 26, 2018. Businesses would be forced to cease operations; only local residents would be allowed to stay on the island. Throughout April, flights were cancelled and tourists turned away as the government prepared for lockdown. To coordinate the closure, the central government created the Boracay Interagency Task Force – an ad hoc body composed of representatives from central departments and the national police – to ensure that local actions aligned with central orders. On the day of the closure, 600 members of the security forces (including the Police and Coast Guard) were sent to patrol the area and enforce the closures.[9]

Boracay's closure has all the hallmarks of blunt force regulation. The president imposed an inflexible ban on an entire jurisdiction despite the enormous toll it would have on the local economy and livelihoods. Duterte offered limited compensation to local residents, which was barely enough to cover their losses.[10] He used coercive tactics to implement this ban, forcibly closing down businesses, tearing down illegal structures, even engaging state security forces to enforce it. The ban was also perceived as arbitrary. Local environmental officials argued that with the entire industry banned from operating, they would not be able to test whether hotels were improving their sewage treatment facilities as instructed.[11] Regulators would also be prevented from carrying out checks on polluters, despite their painstaking efforts throughout February and March to investigate and document noncompliance. Even the environment secretary acknowledged that continued investigations were more desirable than a complete ban, because they would allow the tourist industry to stay afloat while regulators fixed local sewage problems.[12]

Some environmental experts insisted that a full ban was still necessary to rehabilitate the local environment and give the beaches a chance to recover. However, 2 months into the lockdown, the environment undersecretary acknowledged (under pressure from environmental organizations) that the government had yet to finalize its rehabilitation plans.[13] This suggests the ban was not undertaken merely to carry out environmental rehabilitation.

Boracay residents grumbled that Duterte's personal interests were driving the closure. They suggested that the government had imposed the ban *not* to protect the environment, but to eliminate small businesses and clear land to make way for a multimillion-dollar international casino project to be built in partnership with Galaxy, a Macau-based gambling company.[14] Indeed, Duterte has become known for an ad hoc, personalistic style of rule in which he uses "extreme language to justify extreme interventions".[15] These claims reflect the belief that blunt force regulation is a manifestation of despotic power, in which powerful presidents take draconian measures because they can get away with it.

Yet to understand why Duterte closed Boracay, one must also take into account the state's fragmented authority, and the ruling elite's struggle to control local officials in the region. In the Philippines, just as in China, regional governments are granted greater enforcement authority than the functional departments that oversee environmental issues. Thus, local leaders are responsible for enforcing pollution regulation *and* encouraging local business development; given a choice between the two, they often opt for development. Indeed, 17 officials from Aklan Province (where Boracay is located) were later investigated for approving major developments on protected land, and for turning a blind eye to the proliferation of illegal businesses. Investigations by the Department of Interior and Local Government (DILG) revealed that over half of the 2,269 businesses investigated lacked the necessary permits.[16] These investigations suggest that even if Duterte had avoided a ban and delegated the clean-up to local authorities and government departments, state–business collusion may have scuppered the central government's efforts to rectify Boracay's sewage problems. Through a centrally managed blunt force campaign, Duterte at least ensured that local politicians would temporarily comply with his goal to clean up the beaches. Not all arbitrary enforcement action can be attributed to despotic power.

Moreover, this case shows that even in states with low resource capabilities, leaders can amass the resources required to impose costly efforts like blunt force regulation precisely because it is a short-term intervention. Duterte's actions in Boracay remind us that states are designed for just this purpose: to enable leaders to quickly redirect available resources to act against elements in society that are deemed threatening or problematic to their goals (Saffon and González-Bertomeu 2019, 9–10; Holland 2017). They can call on the national police to enforce non-security issues, redirect the nation's environmental inspectors to rectify polluted waters, and create central task forces to temporarily override the authority of corrupt or noncompliant local officials. In short, even resource-poor leaders can marshal startling levels of capacity in unexpected times or places.[17] Blunt force regulation does not require resource capabilities on the level of China.

However, this case also suggests that while states with more limited resources are capable of carrying out blunt force regulation, they will have to be more selective in the *scope* of enforcement because they can only carry out such interventions by diverting resources from other efforts. In Chapter 2, I describe a case in which the Chinese government responded to a chemical explosion in one industrial park by imposing a production ban on all chemical companies in the region. In the Philippines, by contrast, the central government could only take on the problem of sewage treatment on a site-by-site basis. In 2019, following the success of the Boracay closure, Roy Cimatu moved on to a cleanup of Manila Bay.[18] Moreover, reports suggest that while the spotlight was trained on Boracay's sewage problem, pollution problems were allowed to fester elsewhere. For instance, the government was unable to enforce suspension orders issued against the mining industry, in part because the bulk of the DENR's personnel had been diverted to carry out the measures in Boracay.[19]

The case of the Philippines therefore suggests that *low resource capabilities do not prevent the use of blunt force regulation. However, they may constrain the scope and severity of the measures undertaken. States with limited personnel, funds, or enforcement infrastructure will have to apply blunt force regulation more selectively, leading to smaller-scale interventions.*

However, this case leaves important questions unanswered. How important are despotic powers in the decision to undertake blunt force regulation? In both China and the Philippines, the leadership imposed draconian solutions despite considerable opposition from local residents, businesses, and even high-ranking environmental officials. Are despotic powers a precondition for blunt force regulation? If constraints on arbitrary action are strong, would leaders still be able to undertake such measures? In the next section I evaluate a case from India to show that blunt force regulation does still happen in these conditions.

8.2.2 India: Blunt Force Regulation in Delhi

India is classified as a much more stable democracy than the Philippines (Tudor 2013) with stronger institutional and political constraints on the ruling elite's despotic powers. However, like the Philippines, India is often classified as a low-capacity state because of its limited fiscal and administrative resources, especially at the local state level (Auerbach 2020; Ghertner 2015; Heller 2017). Yet, despite these constraints on executive power and resource capabilities, it still has a history of implementing blunt force regulation, such as the 1996 Delhi pollution plan.

In July 1996, the Supreme Court of India ordered Delhi's municipal government to close 1,328 heavy polluting industries by the end of the year, relocate a further 90,000 light industry units outside the city's borders within 3 years, and force all remaining factories in the area to set up central effluent plants to treat their waste. These orders were issued on the basis of the Delhi Master Plan 2001, which was drawn up by the Delhi government in 1990 to tackle the city's escalating pollution problems (Dasgupta 2000, 954–55).

Officials in Delhi have a long history of dragging their feet on implementing pollution plans. The first plan was issued in 1962, when the Delhi Developmental Authority ordered 2,000 industries to relocate outside the region, but to no avail; industry continued to expand in the city (Bell and Narain 2005). A new plan was developed in 1990, which required all heavy industry in the region to close down by 1993, but the deadline passed with few discernible improvements. Polluting industries grew throughout the 1990s until an estimated 150,000 units were operating in the region in 1997 (Dasgupta 2000, 956).

Delhi's enforcement failures are often blamed on its noncompliant bureaucrats, who protect industries under the cover of fragmented authority and an unclear distribution of responsibilities. Enforcement duties are split between central and state pollution control boards, as well as local health, development, and water departments (Greenstone and Hanna 2014, 3066). Local inspectors also lack the training and technical knowledge to oversee the greening of dirty industry (Dasgupta 1997, 295), which (as in the case of China) makes it easier to blame enforcement failures on resource shortages. Finally, local officials are reluctant to implement pollution policies for fear of alienating powerful industrial interests (Rosencranz and Jackson 2003, 249; Heller 2017). Since the government cannot afford to compensate industries for closures, factory owners are forced to cover the costs of relocating or laying off workers (Dasgupta 2000). But while governments in both China and India share this challenge of uncooperative local industry, China's officials can leverage the central state's coercive apparatus to bring about industry compliance. By contrast, the Indian state's lack of despotic powers means that local officials often struggle to challenge local industry.

However, under the Supreme Court's order in 1996, local officials did finally succeed in eliminating part of the city's polluting industry. By February 1998, the commissioner of industry confirmed that all 1,328 heavy industries had been closed as instructed. Shortly after the plan was implemented, 52,000 factories in the light industry sector had begun the process of relocation and were waiting to hear back from the government for available land (Dasgupta 1998). Factories that had survived the shutdowns began developing local effluent plants in accordance with the Supreme Court's instructions (Dasgupta 1998). Thus, after years of weak enforcement, local officials were finally able to force industry to comply with environmental orders.

On the surface, the events in Delhi look very different from the cases of blunt force regulation described in China and the Philippines. The industry shutdowns in Delhi were enacted fully *within* the law; court orders were based on existing city government plans. Thus, while the timing may have been a surprise to local industry, there was nothing inherently arbitrary about the restrictions imposed. In this sense the case was different from that of China, where the state selects industries for shutdown without explaining why they were chosen or how they can improve compliance, as well as events in the Philippines, where Duterte overrode existing regulation and overturned existing structures of authority to lock down Boracay.

In Delhi, civil society also played an important role in driving forward implementation. With the introduction of public interest litigation in the 1980s, citizen activists had started using the courts to sue the government for failing to enforce pollution laws; they pushed the government to issue a spate of new pollution legislation in the 1980s and 1990s (Bell and Narain 2005; Greenstone and Hanna 2014; Dasgupta 1997), culminating in the 1996 Supreme Court order. Thus, in contrast to China and the Philippines, the state was able to draw on voluble support from civil society to legitimize its extreme measures against polluting industries.

Yet a closer look at this case demonstrates that it did follow the logic of blunt force regulation: The central state used its concentrated authority (in this case, the Supreme Court) to cut through local bureaucratic intransigence and temporarily increase enforcement effectiveness. In effect, the Supreme Court order served the same function as central leaders in China and the Philippines, embodying the high-level scrutiny and sudden threat that convinces local actors to finally comply with existing laws. For a while, there was even a debate over whether the Supreme Court went too far in exerting its powers in India's environmental policy implementation (Bell and Narain 2005), especially in trying to counterbalance a legislature that had been captured by the interests of local industry (Rosencranz and Jackson 2003, 249). Crucially, this central state intervention also gave Delhi's officials the leverage to turn against powerful industries, because it is harder for businesses to confront or buy off the Supreme Court (Greenstone and Hanna 2014; Bell and Narain 2005).

Moreover, as with blunt force regulation in China and the Philippines, local industry experienced the sudden imposition of restrictions as highly inflexible, coercive, and arbitrary. Polluting industries were forced to close immediately, with little offer of compensation for the approximately 125,000 workers who were laid off (Dasgupta 2000, 955). While the government agreed to help relocate the 90,000 light industries, its approach was highly arbitrary. Factory owners were required to pay a 10% deposit for land outside the city limits, but then sometimes waited years to be allotted their parcel of land. Others found that the land offered was inadequate; with some large factories allocated plots of land that were too small to encompass their operations. Environmental experts were also surprised that firms relocating outside Delhi were not required to upgrade their infrastructure, which meant that polluting activity was simply transported from one region to another. Finally, while Delhi's remaining factories were mandated to set up central effluent treatment plants, officials offered little advice on how different sized factories should share the operating costs, or how a shared plant should be designed to process the variety of pollutants from different factories. These arbitrary measures contributed to findings that the measures enacted through Delhi's pollution plan were unnecessarily costly and counterproductive for long-term pollution control in the region (Dasgupta 1998).

This example of extreme pollution enforcement in Delhi confirms that even states with weak despotic powers may use blunt force regulation to counteract noncompliance. This case shows that in nonauthoritarian contexts, blunt force regulation is more likely to be circumscribed by existing institutions – such as the law – and may require a stronger coalition of support from civil society to bolster the legitimacy of executive action. Unlike in states with high despotic powers, leaders cannot simply upend existing authority structures to achieve their goals. Indeed, in a similar case of blunt force regulation against slum dwellings in Delhi, the state had to pass a new law in the courts to justify razing semilegal dwellings (Ghertner 2015).

Moreover, in the Delhi pollution plan case, while the Supreme Court did finally convince local authorities to take action, the scope of their enforcement actions was limited by law, leading to more truncated and discriminating actions against polluters. The court could not unilaterally create a central task force (as in the Philippines) or mobilize party disciplinary structures (as in China) to ensure local officials shut down all industry in the region. Instead, they had to follow the guidelines in existing pollution plans. Enforcement was also delegated to the same ill-equipped, underresourced, fragmented bureaucracy that had previously failed to implement the policies. This may explain why short-term, highly visible measures (like closing down the 1,328 big polluters) succeeded, whereas longer-term measures (such as relocating light industry) were less effective. Later studies indicate that half of the factories designated for relocation simply did not respond to orders because they fell into gray areas (such as already being illegal or operating on government land) (Dasgupta 2000, 955). Several of these remaining factories also failed to comply with orders to install new pollution infrastructure (Dasgupta 1998), which likely helps explain why later studies found that India's pollution action plans did not have a lasting effect on the country's pollution levels (Harrison et al. 2015).[20]

In sum, the case of Delhi pollution closures offers further preliminary conclusions about how different dimensions of state capacity shape the character of blunt force regulation. It suggests that *constraints on executive power do not prevent the use of blunt force regulation. Draconian enforcement can still be carried out through a sudden concentration of authority. However, in strong, stable democracies, the need to legitimize such measures may require closer adherence to the law and written policies. This may lead to less ad hoc, indiscriminate enforcement.*

8.3 IS BLUNT FORCE REGULATION UNIQUE TO DEVELOPING COUNTRIES?

The cases described so far vary on two key dimensions of state capacity – despotic power and resource capabilities. I show that blunt force regulation is used irrespective of these differences. Variations in these dimensions may alter the scale or severity of blunt force regulation, but they do not prevent its use.

Yet the cases of China, India, and the Philippines all share one variable in common – weak enforcement powers due to a weak weight of the state. Whether because of noncompliant local officials, historically weak party infrastructure, or powerful industry groups, central leaders cannot shape society according to their will, or implement policies based on their plans. This aligns with the book's central argument: that blunt force regulation is a response to weak enforcement effectiveness.

This theory suggests that blunt force regulation would be highly unlikely in states where strong courts and enforcement institutions have produced widespread norms of compliance, preempting the need for costly, quick-fix measures. How, then, does one explain the emergence of blunt force regulation in high-capacity states, which enjoy both high resource capabilities and strong enforcement effectiveness?

Does the occurrence of blunt force regulation in these contexts under-mine the book's central theory?

Consider, for instance, the COVID-19 lockdowns in Western Europe. As the virus spread around the world in the spring of 2020, France, Italy, Spain, and the UK all imposed national lockdowns. These countries are institutionally sophisticated and have considerable resource capabilities and enforcement power. One need only compare the state of pandemic control in places like India (where information-gathering and enforcement capacity are weak) to places like the UK (where extensive testing, tracking, and policing is used where man-dated) to understand why the latter is considered a "high-capacity state." Theoretically, these institutional advantages should have allowed leaders to apply more targeted enforcement measures. Instead, in March 2020, the national governments of all four countries successively chose to impose blunt, society-wide restrictions to control the spread of the pandemic.

Lockdowns are a classic example of blunt force regulation: States forcibly change their subjects' behavior through *inflexible*, one-size-fits-all rules that severely limit the range of acceptable actions. People in many Western European countries were ordered to stay at home; they were only permitted to leave for essential actions such as grocery shopping, exercise, or medical needs. In other high-capacity countries such as Australia, mass quarantines were imposed on neighborhoods where an outbreak of the disease was suspected.[21]

This solution is also *coercive*. In Europe especially, these actions defied established norms on the state's respect for civil liberties. In many cases, governments had to invoke legally questionable emergency powers to impose a near-total confinement of their societies. For example, the Spanish high court overturned lockdown orders in Madrid in October 2020, ruling that they violated fundamental rights and lacked legal foundation.[22] Enforcing lockdowns also required an extraordinary mobilization of resources to police noncompliance. For instance, France deployed an additional 100,000 police to patrol the streets to verify that citizens were only leaving their houses for the allowed reasons.[23]

Finally, the restrictions issued during lockdown were perceived as *arbitrary* due to the inordinate cost to businesses and services. Instead of restricting only the areas or populations most likely to exacerbate the risk of infection, entire populations were forced to cease nonessential activities, devastating the industrial and services sectors. By the fall of

2020, several countries that imposed nationwide lockdowns had entered recessions for the first time in years, especially in countries like the UK,[24] which were highly dependent on a service economy. Yet in many cases, lockdowns were credited with stopping the transmission of the virus, allowing societies to escape the fate of the United States, where a reluctance to impose more severe restrictions resulted in one of the worst coronavirus outbreaks in the world.[25]

Why did such institutionally advanced countries, known for their high state capacity, impose lockdowns? Public health experts argue that lockdowns were a *necessary* response to the pandemic because the risk was so dispersed and difficult to control. In contrast to risks where noncompliance only harms the individual (such as not wearing a seatbelt), the spread of the COVID-19 virus had a network effect: One individual's noncompliance could put many other people at risk. With the virus spreading so quickly, and with so many unknowns about this new disease, experts argued that the only way to protect public health was to use lockdowns to disrupt its transmission. According to this perspective, even governments armed with the most well-informed and well-funded bureaucracies would be unable to manage this risk without a lockdown.

This argument highlights the relational aspect of state capacity, and how important it is for enforcement effectiveness. A state's ability to implement policies depends not just on its resources and institutions, but on how society responds to interventions, and whether they perceive a state's actions as legitimate. Ordinarily, leaders in these Western European countries are spared more extreme enforcement uncertainties because public norms of compliance with intrusive laws or practices have developed and stabilized over time (Gunningham et al. 2005; Kagan et al. 2003). Enforcement will always entail compliance uncertainties, but these are generally "known unknowns": States can predict and preempt severe compliance obstacles (Yasuda 2020, 4).

However, when COVID-19 first emerged, many of the public health risks had not yet been discovered; leaders were thus forced to regulate "unknown unknowns." Controlling the virus demanded extraordinary levels of public compliance with restrictions that compromised other widely held public norms, such as the right to civil liberties. While public trust in the government has been proven essential to voluntary compliance with public health interventions (see Blair, Morse, and Tsai 2017), several Western governments lost legitimacy by downplaying the infectiousness of the virus[26] or dismissing the need for mask wearing, only to mandate it months later. Faced with escalating public noncompliance, leaders of these countries struggled to control the virus through more targeted means.

The UK government's vacillation between containment strategies illustrates this sudden inability to regulate amid unknown unknowns. When the virus first came to the UK in the spring of 2020, the government started out with a more flexible approach, resisting the need to impose blanket restrictions due to fears they would place a huge burden on people who could not afford to stay at home. Thus, leaders initially planned to emulate Singapore's flexible (and initially highly effective) virus response strategy[27] in which the state altered restrictions in response to fluctuations in the outbreak. With the help of extensive testing and tracking starting from the outbreak of the virus, governments in Singapore, Taiwan, South Korea, and Hong Kong were all able to refrain from blanket closures. They imposed basic restrictions on public gatherings, but otherwise issued advisories for people to work from home, leaving it up to companies or individuals to decide how to respond to these exhortations.[28]

Government documents[29] from the early stages of decision-making show that the UK's Scientific Advisory Group for Emergencies (SAGE) (the government group tasked with handling the virus) decided to impose restrictions on only the highest-risk populations[30] and pursue a strategy of voluntary compliance for the rest of the public. A March 13 SAGE report stated, "citizens should be treated as rational actors, capable of taking decisions for themselves and managing personal risk."[31] To help citizens make these decisions, the government would release regular information on the virus outbreak and infection patterns, but would leave it to citizens to assess their personal risks and engage in social distancing accordingly.

However, by mid-March the government realized the virus was spreading faster than expected, and that compliance rates were insufficient to prevent a pandemic.[32] On March 18, data on compliance levels suddenly became a "priority."[33] On March 23, decision-makers noted that "social distancing behaviors have been adopted by many but there is uncertainty whether they are being observed at the level required to bring the epidemic within [the National Health Service's] capacity."[34] That evening, the prime minister announced a nationwide lockdown, stating, "From this evening I must give the British people a very simple instruction – you must stay at home."[35]

As the need for compliance became acute and uncertainty around levels of voluntary compliance mounted, leaders came to the conclusion that a lockdown was the most effective way to protect the nation's health and public services. Though coercive and legally questionable,[36] a lockdown was more likely to achieve the necessary levels of social distancing than continuing to pursue a risk-based approach. Moreover, while deferring to citizens as "rational actors" could minimize the costs to society, UK leaders no longer trusted citizens to comply.

By contrast, Hong Kong's government applied flexible, risk-based measures at the start of the pandemic, largely due to widespread voluntary compliance with social distancing and precautionary public health practices bolstered by recent experience with deadly viruses such as SARS and MERS.[37] It kept transit and public spaces open, and merely imposed limits on large gatherings such as weddings. Almost all residents wore masks in public by January 2020, a full 6 months before the government required it. They also began to socially distance, cancelling group gatherings and avoiding big events, long before the government imposed these restrictions. In Taiwan, the public (rather than the government) similarly introduced high levels of social distancing.[38]

The UK government's uncertainty over public compliance prompted a sudden shift from flexible measures to a blunt lockdown. Leaders in the UK justified their blunt response by claiming that they lacked the resources and personnel to adopt the community-level testing or tracking strategies used in Hong Kong and South Korea.[39] Yet the comparison between Hong Kong and the UK shows that the divergent responses of these high-capacity states can be attributed to more than just strong information-gathering capacity or a quick initiative to test, track, and trace virus transmission from the outset.[40] It also can be explained in terms of the level of voluntary public compliance, and how this affected the tools that each state could use to control the spread of the virus.

In sum, the COVID-19 lockdowns in Europe indicate that blunt force regulation is not unique to developing countries because enforcement effectiveness is ultimately a relational process. In ordinary times, leaders can draw on strong, stable institutions to help monitor and mitigate principal–agent problems. They can rely on free and fair elections to help control local politicians who fail to deliver public goods; they can leverage the bureaucracy's high technical capacities to identify and address enforcement problems; and they can lean on strong independent courts to provide a credible threat to punish poor compliance. Over time, these threats build up widespread norms of compliance that preclude the need for drastic action.

However, these threats tend to work in the medium to long term. *During unexpected crises, leaders might be plunged into situations in which institutions are inadequate, or the regulated have not yet been socialized into compliance, forcing leaders to find ways to bring about compliance via other means.* And just as pervasive uncertainty over bureaucratic compliance drives leaders in Beijing to enact blunt force pollution regulation, uncertainty over compliance in the face of unknown risks drove leaders around the world to implement blunt force COVID-19 lockdowns.

Indeed, throughout history, political leaders have resorted to information shortcuts to regulate and control society. By creating standardized rules to interpret citizens' activities, states find it easier to process abundant information and to police and control diverse threats across their territories (Downs 1967, 144–53; Migdal 2001, 68–70; Weinberg 2017, 1106; Weber 1978, 975–79). Thus, street-level bureaucrats are taught to use arbitrary categories (such as black versus white, or poor versus rich) rather than informed, on-the-ground knowledge to determine the "likelihood" of illegal behavior (Lipsky 1980, 395–96); thus regulators are forced to assess businesses' compliance with blunt, standardized rules – rather than respond to specific, on-the-ground risks – to make it easier for governments to prevent market monopolies or manage negative externalities like pollution (Coglianese and Kagan 2008, 19).

Blunt force regulation is not the hallmark of an authoritarian or institutionally weak state. Rather, it is an age-old strategy of regulation in which the state bluntly categorizes citizens' private activities to facilitate control from "a god's eye view, or the view of an absolute ruler" (Scott 1998, 57).

8.4 CONCLUSION

This chapter argues that blunt force regulation is not unique to China. Nor is it an exclusively authoritarian strategy. Cases from the Philippines and India remind us that over short periods, leaders can quickly generate startling levels of capacity. Moreover, when leaders have control over the security apparatus (such as the national police or the military), they will have the potential to coerce actors into immediate compliance. These countries share the problem of weak enforcement effectiveness. Moreover, because enforcement effectiveness is a relational variable, dependent on society's response, blunt force regulation can happen in a variety of contexts.

This chapter also offers preliminary insights into how the character of blunt force regulation might change depending on the type of state or the level of state capacity: It may be more draconian and last longer in authoritarian states because leaders can use coercive powers to sustain enforcement despite public pushback. Elected leaders of democratic countries might be forced to truncate their use of blunt force regulation due to institutional constraints on their power. The cases discussed here also suggest that weak resource capacities can limit the scale of blunt force regulation; otherwise, leaders will find that their resources are spread too thin. Thus China's unusual combination of high coercive power (leading to more severe blunt force regulation) and weak infrastructural power (leading to a more frequent need for blunt force regulation) means that it may be distinctive in the severity, breadth, and length of its blunt force campaigns. More research is needed to examine whether these preliminary observations apply more broadly.

This chapter also shows that while blunt force regulation can happen anywhere, leaders do not pursue such a strategy lightly. Blunt force regulation exposes the state to greater risks (like protests) and a broader range of unintended consequences (such as prolonged economic slowdowns or declining foreign investment). This may be why leaders who use these measures are often criticized for prioritizing short-term, quick-fix solutions over long-term behavioral changes (Dasgupta 2000; Wengle 2015), or for resorting to blunt instruments of coercion because more proportionate, targeted approaches[41] would require too much information and effort (Chaudhry 1993).

Yet in every case described here, government officials first tried to solve problems through more flexible, responsive regulatory measures before turning to the inflexible solution of blunt force regulation. In other words, blunt force regulation is a last resort – a suboptimal solution that leaders use *not* because they have the means to push through draconian measures but because they cannot manage the less costly alternatives.

NOTES

1 BBC, "China's Xi allowed to remain 'president for life' as term limits removed," March 11, 2018, www.bbc.co.uk/news/world-asia-china-43361276.

2 Soifer calls this "national capabilities" (2008, 236), but I use the term "resource capabilities" to highlight that this is the dimension most focused on resources.

3 Duterte as quoted in *Manila Times*, "Duterte warns of closure of 'cesspool' Boracay," February 11, 2018, www.manilatimes.net/2018/02/11/news/top-stories/duterte-warns-closure-cesspool-boracay/379532.

4 *Wall Street Journal*, "Heavy police presence to close idyllic Philippine island under ecological strain," April 26, 2018, www.wsj.com/articles/heavy-police-presence-to-close-idyllic-philippine-island-under-ecological-strain-1524721113.

5 In early 2018, the Japan International Cooperation Agency published a study showing that untreated sewage in Boracay's waters had reached "unsafe" and "alarming" levels. See *Business Mirror*, "Government addresses major problems in Boracay," February 1, 2018, https://businessmirror.com.ph/2018/02/01/government-addresses-major-problems-in-boracay-3/.

6 *Business Mirror*, "New DENR list reveals more Boracay businesses violated environment laws," May 2, 2018, https://businessmirror.com.ph/2018/05/02/new-denr-list-reveals-more-boracay-businesses-violated-environment-laws/.

7 *South China Morning Post*, "Duterte's 'cesspool' Boracay Island set for closure. Or is it?," March 20, 2018, www.scmp.com/magazines/post-magazine/travel/article/2138014/dutertes-cesspool-boracay-island-set-closure-or-it.

8 *Business Mirror*, "DENR chief wants to keep Boracay open," March 3, 2018, https://businessmirror.com.ph/2018/03/03/denr-chief-wants-to-keep-boracay-open/.

9 *Wall Street Journal* 2018.

10 *South China Morning Post*, "Is there more to President Rodrigo Duterte's Boracay closure and drug war than meets the eye?," May 1, 2018, www.scmp.com/comment/insight-opinion/article/2144058/there-more-dutertes-boracay-closure-and-drug-war-meets-eye.

11 "DENR chief wants to keep Boracay open," *Business Mirror*, March 3, 2018.

12 *Ibid.*

13 *Philippines Star*, "Greenpeace: Butanding off Boracay no indicator of cleanup success" June 26 2018, www.philstar.com/headlines/2018/06/26/1828116/greenpeace-butanding-boracay-no-indicator-cleanup-success.

14 *South China Morning Post*, "Is Duterte putting thousands out of work in Boracay to clean it up for Chinese gamblers?" April 7, 2018, www.scmp.com/week-asia/business/article/2140668/duterte-putting-thousands-out-work-boracay-clean-it-chinese.

15 *South China Morning Post.* May 1 2018.

16 *Philippine Daily Inquirer*, "DILG sues 17 Aklan execs for 'neglecting' Boracay," June 28, 2018, https://newsinfo.inquirer.net/1004891/dilg-sues-17-aklan-execs-for-neglecting-boracay.

17 For instance, in the mid-1850s, the liberal Mexican state was able, in the midst of war, to force a powerful church to divest its lands around the

country, even while its attempts to redistribute land from other actors were less successful (Saffon and González-Bertomeu 2019).

18 *The Philippine Star*, "DENR Yearend Report 2019: Saving Manila Bay," January 2, 2020, www.philstar.com/business/science-and-environment/2020/01/02/1981302/denr-yearend-report-2019-saving-manila-bay.

19 *Business Mirror*, "DENR in 2018: Exceeding targets, Boracay as biggest accomplishment," January 7, 2019, https://businessmirror.com.ph/2019/01/07/denr-in-2018-exceeding-targets-boracay-as-biggest-accomplishment/.

20 Note, however, that this study does not include Delhi in its analysis, because it was the first city in India to implement an action plan.

21 *The New York Times*, "Australia thought the virus was under control. It found a vulnerable spot," July 2, 2020, www.nytimes.com/2020/07/02/world/australia/melbourne-coronavirus-outbreak.html.

22 *Financial Times*, "Spanish high court strikes down Madrid coronavirus curbs," October 9, 2020, www.ft.com/content/b041cc5d-f545-4f6a-a475-54ba3c5b269b.

23 France 24, "France to deploy 100,000 police to enforce coronavirus lockdown," March 17, 2020, www.france24.com/en/20200317-france-to-deploy-100-000-police-to-enforce-its-war-on-coronavirus.

24 BBC, "UK officially in recession for first time in 11 years," August 12, 2020, www.bbc.com/news/business-53748278.

25 Dr Anthony Fauci, Advisor to the White House on the Coronavirus, as quoted in CNBC, "The U.S. has the worst coronavirus outbreak in the world: 'The numbers don't lie,' Dr. Fauci says," August 5, 2020, www.cnbc.com/2020/08/05/dr-fauci-agrees-the-us-has-the-worst-coronvirus-outbreak-in-the-world-the-numbers-dont-lie.html.

26 *The Times*, "Boris Johnson failed to take coronavirus threat seriously," June 3, 2020.

27 SAGE, "SAGE 15 minutes: Coronavirus (COVID-19) response," March 13, 2020, https://assets.publishing.service.gov.uk/government/uploads/system/uploads/attachment_data/file/888783/S0383_Fifteenth_SAGE_meeting_on_Wuhan_Coronavirus__Covid-19__.pdf.

28 *The Regulatory Review*, "Comparing nations' responses to COVID-19," www.theregreview.org/2020/04/20/comparing-nations-responses-covid-19/.

29 The collection of documents that record the minutes of the SAGE meetings throughout the pandemic can be found at www.gov.uk/government/collections/sage-meetings-march-2020.

30 SAGE, "SAGE 13 minutes: Coronavirus (COVID-19) response," March 5, 2020, www.gov.uk/government/publications/sage-minutes-coronavirus-covid-19-5-march-2020/sage-13-minutes-coronavirus-covid-19-response-5-march-2020.

31 SAGE, "SAGE 15 minutes: Coronavirus (COVID-19) response," March 13, 2020.

32 *Ibid.*

33 *Ibid.*

34 SAGE, March 23, 2020.

35 "Prime Minister's statement on the coronavirus (COVID-19)," March 23, 2020, www.gov.uk/government/speeches/pm-address-to-the-nation-on-cor onavirus-23-march-2020.

36 See for, example, a report by lawyers in the UK, led by Dr. Tom Hickman QC questioning whether the regulations exceeded statutory authority (file:///Users/aispts/Downloads/Coronavirus_and_Civil_Liberties_in_the_ UK.pdf). See also the criticisms against the French Constitutional Court's decision to uphold emergency laws, https://blogs.mediapart.fr/paul-cassia/ blog/270320/le-conseil-constitutionnel-dechire-la-constitution.

37 *The Regulatory Review* 2020.

38 For more details on how this process unfolded in Taiwan, see Cheng-Yi Huang, "Soft regulation and hard compliance in Taiwan," *The Regulatory Review* 2020, June 11, 2020, www.theregreview.org/2020/06/11/huang-soft-regulation-hard-compliance-taiwan.

39 "Prime Minister's statement on the coronavirus (COVID-19)," March 23, 2020.

40 Jason Beaubien, "How South Korea reined in the outbreak without shutting everything down," National Public Radio, March 26, 2020, www.npr.org/ sections/goatsandsoda/2020/03/26/821688981/how-south-korea-reigned-in-the-outbreak-without-shutting-everything-down.

41 For an example of this argument, see Frieden, Tom and Kelly Henning, May 5 2020, *New York Times*, "Lockdown Is a Blunt Tool. We Have a Sharper One." www.nytimes.com/2020/05/05/opinion/coronavirus-con tact-tracing.html

CHAPTER 9

CONCLUSION

Blunt force regulation is a striking phenomenon. Anyone who has witnessed roads of empty factories, the owners standing amid their dead assets, or the abrupt suspension of smokestacks, would have a hard time doubting China's commitment to its "war on pollution." The impact of its blunt force approach shows us what can be achieved when a state sets its mind (and resources) to the task of fixing pollution problems.

However, the logic of blunt force regulation can also seem perverse. Why does the state punish the *ruled* for the disobedience of local *rulers*? Why punish the *compliant* for the misdeeds of *noncompliers*? Imposing standardized reactions to complex problems can seem unreasonable. Far from limiting risks or facilitating markets, regulation is experienced as a form of violence (Weinberg 2017). Indeed, like all processes designed to make citizen actions more identifiable or "legible" to state authorities, blunt force regulation operates by simplifying rather than understanding diverse risks (Lindblom 1959; Scott 1998, 2). It creates systems with "strong thumbs and no fingers" (Lindblom 1977, 65) and can produce serious unintended consequences (Bates 2005; Chaudhry 1993; Van de Walle 1989; Zhou et al. 2013).

Yet this perverse logic reveals just how hard it is for states to control the private actions of individuals or local authorities across their territory. We sometimes take for granted – especially in societies with strong institutions – that policies formulated on paper will be implemented, or that those who follow the rules will be rewarded. And yet, as the coronavirus crisis revealed, when political leaders are forced to regulate complex issues without cooperation from society, they sometimes break the social contracts or legal commitments they promise to uphold. Whether authoritarian or democratic, developed or developing, states resort to the clumsy solution of using their coercive powers to impose uniform restrictions. China therefore deals with pollution violations by subjecting all potential violators to blunt force regulation. And leaders in Europe respond to pockets of public health noncompliance with indiscriminate lockdowns.

Blunt force regulation also illustrates what can happen when a strong, experienced authoritarian state sets its mind (and resources) to the task of fixing pollution problems. Yet the scale and persistence of blunt force regulation in China also reveal at least two central weaknesses of the authoritarian state: its fear of popular participation and its reluctance to cede power to institutions that could strengthen environmental governance in the long term. If the Chinese leadership was not so wary of leveraging the powers of civil society to improve its regulatory efforts, or so committed to preventing the courts from acting independently, it could have applied the more incremental, bottom-up, positive-sum regulatory strategies that weak states are using elsewhere.

In this way, blunt force regulation demonstrates both the extraordinary reach and inescapable limits of governing in strong, authoritarian states. This paradox of authoritarian strength and weakness is not limited to pollution control in China. It can also be observed in its policing of protestors: The state expends an enormous amount of resources to demobilize ordinary protestors, sometimes resorting to "man-to-man coverage" (O'Brien and Deng 2017, 92) or outsourcing coercion to private actors (Ong 2018). That the regime is able to apply these methods on such a large scale is a sign of strength. That it is so wary of contention from ordinary citizens is a sign of its weakness.

In this final chapter, I explore how China's authoritarian underpinnings may affect the trajectory of its environmental regulation. How will the regime's current preference for a flexible, adaptive mode of governance impact the future of pollution control?

9.1 THE END TO "GROWTH AT ALL COSTS"

A major conclusion of this book is that China must develop stronger norms of societal compliance before it can achieve sustainable, lasting solutions to its pollution problems. Regulating all industry out of existence is no longer a viable option. Moreover, blunt force regulation is a clumsy vehicle for strengthening these norms, because it punishes compliant firms and focuses on short-term outcomes at the expense of more sustainable, cooperative relations between the regulators and the regulated.

And yet, the frequency of blunt force regulation does signal Beijing's resolve to fix China's pollution problems. Gone are the days of toothless, underfunded environmental agencies engaged in a symbolic fight against indifferent industries. Gone also are the days when the regime treated pollution problems as an unavoidable but tolerable consequence of rapid economic growth.

Meanwhile, the accumulation of harsh environmental enforcement over the years is changing polluters' perceptions of the risks of unbridled pollution. They know the state's discretionary powers can protect them from the law, but they also see fewer opportunities to disregard the central governments' policies. As a company executive explained to me:

> We used to make a big effort to build connections with city officials because they were the ones who could help us with permits or protect us from harsh new regulations. But now these connections are not so useful because Beijing is so determined to clean up the environment that even city officials can't protect us [from these enforcement measures]. Now we have to seek out connections at the higher level because the orders are coming from there.[1]

Exposure to international trade and capital is also changing environmental compliance norms. International companies – which are under pressure from home-country governments and lobby groups to green their supply chain – are pushing Chinese suppliers to meet high environmental standards (Laari et al. 2016; Li, Shao, and Zhang 2019), and Chinese companies are innovating to meet new market opportunities in renewable energy (Nahm and Steinfeld 2014). This reflects a common pattern in global norm diffusion, in which international actors gain leverage in domestic politics or domestic markets and influence local actors to adapt to new norms (Keck and Sikkink 2014).

These norms are also changing the government's attitude towards foreign investment. China no longer appeals to foreign companies as a pollution haven in which manufacturers can take advantage of stripped-down regulations and half-hearted enforcement to increase their profit margins. Instead, the government is moving to upgrade its economy by attracting cleaner investors and introducing new bans to protect its natural environment from this type of predation. For instance, in 2017, China – once the world's largest importer of waste – imposed a ban on waste imports,[2] forcing countries to either change their waste processing habits or dump their garbage elsewhere.[3]

After decades wedded to a "growth at all costs" model, there are signs that local officials may be coming round to an economic model that prioritizes cleaner, greener, high-tech growth, even if it requires painful economic restructuring.

Readers acquainted with the politics of bureaucratic promotion and corruption in China might still ask why a rational, ambitious local official would ever forsake growth to protect the environment. But perhaps a new rationality is driving the calculations of these local officials. Evidently, officials who resolutely destroy pillar industries in the hope that their county or city might become a "rural tourism hub" (as occurred in Luquan County, see Chapter 3)[4] or a "center for ceramics research and development" (see the Foshan city case described in Chapter 1)[5] are not only seeking to fill public (or private) coffers. There seems to be a genuine aspirational element to their actions – a desire to become part of an elite club of clean, green cities with innovative industries and skilled, contented workers (Nahm 2017; van der Kamp et al. 2017). There are more frequent examples of former industrial hubs planning to transform – somewhat improbably – into major tourism destinations.[6] Similar aspirational thinking can be observed in the emergence of China's "ghost cities" – vast urban developments built (partly) in anticipation of a migration and developmental boom that never occurred (Looney and Rithmire 2017; Woodworth and Wallace 2017).

Of course, some officials might still be wedded to the easy prosperity of dirty development. As one man declared to me while surrounded by pools of factory effluent: "I've been eating and sleeping amid this waste for 30 years now! Do you really think I care that much about pollution?"[7] However, others might tire of endless gray skies and smoggy air and decide, irrespective of the cost, to undertake a complete economic turnaround that could set their city on a "clean growth" trajectory. Thus, beyond the purely economic, cost–benefit reasons why local bureaucrats follow central orders to destroy their economies, there is an aspirational element that helps explain the more extreme or irreversible versions of blunt force regulation.

These developments may indicate that compliance is building within society, and that China is finally moving beyond the era of dirty growth. Blunt force regulation does not bolster institutions, and governing loosely by the rules does not strengthen rule following. Yet new norms may still form and consolidate through other social and economic processes, which might in turn move China towards greener growth.

9.2 IS THIS JUST A TRANSITION PHASE?

This book argues that blunt force regulation is not sustainable in the long term, yet it has been effective at implementing an immediate solution to one of the most pressing problems in the developing world – environmental pollution. As the results in Chapter 5 show, blunt force regulation *is* currently more effective at improving air quality than conventional enforcement measures. If the regime had pursued a rules-based legal approach to reduce pollution exclusively through inspections and penalties (instead of through ad hoc, extralegal closures), it may have been trapped in a quagmire of attempting to use inadequate institutions to control escalating pollution levels.

Moreover, observers often suggest that blunt force regulation may be just a transition phase. As norms of compliance build in society, as the legal system matures, and as monitoring technology develops, the state will be able to move towards a more stable, transparent, conventional approach to regulating pollution. After all, few countries set out to build their regulatory systems with strong legal institutions or compliance norms already in place. These institutions often end up developing or "coevolving" in tandem (Dubash and Morgan 2013).

Indeed, China's startling economic successes in the 1990s and 2000s have been attributed to just such a process of "coevolution" (Ang 2016). Lacking the property rights institutions that were considered essential for market reforms, Beijing gave local officials free rein to develop policies that might encourage businesses to invest even without formal property rights guarantees (Naughton 1995; Oi 1999). Amid a severe shortage of fiscal resources, Beijing also encouraged local officials to come up with their own development funds, guaranteeing that a portion of the profits could be kept in local coffers (Ang 2016; Pei 2009, Tsai 2002). Successful experiments were then rolled out on a national level (Heilmann 2008b), leading to the incremental buildup of stable but unexpected market governing institutions that aligned with party leaders' core priorities (Eaton 2013; Tsai 2011).

Perhaps the same process will unfold in the sphere of environmental governance, reaffirming the value of China's adaptive governance model. The success of the country's early economic reforms demonstrated that one can never underestimate local bureaucrats' capacity for innovation, especially when conjuring up solutions to resource shortages or institutional handicaps (Chen 2014). Indeed, China's ability to deliver strong growth in a context of high bureaucratic discretion is why it is often referred to as a "high-capacity state" (Edin 2003; Fukuyama 2013; Rothstein 2015) – a label usually reserved for states with strong, disciplined bureaucratic institutions. Perhaps, then, local experimentation will again produce an unexpected but effective set of institutions that can enforce sustainable solutions to pollution, even without the rule of law or independent regulatory bodies.

If China's adaptive mode of governance proves to be effective at managing pollution in the long term, it will challenge a long-held view in political science that rule-abiding bureaucracies are the key to developmental success. Drawing on Weber's seminal theories, scholars argue that only bureaucrats who are recruited and rewarded based on merit will refrain from using their powers to further personal, corrupt aims (Evans and Rauch 1999). Moreover, only bureaucrats who are offered stable, predictable career paths will apply their technical expertise to long-term developmental goals (Evans 1995; Woo-Cummings 1999). Thus, one thread that unites scholarly prescriptions for well-regulated markets (Bates 2005), sustained growth (Skocpol 1985), improved public good provisions (Herbst 2000), and improved environmental governance (Economy 2014) is the need to foster disciplined, rational, and meritocratic bureaucracies.

If China can develop a workable alternative despite featuring none of these bureaucratic ideals, then this adaptive mode of governance could offer a more attractive, attainable model than the Weberian model held up by advanced western democracies.

9.3 CLEAN AIR AT WHAT COST?

However, Xi Jinping's recent anticorruption campaign has revealed a major hurdle in this hypothetical trajectory in which local bureaucrats develop a sustainable environmental governance model through a process of experimentation. Prior research has noted that while the anticorruption campaign has successfully reduced corruption, one side effect is that it has made even the most experimental, risk-taking bureaucrats more wary of innovating (Hasmath et al. 2019; Ang

2020, 176). This is because bureaucrats need high levels of discretion to come up with ad hoc solutions to unexpected problems, and these solutions often require a greasing of the wheels or an exchange of access money to induce cooperation from powerful local actors. In other words, corruption is a corollary of discretion, and amid the heightened fear and uncertainty surrounding the anticorruption campaign, bureaucrats have decided that the best way to stay safe is to avoid using their discretion altogether (Wang 2021).

The problem is that bureaucratic discretion is still the lynchpin of China's adaptive governance model. Moreover, the party's resilience when faced with seemingly insurmountable social and economic challenges has often been attributed to this built-in discretion, because it allows local officials to develop clever ways to defuse public grievances (Perry 2007; Heilmann and Perry 2011b; Mattingly 2020). Recall, for instance, how deftly local officials used their powers of discretion in the case of Luquan (documented in Chapter 7) to soften the blow of blunt force regulation and to smooth over social tensions generated by mass unemployment. Through a skillful combination of "face work" (Ding 2020, 539), moral appeals, and carefully targeted compensation, local officials managed to cajole even the most powerful factory owners to accept the destruction of their own factories and to cooperate in demobilizing their workers.

However, in the past few years, Xi Jinping has begun to concentrate decision-making power in leading small groups in Beijing (Hasmath et al. 2019; Minzner 2018, 92), chipping away at this much-vaunted discretion. Meanwhile, investigations by the powerful party organ tasked with carrying out the anticorruption campaign, the Central Commission for Discipline Inspection, continue to instill fear and apathy in local officials. In this new environment, it remains to be seen whether local bureaucrats will retain the will or the means to innovate towards more sustainable regulatory solutions, or to implement creative ways to defuse unrest.

This leads to one final, intractable problem with China's adaptive governance model. In environments with high levels of discretion and fluid rules, leaders may act more decisively, and bureaucrats more innovatively. On the other hand, bureaucrats who are bound by legal-contractual obligations or observed by independent judicial institutions are far more likely to take public costs into account when implementing policies (Evans and Rauch 1999; Geddes 1996; North and Weingast 1989; Root 1989; Weber 1978). By choosing fluidity over rules, China's mode of governance sacrifices greater political accountability for greater political discretion.

As I show in Chapter 6, this preference for discretion becomes problematic when it is used in a one-side manner. As the public becomes aware that party or state interests often override the public interest, the use of discretion breeds distrust, which can lead to more adversarial relations between the state and society. Rather than building the relationships, linkages, and cooperative institutions that help societies solve coordination problems and deliver collective benefits, political discretion can contribute to a more ad hoc, fractious engagement between the state and society.

Moreover, while growing norms of compliance among polluters will help improve overall levels of pollution, this does not guarantee that they will ease or alleviate levels of distrust in society. For instance, if norms are changing and the overall trajectory is moving towards better compliance, why is there a rising tide of adversarial environmental activism in China (Zhong and Hwang 2016; Li 2019)? Why have citizens not been appeased by the state's drastic attempts to reduce pollution through blunt force regulation? Gunningham et al. (2004) found that communities' distrust of polluters and regulators can undermine an industry's "social license"; citizens may continue to protest or disrupt production processes, even when a factory is compliant. The failure to address or ease this distrust can therefore lead to a much more chaotic, crisis-based regulation, exacerbating uncertainty costs (Alkon and Wang 2018; McAllister 2008; O'Rourke 2004).

The consequences of this distrust are evident in a series of protests against waste incineration plants in China over the last decade. Citizens from Guangzhou to Zhengzhou, and Beijing to Shenzhen have participated in demonstrations and protests to adamantly oppose the construction of new plants.[8] Waste incineration plants are part of a new nationwide policy to simultaneously fix China's energy shortages and save overflowing landfills by burning waste (as cleanly as possible) to generate electricity. The state has invested vast amounts of money and technology into building these state-of-the-art plants, even inviting supervision from Danish and German companies.[9] Yet, despite repeated official assurances about the safety of these plants, China's middle class continues to be deeply suspicious, convinced that waste incineration will poison a city's air and water.

It seems strange that China's urban middle class would fixate on these high-tech, well-funded waste incineration plants when the air, water, and soil of these cities is already being poisoned by poorly regulated, outdated industrial factories.[10] However, given citizens' general distrust of the government's ability to regulate pollution and enforce safety checks, it is understandable that they would be suspicious of repeated government assurances and seek to prevent new projects where possible (Johnson 2016). This state of affairs has proven incredibly frustrating to policymakers, who have expended vast amounts of political and scientific resources to win citizen support for this policy (Johnson, Lora-Wainwright, and Lu 2018). As one official from the Ministry of Environmental Protection grumbled:

> The problem is, ordinary people only react to pollution that they can see, smell or hear... we made this big effort to close down small, polluting factories, but now citizens want us to close down the big factories because they seem "more polluting." I have seen people protest when they see a factory emitting white-colored water, and then when regulators conduct tests it turns out this water is actually clean! But because citizens lack trust in the government, they don't believe us when we show that the water is clean or that these big factories are compliant.[11]

This kind of deep distrust makes it very hard for the state to appease protestors. It is telling that construction on several waste incineration projects had to be postponed following public protests.[12] Thus, despite China's success in reducing overall emissions through blunt force regulation, widespread distrust in the regulatory system remains. Blunt force regulation may have reduced pollution, but it has not stopped pollution protests.

Moreover, China does not always succeed at containing opposition to blunt force regulation and may sometimes have to reverse its approach mid-campaign, as happened with the government's blunt force regulation of coal stoves in 2017. In August 2017, in an effort to reduce its reliance on coal, Beijing ordered local officials to remove 300 million coal stoves from small businesses and homes all over northern China, and replace them with more environmentally friendly gas furnaces.[13] Targets were set, backed by the threat of punishment and fines,[14] and cadres responded vigorously, even exceeding targets in some regions.[15] However, the intervention happened so quickly that some areas were not connected to gas heating in time to replace the stoves. In other areas, gas prices surged, so people could not afford to pay for heating and reverted to illegally burning coal. As a result, tens of thousands of people in schools, homes, and businesses were left freezing.[16] The impact was so severe that the central government eventually reversed its decree, allowing some places to continue using coal.[17] Even Beijing's municipal government (which adamantly opposed coal usage) eventually had to reopen a coal-fired power plant to sustain the city through the winter.

The state does not seem to be learning from such mistakes. In 2021, provinces around China (including Guangdong, Jilin, Liaoning, and Heilongjiang) were again plunged into extended energy blackouts.[18] Factories had to reduce their production schedules, schools and hospitals were closed, and residential buildings were left without power, causing netizens to erupt in anger.[19] Reports later revealed that these shortages were partly caused by blunt force regulation. Local officials, spurred on by stringent emissions reduction targets, had decided to enforce widespread closures of coal mines over the summer. This sudden shortage of coal, combined with an unexpected surge in energy demand as the economy recovered, left governments in some provinces scrambling to make up for energy shortages.[20] Eventually, in the face of a public outcry, the central government was forced to reopen mines and increase coal production to ride out the storm.[21]

These cases point to a different interpretation of China's path ahead, one in which distrust between the state and society drives the leadership towards a pervasive "short-termism" in environmental governance. Policy implementation is contested and crisis-ridden, and the state must repeatedly return to a low-level equilibrium of "putting out fires" (Naughton and Tsai 2015, 28). The Chinese government can solve problems quickly, but nothing is gained in the long term.

Proponents of China's adaptive mode of governance may argue that the regime is willing to tolerate occasional policy reversals or chaotic civil society battles if it allows the rules to stay fluid, and the regime to remain adaptive. Leaders will accept the need to shut down industries, silence protestors, and sacrifice growth if it means they can preserve leadership discretion. They will tolerate a degree of bureaucratic corruption and disobedience if they can continue experimenting with policy implementation. And they will forge ahead with short-term solutions so long as they have the coercive tools to rectify any problems that may arise.

Others may argue that leaders have been forced into this suboptimal solution. Perhaps the state can control corruption, silence the opposition, and sustain its guerilla-style policy. However, the frequent outbreak of regulatory crises and the revival of polluting activities suggests that the costs of governing without clear rules will be high. Instead of investing in enduring systems to prevent crises, the regime will be caught in the more expensive, exhausting mode of responding to crises after they have occurred. If China's increasing tendency towards top-down, state-centered solutions to governance problems indeed reflects a short-termist mindset, its governance style begins to seem less experimental, less adaptive, and more careworn. In this way, China may eventually find that with blunt force regulation, it is paying too high a cost for clean air.

NOTES

1 Interview X10231019 with company executive, Hong Kong (October 2019).
2 Xinhua, "China tightens ban on solid waste imports," November 19, 2018, www.xinhuanet.com/english/2018-11/19/c_137615850.htm.
3 *East Asia Forum*, "Will China's waste ban force a global cleanup?" December 7, 2018, www.eastasiaforum.org/2018/12/07/will-chinas-waste-ban-force-a-global-clean-up/.
4 *Economic Daily* (经济日报), "Farewell to the 'Cement Corridor'" (告别"水泥走廊), December 17, 2014, www.ce.cn/xwzx/gnsz/gdxw/201412/17/t20141217_4138023.shtml.
5 Xinhua net (新华网), "Can closures bring about economic transformation?" (关停能否带来转型？佛山整治传统陶瓷业引发震撼), May 7 2008, http://news.xinhuanet.com/energy/2008-05/07/content_8121660.htm.
6 *South China Morning Post*, "Chinese city lauded as model of economic transformation struggling as nation's economy cools," August 22, 2016, www.scmp.com/news/china/economy/article/2007253/chinese-city-lauded-model-economic-transformation-struggles; *The Economist*, "You're stir-fried squid," June 18, 2016, www.economist.com/news/china/21700687-youre-fired-chinese-officials-meet-apprentice-youre-stir-fried-squid.
7 Interview X7a190416a with owner of small recycling factory, Guangdong Province (April 2016).
8 Michael Standaert, "As China pushes waste-to-energy incinerators, protests are mounting," April 20, 2017, http://e360.yale.edu/features/as-china-pushes-waste-to-energy-incinerators-protests-are-mounting.
9 Interview X1a160516; *China Dialogue*, "China waste: the burning issue," January 26, 2012, www.chinadialogue.net/article/show/single/en/4739-Chinese-waste-the-burning-issue.
10 For more on the dynamics of these waste incinerator protests, see Johnson 2013, 2020.
11 Interview X1120516 with Ministry of Environmental Protection official, Beijing (May 2016).
12 Specific cases include Hangzhou city in 2014 (*Financial Times*, "China waste incineration protest turns violent," May 11, 2014, www.ft.com/

content/7035866e-d8ca-11e3-a1aa-00144feabdc0) and Hunan Province in 2016 (Reuters, "China shuts down waste-burning plant project over protests," June 27, 2016, www.reuters.com/article/us-china-protests-idUSKCN0ZD0HU).

13 See Ministry of Environmental Protection, 《京津冀及周邊地區2017–2018年秋冬季大氣污染綜合治理攻堅行動方案》, August 24, 2017.

14 *New York Times*, "In China's coal country, a ban brings blue skies and cold homes," February 10, 2018, www.nytimes.com/2018/02/10/world/asia/china-coal-smog-pollution.htm.

15 *The Paper* (澎湃新闻), 《环保部：今年北方将完成煤改400万户，前提确保百姓不受冻>, February 11, 2018; *The Initium*, 中國強推煤改氣惹民怨，為什麼環保與溫暖不可兼得?>, December 6, 2017.

16 *Caixin Global*, "Thousands in rural China secretly burn coal as gas prices soar," December 9, 2017, www.caixinglobal.com/2017-12-08/thousands-in-rural-china-secretly-burn-coal-as-gas-prices-soar-101182697.html.

17 See *Global Times*, 单仁平: 煤改气，国家不是要让部分群众冻着, December 4, 2017; *China Environment News* (中国环境报), November 7, 2013, 《国家发改委连发通知强调 "煤改气"不能一哄而上》

18 BBC, "China power cuts: What is causing the country's blackouts?" September 30, 2021, www.bbc.co.uk/news/business-58733193.

19 *New York Times*, "Power outages hit China, threatening the economy and Christmas," September 27, 2021, www.nytimes.com/2021/09/27/business/economy/china-electricity.html.

20 *Los Angeles Times*, "Traffic lights gone dark. Factories shut down. What caused China's power crisis?" October 2, 2021, www.latimes.com/world-nation/story/2021-10-02/china-power-shortage-energy-coal-climate.

21 Reuters, "China's state planner says coal supply improving, prices stabilising," November 1, 2021, www.reuters.com/business/energy/chinas-state-planner-says-coal-supply-improving-prices-stabilising-2021-11-01/.

Appendix

CHAPTER 4

TABLE A4.1. Definition of variables for Chapter 4

Variable	Definition
Blunt force regulation	The annual total tons of industrial production ordered by Beijing to be reduced in each city, for 2010–2014. This variable only reflects orders for capacity reduction in industries that contribute to air pollution. It does not include tons of production reduced through market slowdowns or individual firm decisions. This data was hand collected using documents from MEP and MIIT.
Revenue per capita	This is the annual sum of own-source revenue (i.e., the sum of all taxes and fees collected and kept at the local level) divided by a city's population. Revenue is measured in RMB (millions). I focus on own-source revenue because in countries such as China, where fiscal transfers to cover budget shortfalls are politicized, this is the best measure of a local government's revenue autonomy (Rodden 2004). The ratio of own-source revenue to a city's population therefore captures how effectively a city can cover its own budget, or how desperately local officials need to raise additional revenue.
SO_2 air pollution level	I use satellite measures of ground-level SO_2 to calculate SO_2 air pollution levels (in Dobson Units). This data is obtained from NASA's OMSO2e dataset (Li et al. 2015). Based on expert advice, I use the Fioletov et al. (2011) method to calculate SO_2 atmospheric levels, which includes averaging only for the summer

Table A4.1. (*cont.*)

Variable	Definition
	months of May–September (when there is no snow coverage). Given that central and provincial officials may also lack accurate data on air pollution when making decisions, I run the same tests with government-reported levels of SO_2, obtained from the *China Environment Yearbook*. The results remain the same.
GDP services*	The total annual GDP (RMB billions) from services industries.
Real estate investment*	The total revenue (in RMB millions) that a city obtains from the real estate industry.
Gross industrial output/No. of industrial firms*	Annual gross industrial output (in RMB millions) for each city scaled by the number of industrial firms for each city.
Steel output*	Annual steel production (in million tons) for each city. Data on steel output is only available at the provincial level. Given that variation in policy enforcement actions cluster at the provincial level, I impute this data to the city level.

*Data for these variables was obtained from the National Bureau of Statistics' city yearbooks.

Data Notes

1. PITI Transparency Data

Data assessing the transparency scores of different cities is obtained from the Institute of Public and Environmental Affairs, a well-respected environmental NGO in China that produces the PITI scores. This NGO evaluates the implementation of pollution transparency in 113 cities. Values range from 0 (poor transparency) to 100 (excellent transparency) and include criteria such as local officials' performance on 1) complying with daily emissions standards, 2) monitoring polluters, 3) disclosing data on emissions levels, and 4) responding to public petitions on pollution.

2. Table 4.3: Effect of Bureaucratic Noncompliance on Blunt Force Regulation

Model specifications: The dependent variable (*Blunt Force Regulation (logged)*) is measured for the years 2010–2014, whereas the independent variables are measured for 2009–2013. I lag the independent variables because blunt force orders are issued at the beginning of the year, so decisions about how much production each city will be forced to reduce depends on the previous year's performance. This model uses city-level fixed effects. I also include province-year fixed effects to account for province-wide common shocks, and because provinces are responsible for allocating and enacting enforcement targets. Finally, I control for the impact of blunt force regulation assigned in the previous year by including blunt force outcomes for t–1, t–2, t–3, and t–4 in the model.

3. A Note on the Use of SO_2 as a Measure of Industrial Pollution

I use sulfur dioxide (SO_2) to measure air pollution for two reasons. First, SO_2 is the best measure of industrial air pollution, whereas other airborne pollutants (such as PM2.5 and NOx) are also produced by car and ship exhaust. Second, SO_2 is not prone to secondary chemical reactions in the air, so the amount of SO_2 in the atmosphere is a direct product of industrial emissions. PM2.5 is often produced by secondary reactions in the air. Thus the levels of SO_2 in the atmosphere are more directly related to industrial pollution than either PM2.5 or NOx. This decision is based on advice from atmospheric science experts at Tsinghua University and information on atmospheric pollution in *Clearer Skies Over China* (Nielsen and Ho 2013). The same reasoning applies for analysis in Chapter 5.

4. A Note on the Use of SO_2 Remote Sensing Data

Estimates of ground-level SO_2 from satellite data can now be pinned down to an area of approximately 27 x 27 km^2 at the equator, approximately the area of a Chinese city and its surrounding counties. Given that city officials usually exercise direct authority over large factories in surrounding counties, it is useful to include SO_2 levels from these areas. To calculate each city's SO_2 level, I overlay the SO_2 values from satellite data onto the city geocoordinates. I take the average of all SO_2 values that overlap the city grid.

SO_2 emissions are measured in Dobson Units (DU). 1 DU is equal to $2.69 \cdot 1026$ molec·km−2. Scientifically, this means "if you were to compress all of the sulfur dioxide in a column of the atmosphere into a flat layer at standard temperature and pressure ($0°$ C and 1013.25 hPa), one Dobson Unit would be 0.01 mm thick and would contain

0.0285 grams of SO_2 per square meter" (see NASA, https://so2.gsfc
.nasa.gov/so2intro.html). To put this into context, Zibo city
(Shandong Province), one of the most polluted cities in China,
recorded a mean SO_2 level of 48.140 DU in 2010–2012 for May to
September. Lincang (Yunnan Province), one of the least polluted
cities in China, recorded a mean SO_2 level of 1.598 DU for same
period.

TABLE A5.1. Effect of enforcement measures on air pollution levels
(with standardized variables)

	SO$_2$ levels			
	(1)	(2)	(3)	(4)
Blunt force regulation	−0.149***	−0.145***	−0.162***	−0.181*
	(0.042)	(0.042)	(0.042)	(0.094)
Pollution inspections			−0.005	
			(0.010)	
Pollution fines			−0.022	
			(0.023)	
Pollution transparency score				−0.039
				(0.035)
Neighbor SO$_2$ levels		0.655***	0.646***	0.674***
		(0.106)	(0.112)	(0.104)
Electricity consumption		0.321***	0.342***	0.230*
		(0.099)	(0.106)	(0.119)
GDP		−0.142**	−0.134	0.071
		(0.083)	(0.084)	(0.123)
Observations	1,410	1,384	1,209	548
Number of cities	282	281	271	116
City fixed effects	✓	✓	✓	✓
Year fixed effects	✓	✓	✓	✓
Adjusted R-squared	0.25	0.35	0.34	0.43

Note: Robust standard errors are in parentheses. Variables are standardized.
Significance: *$p < 0.1$; **$p < 0.05$; ***$p < 0.01$. The dependent variable is
the absolute change (reduction or increase) in SO_2 levels between 2012
and 2015.

CHAPTER 5

Data Notes for Chapter 5

1. Measurement of Enforcement Variables in Tables 5.1 and A5.1, and Figures 5.5 and 5.6

I assess the impacts of conventional regulation differently from those of blunt force regulation because they operate differently. For conventional regulation, I look at how the *change in* the number of inspections or penalties between the two periods impacts shifts in pollution levels because documents from provincial-level Environmental Protection Bureaus indicate that administrative penalties are often levied against the same companies for several consecutive years. Thus the intensity of penalties must be measured against the baseline of previous penalties. If this practice is widespread, then unlike blunt force regulation, a given administrative punishment will not have a one-off impact on reducing pollution. Instead, it is the *change* in the number of penalties over time that is associated with changes in pollution levels.

By contrast, blunt force regulation directly reduces pollution levels because it is enacted through factory closures and forced reductions. Moreover, enforcement actions will have a lasting impact on pollution reduction, because units subjected to blunt force regulation will disappear from the population of polluters the following year. Blunt force regulation imposed in t1 (e.g. in the first year) cannot be imposed again in t2 (e.g. in the second year) against those same units. Measuring the change in total tons across periods will obscure this impact. For instance, even if the intensity of blunt force regulation in Shijiazhuang decreased between t1 and t2, blunt force reductions in t2 will still have an absolute impact on pollution levels. This means that blunt force regulation has an additive impact on air pollution over time. Thus, in contrast to the conventional enforcement variables, I examine how the *total* tons reduced so far affects the change in pollution levels in the following year, not the *change in* tons reduced between the 2 years. I achieve this by adding each year's total blunt force regulation (in tons) to the sum of the previous years.

2. Using SO$_2$ Remote Sensing Data and the Use of SO$_2$ as a Measure of Industrial Pollution

See data notes in for Chapter 4 (appendix) for explanations on how SO$_2$ measures were obtained and why I chose to use SO$_2$ to measure industrial pollution.

TABLE A5.2. Definition of variables for Chapter 5

Variable	Definition
SO$_2$ levels	The annual level of sulfur dioxide (SO$_2$) recorded in a city for the years 2010–2015. Data was obtained from the OMSO2e dataset on the NASA website. Based on expert advice, I used Fioletov et al.'s (2011) method to calculate SO$_2$ atmospheric levels, which includes averaging only the summer months of May–September (when there is no snow coverage), and then averaging across 3 years to reduce measurement error from severe cloud cover and extreme weather patterns. Unit = Dobson Units (DU)
Blunt force regulation	The annual total tons of industrial production ordered by Beijing to be forcibly reduced in each city for the years 2009–2014. This variable only measures orders for capacity reduction in industries that contribute to air pollution. It does not include tons of production reduced through market slowdowns, or as a result of individual firm decisions. Nor does it include blunt force measures that took place against coal-fired power plants (which are regulated separately). This data was hand collected using documents from the MEP and MIIT. Unit = million tons
Pollution fines	The annual total amount of pollution fees (排污费) and administrative fines (罚款) collected by city-level governments for the years 2009–2014. Data on pollution fines was hand collected from city yearbooks (城市年检), which record pollution fines in their "environmental protection" section. Unit = RMB million
Pollution inspections	The annual total number of inspections (检查) and monitoring visits (监察) conducted by city-level governments for the years 2009–2014. Data on inspections was hand collected from city yearbooks (城市年鉴), which record inspections in their "environmental protection" section. Unit = 1,000 inspections
Pollution transparency score	The annual pollution transparency score assigned to each city for the years 2009–2014. This score is assigned based on each city's performance on monitoring polluters, disclosing their emissions levels, and responding to public petitions related to pollution. Theoretically, it puts pressure on firms to improve their

Table A5.2. (*cont.*)

Variable	Definition
	compliance in the following year. This data is obtained from the Institute of Public and Environmental Affairs, a well-respected environmental NGO in China that produces the PITI scores. This NGO evaluates the implementation of pollution transparency in 113 cities. Values range from 0 (poor transparency) to 100 (excellent transparency). Unit = Score/100
Neighbor SO2 emissions	The annual mean SO2 levels of all neighboring cities (within 100km) of each of the 282 cities in the dataset for the years 2010–2015. This variable is weighted by the inverse distance, so the closer the neighbor, the stronger the weight. It is also additive, so for cities with multiple neighbors, this variable represents the sum of neighbor SO2 levels (weighted by distance). This variable is calculated using the same NASA satellite dataset used to calculate SO2 levels. Unit = Dobson Units (DU)
Electricity consumption	The annual total consumption of electricity in each city for the years 2009–2014. This variable is intended to control for changes in emissions from coal-fired power plants, which are a key source of emissions, but are not included as blunt force regulation targets. This data was obtained from the National Bureau of Statistics. Unit = kilowatt hours (billion)
GDP	The annual GDP of each city for the years 2009–2014. This data was obtained from the National Bureau of Statistics. Unit = RMB billion

BIBLIOGRAPHY

Alkon, M., & Wang, E. H. (2018). Pollution lowers support for China's regime: quasi-experimental evidence from Beijing. *The Journal of Politics*, 80(1), 327–31.

Almond, D., Du, X., Karplus, V. J., & Zhang, S. (2021). Ambiguous air pollution effects of China's COVID-19 lock-down. *AEA Papers and Proceedings*, 111, 376–80.

Amengual, M. (2013). Pollution in the garden of the Argentine republic: building state capacity to escape from chaotic regulation. *Politics & Society*, 41, 527–60.

(2016). *Politicized Enforcement in Argentina: Labor and Environmental Regulation*. Cambridge University Press.

Amengual, M., & Dargent, E. (2020). The social determinants of enforcement. In Daniel M. Brinks, Steven Levitsky, and María Victoria Murillo, eds., *The Politics of Institutional Weakness in Latin America*. Cambridge University Press, pp. 161–82.

Ang, Y. Y. (2016). *How China Escaped the Poverty Trap*. Cornell University Press.

(2017). Beyond Weber: conceptualizing an alternative ideal type of bureaucracy in developing contexts. *Regulation & Governance*, 11(3), 282–98.

(2020). *China's Gilded Age: The Paradox of Economic Boom and Vast Corruption*. Cambridge University Press.

Ang, Y. Y., & Jia, N. (2014). Perverse complementarity: political connections and the use of courts among private firms in China. *The Journal of Politics*, 76(2), 318–32.

Auerbach, A. M. (2020). *Demanding Development: The Politics of Public Goods Provision in India's Urban Slums*. Cambridge University Press.

Auyero, J., & Swistun, D. A. (2009). *Flammable: Environmental Suffering in an Argentine Shantytown*. Oxford University Press.

Ayres, I., & Braithwaite, J. (1992). *Responsive Regulation: Transcending the Deregulation Debate*. Oxford University Press.

Badran, A. (2013). Understanding the Egyptian regulatory state: independent regulators in theory and practice. In N. K. Dubash and B. Morgan, eds., *The Rise of the Regulatory State of the South: Infrastructure and Development in Emerging Economies*. Oxford University Press, pp. 53–74.

Baker, S. R., Bloom, N., & Davis, S. J. (2016). Measuring economic policy uncertainty. *The Quarterly Journal of Economics*, 131(4), 1593–636.

Bakken, B. (2005). *Crime, Punishment, and Policing in China* (Asia/Pacific/ perspectives). Rowman & Littlefield.

Bardach, E., & Kagan, R. A. (1982). *Going by the Book: The Problem of Regulatory Unreasonableness*. Temple University Press.

Bardhan, P., & Mookherjee, D. (2006). Decentralisation and accountability in infrastructure delivery in developing countries. *The Economic Journal*, 116(508), 101–27.

Bates, R. H. (2005). *Markets and States in Tropical Africa: The Political Basis of Agricultural Policies*. University of California Press.

Beeson, M. (2010). The coming of environmental authoritarianism. *Environmental Politics*, 19(2), 276–94.

Bell, R., & Narain, U. (2005). Who changed Delhi's air? The roles of the court and the executive in environmental decisionmaking. Discussion Papers dp-05-48, Resources For the Future. https://ideas.repec.org/p/rff/ dpaper/dp-05-48.html.

Bernstein, T. P., & Lü, X. (2000). Taxation without representation: peasants, the central and the local states in reform China. *The China Quarterly*, 163, 742–63.

Berwick, E., & Christia, F. (2018). State capacity redux: integrating classical and experimental contributions to an enduring debate. *Annual Review of Political Science*, 21(1), 71–91.

Biddulph, S., Cooney, S., & Zhu, Y. (2012). Rule of law with Chinese characteristics: the role of campaigns in lawmaking. *Law & Policy*, 34 (4), 373–401.

Birney, M. (2014). Decentralization and veiled corruption under China's "rule of mandates." *World Development*, 53, 55–67.

Black, J. (2010). *Risk-Based Regulation: Choices, Practices and Lessons Being Learnt*. OECD.

Blackman, A. (2000). Informal sector pollution control: what policy options do we have?. *World Development*, 28(12), 2067–82.

(2009). Alternative pollution control policies in developing countries: informal, informational, and voluntary. Discussion Papers dp-09-14- efd, Resources For the Future.

Blackman, A., Afsah, S., & Ratunanda, D. (2004). How do public disclosure pollution control programs work? Evidence from Indonesia. *Human Ecology Review*, 11, 235–46.

Blair, R. A., Morse, B. S., & Tsai, L. L. (2017). Public health and public trust: survey evidence from the Ebola virus disease epidemic in Liberia. *Social Science & Medicine*, 172, 89–97.

Blecher, M. J. (2002). Hegemony and workers' politics in China. *The China Quarterly*, 170, 283–303.

Braithwaite, J. (2006). Responsive regulation and developing economies. *World Development*, 34(5), 884–98.

Brinks, D. M., Levitsky, S., & Murillo, M. V. (2019). *Understanding Institutional Weakness: Power and Design in Latin American Institutions*. Cambridge University Press.

Brownlee, J. (2007). *Authoritarianism in an Age of Democratization*. Cambridge University Press.

Cai, Y. (2010). *Collective Resistance in China: Why Popular Protests Succeed or Fail*. Stanford University Press.

(2014). Managing group interests in China. *Political Science Quarterly*, 129 (1), 107–31.

Cao, X., Deng, Q., Li, X., & Shao, Z. (2021). Fine me if you can: fixed asset intensity and enforcement of environmental regulations in China. *Regulation & Governance*. https://doi.org/10.1111/rego.12406.

Cao, X., Kostka, G., & Xu, X. (2019). Environmental political business cycles: the case of PM2.5 air pollution in Chinese prefectures. *Environmental Science & Policy*, 93, 92–100.

Carrigan, C., & Coglianese, C. (2011). The politics of regulation: from new institutionalism to new governance. *Annual Review of Political Science*, 14 (1), 107–29.

Centeno, M. A., Kohli, A., Yashar, D. J., & Mistree, D. (2017). *States in the Developing World*. Cambridge University Press.

Chan, A. T., & O'Brien, K. J. (2019). Phantom services: deflecting migrant workers in China. *The China Journal*, 81, 103–22.

Chan, C. K. C., & Ngai, P. (2009). The making of a new working class? A study of collective actions of migrant workers in South China. *The China Quarterly*, 198, 287–303.

Chan, K. N., & Fan, S. (2021). Friction and bureaucratic control in authoritarian regimes. *Regulation & Governance*, 15(4), 1406–18.

Chan, K. N., & Lam, W. F. (2018). Bureaucratic control and information processing: an institutional comparison. *Governance*, 31(3), 575–92.

Chaudhry, K. A. (1993). The myths of the market and the common history of late developers. *Politics & Society*, 21(3), 245–74.

Chen, J., Jiang, F., & Tong, G. (2017). Economic policy uncertainty in China and stock market expected returns. *Accounting & Finance*, 57(5), 1265–86.

Chen, L. (2014). Varieties of global capital and the paradox of local upgrading in China. *Politics & Society*, 42(2), 223–52.

Chen, L., & Hollenbach, F. M. (2022). Capital mobility and taxation: state–business collusion in China. *International Studies Quarterly*, 66(1), sqab096.

Chen, X. (2012). *Social Protest and Contentious Authoritarianism in China*. Cambridge University Press.

Chng, N. R. (2012). Regulatory mobilization and service delivery at the edge of the regulatory state. *Regulation & Governance*, 6(3), 344–61.

Coglianese, C., & Kagan, R. A. (2008). Regulation and regulatory processes (SSRN Scholarly Paper ID 1297410). Social Science Research Network.

Coglianese, C., & Lazer, D. (2003). Management-based regulation: prescribing private management to achieve public goals. *Law & Society Review*, 37(4), 691–730.

Cole, D. H., & Grossman, P. Z. (2003). When is command-and-control efficient? Institutions, technology, and the comparative efficiency of alternative regulatory regimes for environmental protection. In P. Berck and G. E. Helfand, eds., *The Theory and Practice of Command and Control in Environmental Policy*. Routledge, pp. 115–66.

Dasgupta, N. (1997). Greening small recycling firms: the case of lead smelting units in Calcutta. *Environment and Urbanization*, 9(2), 289–306.

(1998). Tall blunders: present strategies do more harm than good. *Down to Earth*, 30, 22–25.

(2000). Environmental enforcement and small industries in India: reworking the problem in the poverty context. *World Development*, 28 (5), 945–67.

De Soto, H. (2001). *The Mystery of Capital: Why Capitalism Triumphs in the West and Fails Everywhere Else*. London: Black Swan.

Deng, G., & Kennedy, S. (2010). Big business and industry association lobbying in China: the paradox of contrasting styles. *The China Journal*, 63, 101–25.

Deng, Y., & O'Brien, K. J. (2013). Relational repression in China: using social ties to demobilize protesters. *The China Quarterly*, 215, 533–52.

Dickson, B. J. (2003). *Red Capitalists in China: The Party, Private Entrepreneurs, and Prospects for Political Change*. Cambridge University Press.

(2008). *Wealth into Power: The Communist Party's Embrace of China's Private Sector*. Cambridge University Press.

Ding, I. (2017). Performative Governance. Ph.D. Dissertation, University of Pittsburgh.

(2020). Performative governance. *World Politics*, 72(4), 525–56.

Distelhorst, G. (2017). The power of empty promises: quasi-democratic institutions and activism in China. *Comparative Political Studies*, 50(4), 464–98.

Distelhorst, G., & Hou, Y. (2017). Constituency service under nondemocratic rule: evidence from China. *The Journal of Politics*, 79(3), 1024–1040.

Downs, A. (1967). *Inside Bureaucracy*. Little, Brown.

Dubash, N. K., & Morgan, B. (2012). Understanding the rise of the regulatory state of the South. *Regulation & Governance*, 6(3), 261–81.

(2013). *The Rise of the Regulatory State of the South: Infrastructure and Development in Emerging Economies*. Oxford University Press.

Duflo, E., Greenstone, M., Pande, R., & Ryan, N. (2013). Truth-telling by third-party auditors and the response of polluting firms: experimental evidence from India. *The Quarterly Journal of Economics*, 128(4), 1499–1545.

Dutton, M. (2005). *Policing Chinese Politics: A History*. Duke University Press.

Eaton, S. (2013). Political economy of the advancing state: the case of China's airlines reform. *The China Journal*, 69, 64–86.

Eaton, S., & Kostka, G. (2014). Authoritarian environmentalism undermined? Local leaders' time horizons and environmental policy implementation in China. *The China Quarterly*, 218, 359–80.

(2017). Central protectionism in China: the "central SOE problem" in environmental governance. *The China Quarterly*, 231, 685–704.

Ebenstein, A., Fan, M., Greenstone, M., He, G., Yin, P., & Zhou, M. (2015). Growth, pollution, and life expectancy: China from 1991–2012. *American Economic Review*, 105(5), 226–31.

Economy, E. (2014). Environmental governance in China: state control to crisis management. *Daedalus*, 143(2), 184–97.

Edin, M. (2003). State capacity and local agent control in China: CCP cadre management from a township perspective. *The China Quarterly*, 173, 35–52.

Evans, P. B. (1995). *Embedded Autonomy: States and Industrial Transformation*. Princeton University Press.

Evans, P., & Rauch, J. E. (1999). Bureaucracy and growth: a cross-national analysis of the effects of "Weberian" state structures on economic growth. *American Sociological Review*, 64(5), 748–65.

Faguet, J.-P. (2012). *Decentralization and Popular Democracy: Governance from Below in Bolivia*. University of Michigan Press.

(2014). Decentralization and governance. *World Development*, 53, 2–13.

Fewsmith, J., & Gao, X. (2014). Local governance in China: incentives & tensions. *Daedalus*, 143(2), 170–83.

Fioletov, V. E., McLinden, C. A., Krotkov, N., Moran, M. D., & Yang, K. (2011). Estimation of SO2 emissions using OMI retrievals. *Geophysical Research Letters*, 38(21).

Friedman, E. (2014). *Insurgency Trap: Labor Politics in Postsocialist China*. Cornell University Press.

Fu, D. (2017). Disguised collective action in China. *Comparative Political Studies*, 50(4), 499–527.

Fukuyama, F. (2013). What is governance? *Governance*, 26(3), 347–68.

Gallagher, M. E. (2002). "Reform and openness": why China's economic reforms have delayed democracy. *World Politics*, 54(3), 338–72.

(2006). Mobilizing the law in China: "Informed Disenchantment" and the development of legal consciousness. *Law & Society Review*, 40(4), 783–816.

Gallo, C. (1991). *Taxes and State Power: Political Instability in Bolivia, 1900–1950*. Temple University Press.

Gandhi, J., & Przeworski, A. (2006). Cooperation, cooptation, and rebellion under dictatorships. *Economics & Politics*, 18(1), 1–26.

García, J. H., Sterner, T., & Afsah, S. (2007). Public disclosure of industrial pollution: the PROPER approach for Indonesia? *Environment and Development Economics*, 12(6), 739–56.

Geddes, B. (1996). *Politician's Dilemma: Building State Capacity in Latin America (1st paperback)*. University of California Press.

Ghanem, D., & Zhang, J. (2014). 'Effortless Perfection': do Chinese cities manipulate air pollution data?. *Journal of Environmental Economics and Management*, 68(2), 203–25.

Ghertner, D. A. (2015). *Rule by Aesthetics: World-Class City Making in Delhi*. Oxford University Press.

Gilley, B. (2012). Authoritarian environmentalism and China's response to climate change. *Environmental Politics*, 21(2), 287–307.

Ginsburg, T., & Moustafa, T. (2008). *Rule by Law: The Politics of Courts in Authoritarian Regimes*. Cambridge University Press.

Goldstone, J. A. (2006). A historical, not comparative method: breakthroughs and limitations in the theory and methodology of Michael Mann's analysis of power. In J. A. Hall & R. Schroeder, eds., *An Anatomy of Power: The Social Theory of Michael Mann*. Cambridge University Press, pp. 263–82.

Goodwin, J. (2001). *No Other Way Out: States and Revolutionary Movements, 1945–1991*. Cambridge University Press.

Grabosky, P. (2013). Beyond responsive regulation: the expanding role of non-state actors in the regulatory process. *Regulation & Governance*, 7(1), 114–23.

Gray, W. B., & Shadbegian, R. J. (2005). When and why do plants comply? Paper mills in the 1980s. *Law & Policy*, 27(2), 238–61.

Greenstone, M., & Hanna, R. (2014). Environmental regulations, air and water pollution, and infant mortality in India. *American Economic Review*, 104(10), 3038–72.

Gunningham, N. A., Thornton, D., & Kagan, R. A. (2005). Motivating management: corporate compliance in environmental protection. *Law & Policy*, 27(2), 289–316.

Gunningham, N., & Holley, C. (2016). Next-generation environmental regulation: law, regulation, and governance. *Annual Review of Law and Social Science*, 12(1), 273–93.

Gunningham, N., Kagan, R. A., & Thornton, D. (2004). Social license and environmental protection: why businesses go beyond compliance. *Law & Social Inquiry*, 29(2), 307–41.

Haber, S. (2006). *Authoritarian government. The Oxford Handbook of Political Economy*. Oxford University Press, pp. 693–707.

Haddad, M. A. (2015). Increasing environmental performance in a context of low governmental enforcement: evidence from China. *The Journal of Environment & Development*, 24(1), 3–25.

Hall, J. A., & Schroeder, R. (2006). *An Anatomy of Power: The Social Theory of Michael Mann*. Cambridge University Press.

Han, D., Currell, M. J., & Cao, G. (2016). Deep challenges for China's war on water pollution. *Environmental Pollution*, 218, 1222–33.

Harrison, A., Hyman, B., Martin, L., & Nataraj, S. (2015). *When Do Firms Go Green?: Comparing Price Incentives with Command and Control Regulations in India*. National Bureau of Economic Research.

Hasmath, R., Teets, J. C., & Lewis, O. A. (2019). The innovative personality? Policy making and experimentation in an authoritarian bureaucracy. *Public Administration and Development*, 39(3), 154–62.

Haufler, V. (2013). *A Public Role for the Private Sector: Industry Self-regulation in a Global Economy*. Carnegie Endowment for International Peace.

Hawkins, K. (1984). *Environment and Enforcement: Regulation and the Social Definition of Pollution*. Clarendon Press.

He, C., & Pan, F. (2013). Decentralization and the environment: industrial air pollution in Chinese cities. In J. Y. Man, ed., *China's Environmental Policy and Urban Development*. Lincoln Institute of Land Policy.

He, B., & Warren, M. E. (2011). Authoritarian deliberation: the deliberative turn in Chinese political development. *Perspectives on Politics*, 9(2), 269–89.

Heilmann, S. (2008a). Policy experimentation in China's economic rise. *Studies in Comparative International Development*, 43(1), 1–26.

(2008b). From local experiments to national policy: the origins of China's distinctive policy process. *The China Journal*, 59, 1–30.

(2009). Maximum tinkering under uncertainty: unorthodox lessons from China. *Modern China*, 35(4), 450–62.

Heilmann, S., & Melton, O. (2013). The reinvention of development planning in China, 1993–2012. *Modern China*, 39(6), 580–628.

Heilmann, S., & Perry, E. J. (2011a). Embracing uncertainty: guerrilla policy style and adaptive governance in China. In S. Heilmann and E. J. Perry, eds., *Mao's Invisible Hand: The Political Foundations of Adaptive Governance in China*. Harvard University Press, pp. 1–29.

(2011b). *Mao's Invisible Hand: The Political Foundations of Adaptive Governance in China*. Harvard University Press.

Heller, P. (2017). Development in the city: growth and inclusion in India, Brazil, and South Africa. In M. Centeno, A., Kohli, D., Yashar, & D. Mistree, eds., *States in the Developing World*. Cambridge University Press, pp. 309–38.

Helmke, G., & Rosenbluth, F. (2009). Regimes and the rule of law: judicial independence in comparative perspective. *Annual Review of Political Science*, 12(1), 345–66.

Hendley, K. (2015). Resisting multiple narratives of law in transition countries: Russia and beyond. *Law & Social Inquiry*, 40(2), 531–52.

Hensengerth, O., & Lu, Y. (2019). Emerging environmental multi-level governance in China? Environmental protests, public participation and local institution-building. *Public Policy and Administration*, 34(2), 121–43.

Herbst, J. (2000). Economic incentives, natural resources and conflict in Africa. *Journal of African Economies*, 9(3), 270–94.

Hillman, B. (2010). Factions and spoils: examining political behavior within the local state in China. *The China Journal*, 64, 1–18.

Hochstetler, K. (2013). Civil society and the regulatory state of the South. In N. Dubash, K. Navroz, and B. Morgan, eds., *The Rise of the Regulatory State of the South: Infrastructure and Development in Emerging Economies.* Oxford University Press, pp. 267–75.

Holland, A. (2017). *Forbearance as Redistribution: The Politics of Informal Welfare in Latin America.* Cambridge University Press.

Holzner, C. (2004). The end of clientelism? Strong and weak networks in a Mexican squatter movement. *Mobilization*, 9(3), 223–40.

Hou, Y. (2019). *The Private Sector in Public Office: Selective Property Rights in China.* Cambridge University Press.

Hsueh, R. (2016). *China's Regulatory State: A New Strategy for Globalization.* Cornell University Press.

Huang, D. (2013). How do entrepreneurs influence local government policy processes: a state-centered categorization and case analysis (企业家如何影响地方 政策过程:基于国家中心的类型建构和案例分析). *Sociological Analysis* (社会学研究), 5, 172–96.

Huang, H. (2015). Propaganda as signaling. *Comparative Politics*, 47(4), 419–44.

(2018). The pathology of hard propaganda. *The Journal of Politics*, 80(3), 1034–38.

Huang, Y. (2008). *Capitalism with Chinese Characteristics: Entrepreneurship and the State.* Cambridge University Press.

Huntington, S. P. (1991). Democracy's third wave. *Journal of Democracy*, 2(2), 12–34.

Hurst, W. (2016). Chinese law and governance: moving beyond responsive authoritarianism and the rule of law. *Journal of Chinese Governance*, 1(3), 457–69.

(2018). *Ruling Before the Law: The Politics of Legal Regimes in China and Indonesia.* Cambridge University Press.

Itahashi, S., Uno, I., Yumimoto, K., Irie, H., Osada, K., Ogata, K., Fukushima, H., Wang, Z., & Ohara, T. (2012). Interannual variation in the fine-mode MODIS aerosol optical depth and its relationship to the changes in sulfur dioxide emissions in China between 2000 and 2010. *Atmospheric Chemistry and Physics*, 12(5), 2631–40.

Jahiel, A. R. (1998). The organization of environmental protection in China. *The China Quarterly*, 156, 757–87.

Jensen, N. (2008). Political risk, democratic institutions, and foreign direct investment. *The Journal of Politics*, 70(4), 1040–52.

Jensen, N. M., Malesky, E., & Weymouth, S. (2014). Unbundling the relationship between authoritarian legislatures and political risk. *British Journal of Political Science*, 44(3), 655–84.

Jia, R. (2017). Pollution for promotion. *21st Century China Center Research Paper* (2017-05).

Jiang, J. (2018). Making bureaucracy work: patronage networks, performance incentives, and economic development in China. *American Journal of Political Science*, 62(4), 982–99.

Johnson, T. (2013). The health factor in anti-waste incinerator campaigns in Beijing and Guangzhou. *The China Quarterly*, 214, 356–75.

Johnson, T. R. (2016). Regulatory dynamism of environmental mobilization in urban China. *Regulation & Governance*, 10(1), 14–28.

(2020). Public participation in China's EIA process and the regulation of environmental disputes. *Environmental Impact Assessment Review*, 81, 106359.

Johnson, T., Lora-Wainwright, A., & Lu, J. (2018). The quest for environmental justice in China: citizen participation and the rural–urban network against Panguanying's waste incinerator. *Sustainability Science*, 13(3), 733–46.

Josephson, P. R. (2004). *Resources Under Regimes: Technology, Environment, and the State*. Harvard University Press.

Kagan, R. A., Gunningham, N., & Thornton, D. (2003). Explaining corporate environmental performance: how does regulation matter? *Law & Society Review*, 37(1), 51–90.

Karplus, V. J., Shen, X., & Zhang, D. (2020). Herding cats: firm noncompliance in China's industrial energy efficiency program. *The Energy Journal*, 41(4), 1–26.

Karplus, V. J., & Wu, M. (2019). Crackdowns in hierarchies: evidence from China's environmental inspections. In *MIT CEEPR Working Paper 2019-017*.

Karplus, V. J., Zhang, S., & Almond, D. (2018). Quantifying coal power plant responses to tighter SO2 emissions standards in China. *Proceedings of the National Academy of Sciences*, 115(27), 7004–9.

Keck, M. E., & Sikkink, K. (2014). *Activists beyond Borders: Advocacy Networks in International Politics*. Cornell University Press.

Kelman, M. (1981). Interpretive construction in the substantive criminal law. *Stanford Law Review*, 33(4), 591–673.

Kennedy, J. J. (2013). Finance and rural governance: centralization and local challenges. *The Journal of Peasant Studies*, 40(6), 1009–26.

Kennedy, S. (2009). *The Business of Lobbying in China*. Harvard University Press.

King, G., Pan, J., & Roberts, M. E. (2013). How censorship in China allows government criticism but silences collective expression. *American Political Science Review*, 107(2), 326–43.

Klitgaard, R. E. (1988). *Controlling Corruption*. University of California Press.

Konisky, D. M. (2009). Inequities in enforcement? Environmental justice and government performance. *Journal of Policy Analysis and Management*, 28(1), 102–21.

Konisky, D. M., & Teodoro, M. P. (2016). When governments regulate governments. *American Journal of Political Science*, 60(3), 559–74.

Kostka, G. (2019). China's social credit systems and public opinion: explaining high levels of approval. *New Media & Society*, 21(7), 1565–93.

Kostka, G., & Goron, C. (2021). From targets to inspections: the issue of fairness in China's environmental policy implementation. *Environmental Politics*, 30(4), 513–37.

Kostka, G., & Hobbs, W. (2012). Local energy efficiency policy implementation in China: bridging the gap between national priorities and local interests. *The China Quarterly*, 211, 765–85.

Kostka, G., & Mol, A. P. J. (2013). Implementation and participation in China's local environmental politics: challenges and innovations. *Journal of Environmental Policy & Planning*, 15(1), 3–16.

Kostka, G., & Nahm, J. (2017). Central–local relations: recentralization and environmental governance in China. *The China Quarterly*, 231, 567–82.

Kuhonta, E. M. (2011). *The Institutional Imperative: The Politics of Equitable Development in Southeast Asia*. Stanford University Press.

Kung, J., Cai, Y., & Sun, X. (2009). Rural cadres and governance in China: incentive, institution and accountability. *The China Journal*, 62, 61–77.

Kuran, T. (1991). Now out of never: the element of surprise in the East European revolution of 1989. *World Politics*, 44(1), 7–48.

Laari, S., Töyli, J., Solakivi, T., & Ojala, L. (2016). Firm performance and customer-driven green supply chain management. *Journal of Cleaner Production*, 112, 1960–70.

Landry, P. F. (2008). *Decentralized Authoritarianism in China: The Communist Party's Control of Local Elites in the Post-Mao Era*. Cambridge University Press.

Lardy, N. R. (2014). *Markets over Mao: The Rise of Private Business in China*. Peterson Institute for International Economics.

Lee, C. K. (2007). *Against the Law: Labor Protests in China's Rustbelt and Sunbelt*. University of California Press.

(2017). *The Specter of Global China: Politics, Labor, and Foreign Investment in Africa*. University of Chicago Press.

Lee, M. M., & Zhang, N. (2017). Legibility and the informational foundations of state capacity. *The Journal of Politics*, 79(1), 118–32.

Leng, N. (2020) *NIMBY? Only to Improve State–business Relations.* Unpublished Paper.

Leutert, W. (2018). The political mobility of China's central state-owned enterprise leaders. *The China Quarterly*, 233, 1–21.

Leutert, W., & Eaton, S. (2021). Deepening not departure: Xi Jinping's governance of China's state-owned economy. *The China Quarterly*, 248(S1), 200–21.

Levi-Faur, D. (2009). Regulatory capitalism and the reassertion of the public interest. *Policy and Society*, 27(3), 181–91.

Levitsky, S., & Ziblatt, D. (2018). *How Democracies Die: What History Tells Us about Our Future.* Viking.

Li, C., Krotkov, N. A., & Leonard, P. (2015). *OMI/Aura Sulfur Dioxide (SO2) Total Column L3 1 day Best Pixel in 0.25 degree x 0.25 degree V3.* Goddard Earth Sciences Data and Information Services Center (GES DISC).

Li, G., Shao, S., & Zhang, L. (2019). Green supply chain behavior and business performance: evidence from China. *Technological Forecasting and Social Change*, 144, 445–55.

Li, H., & Zhou, L.-A. (2005). Political turnover and economic performance: the incentive role of personnel control in China. *Journal of Public Economics*, 89(9), 1743–62.

Li, W., Liu, J., & Li, D. (2012). Getting their voices heard: three cases of public participation in environmental protection in China. *Journal of Environmental Management*, 98, 65–72.

Li, X., & Chan, C. G.-W. (2016). Who pollutes? Ownership type and environmental performance of Chinese firms. *Journal of Contemporary China*, 25(98), 248–63.

Li, Y. (2019). *Playing by the Informal Rules: Why the Chinese Regime Remains Stable Despite Rising Protests.* Cambridge University Press.

Lieberman, E. S. (2003). *Race and Regionalism in the Politics of Taxation in Brazil and South Africa.* Cambridge University Press.

Lieberthal, K., & Lampton, D. M. (1992). *Bureaucracy, Politics, and Decision Making in Post-Mao China.* University of California Press.

Lieberthal, K., & Oksenberg, M. (2020). *Policy Making in China.* Princeton University Press.

Liebman, B. L. (2007). China's courts: restricted reform. *The China Quarterly*, 191, 620–38.

(2014). Legal reform: China's law-stability paradox. *Daedalus*, 143(2), 96–109.

Lindblom, C. E. (1959). The science of muddling through. *Public Administration Review*, 19(2), 79–88.

(1977). *Politics and Markets: The World's Political-Economic Systems.* Basic Books.

Lipsky, M. (1980). *Street-Level Bureaucracy: Dilemmas of the Individual in Public Services.* Russell Sage Foundation.

Liu, N. N., Lo, C. W.-H., Zhan, X., & Wang, W. (2015). Campaign-style enforcement and regulatory compliance. *Public Administration Review*, 75(1), 85–95.

Liu, N., Van Rooij, B., & Lo, C. W.-H. (2018). Beyond deterrent enforcement styles: behavioural intuitions of Chinese environmental law enforcement agents in a context of challenging inspections. *Public Administration*, 96(3), 497–512.

Looney, K. E. (2020). *Mobilizing for Development: The Modernization of Rural East Asia*. Cornell University Press.

Looney, K., & Rithmire, M. (2017). China gambles on modernizing through urbanization. *Current History*, 116(791), 203–9.

Lora-Wainwright, A. (2021). *Resigned Activism: Living with Pollution in Rural China*. MIT Press.

Lora-Wainwright, A., Zhang, Y., Wu, Y., & Van Rooij, B. (2012). Learning to live with pollution: the making of environmental subjects in a Chinese industrialized village. *The China Journal*, 68, 106–24.

Lorentzen, P. (2014). China's strategic censorship. *American Journal of Political Science*, 58(2), 402–14.

Lorentzen, P. L., & Lu, X. (2018). Personal ties, meritocracy, and China's anti-corruption campaign (SSRN Scholarly Paper ID 2835841). Social Science Research Network.

Lorentzen, P., Landry, P., & Yasuda, J. (2014). Undermining authoritarian innovation: the power of China's industrial giants. *The Journal of Politics*, 76(1), 182–94.

Lü, X., & Landry, P. F. (2014). Show me the money: interjurisdiction political competition and fiscal extraction in China. *American Political Science Review*, 108(3), 706–22.

Lust-Okar, E. (2005). *Structuring Conflict in the Arab World: Incumbents, Opponents, and Institutions*. Cambridge University Press.

Magaloni, B. (2006). *Voting for Autocracy: Hegemonic Party Survival and its Demise in Mexico*. Cambridge University Press.

(2008). Credible power-sharing and the longevity of authoritarian rule. *Comparative Political Studies*, 41(4–5), 715–41.

Manion, M. (2004). *Corruption by Design: Building Clean Government in Mainland China and Hong Kong*. Harvard University Press.

(2016). Taking China's anticorruption campaign seriously. *Economic and Political Studies*, 4(1), 3–18.

Mann, M. (1984). The autonomous power of the state: its origins, mechanisms and results. *European Journal of Sociology / Archives Européennes de Sociologie*, 25(2), 185–213.

(2008). Infrastructural power revisited. *Studies in Comparative International Development*, 43(3), 355–65.

Mascini, P. (2013). Why was the enforcement pyramid so influential? And what price was paid? *Regulation & Governance*, 7(1), 48–60.

Mattingly, D. (2020). *The Art of Political Control in China*. Cambridge University Press.

McAllister, L. K. (2008). *Making Law Matter: Environmental Protection and Legal Institutions in Brazil*. Stanford Law Books.

McCubbins, M. D., & Schwartz, T. (1984). Congressional oversight overlooked: police patrols versus fire alarms. *American Journal of Political Science*, 28(1), 165–79.

Mei, C., & Pearson, M. M. (2014). Killing a chicken to scare the monkeys? Deterrence failure and local defiance in China. *The China Journal*, 72, 75–97.

(2017). The dilemma of "managing for results" in China: won't let go. *Public Administration and Development*, 37(3), 203–16.

Meng, T., Pan, J., & Yang, P. (2017). Conditional receptivity to citizen participation: evidence from a survey experiment in China. *Comparative Political Studies*, 50(4), 399–433.

Mertha, A. C. (2005). China's "soft" centralization: shifting tiao/kuai authority relations. *The China Quarterly*, 184, 791–810.

(2009). "Fragmented authoritarianism 2.0": political pluralization in the Chinese policy process. *The China Quarterly*, 200, 995–1012.

(2014). *China's Water Warriors: Citizen Action and Policy Change*. Cornell University Press.

(2017). "Stressing out": cadre calibration and affective proximity to the CCP in reform-era China. *The China Quarterly*, 229, 64–85.

Michelson, E. (2007). Lawyers, political embeddedness, and institutional continuity in China's transition from socialism. *American Journal of Sociology*, 113(2), 352–414.

(2008). Justice from above or below? Popular strategies for resolving grievances in rural China. *The China Quarterly*, 193, 43–64.

Migdal, J. S. (2001). *State in Society: Studying How States and Societies Transform and Constitute One Another*. Cambridge University Press.

Migdal, J. S., Kohli, A., & Shue, V. (1994). Introduction: developing a state-in-society perspective. In J. S. Migdal, A. Kohli, & V. Shue, eds., *State Power and Social Forces: Domination and Transformation in the Third World*. Cambridge University Press, pp. 1–4.

Minzner, C. F. (2011). China's turn against law. *The American Journal of Comparative Law*, 59(4), 935–84.

(2015). Legal reform in the Xi Jinping era. *Asia Policy*, 20, 4–9.

(2018). *End of an Era: How China's Authoritarian Revival is Undermining its Rise*. Oxford University Press.

Moustafa, T. (2007). *The Struggle for Constitutional Power: Law, Politics, and Economic Development in Egypt*. Cambridge University Press.

(2014). Law and courts in authoritarian regimes. *Annual Review of Law and Social Science*, 10(1), 281–99.

Nahm, J. (2017). Renewable futures and industrial legacies: wind and solar sectors in China, Germany, and the United States. *Business and Politics*, 19(1), 68–106.

Nahm, J., & Steinfeld, E. S. (2014). Scale-up nation: China's specialization in innovative manufacturing. *World Development*, 54, 288–300.

Nathan, A. J. (2003). Authoritarian resilience. *Journal of Democracy*, 14(1), 6–17.

Naughton, B. (1995). *Growing Out of the Plan: Chinese Economic Reform, 1978–1993*. Cambridge University Press.

(2014). China's economy: complacency, crisis & the challenge of reform. *Daedalus*, 143(2), 14–25.

(2016). Inside and outside: the modernized hierarchy that runs China. *Journal of Comparative Economics*, 44(2), 404–15.

(2017). Is China socialist? *Journal of Economic Perspectives*, 31(1), 3–24.

Naughton, B., & Tsai, K. S. (2015). *State Capitalism, Institutional Adaptation, and the Chinese Miracle*. Cambridge University Press.

Neaera Abers, R., & Keck, M. E. (2009). Mobilizing the state: the erratic partner in Brazil's participatory water policy. *Politics & Society*, 37(2), 289–314.

Nickolay A. Krotkov, Can Li, and Peter Leonard (2015), *OMI/Aura Sulfur Dioxide (SO2) Total Column L3 1 day Best Pixel in 0.25 degree x 0.25 degree V3*. Goddard Earth Sciences Data and Information Services Center (GES DISC).

Nielsen, C. P., & Ho, M. S. (2013). *Clearer Skies over China: Reconciling Air Quality, Climate, and Economic Goals*. MIT Press.

Niskanen, W. A. (1971). *Bureaucracy and Representative Government*. Aldine, Atherton.

North, D. C., & Weingast, B. R. (1989). Constitutions and commitment: the evolution of institutions governing public choice in seventeenth-century England. *The Journal of Economic History*, 49(4), 803–32.

O'Brien, K. J., & Deng, Y. (2017). Preventing protest one person at a time: psychological coercion and relational repression in China. *China Review*, 17(2), 179–201.

O'Brien, K. J., & Li, L. (1999). Selective policy implementation in rural China. *Comparative Politics*, 31(2), 167–86.

(2006). *Rightful Resistance in Rural China*. Cambridge University Press.

O'Donnell, G. A., Schmitter, P. C., & Whitehead, L. (1986). *Transitions from Authoritarian Rule: Latin America*. Johns Hopkins University Press.

O'Rourke, D. (2004). *Community-driven Regulation: Balancing Development and the Environment in Vietnam*. MIT Press.

Oi, J. C. (1999). *Rural China Takes Off: Institutional Foundations of Economic Reform*. University of California Press.

Olken, B. A. (2007). Monitoring corruption: evidence from a field experiment in Indonesia. *The Journal of Political Economy*, 115(2), 200–49.

Olson, M. (1993). Dictatorship, democracy, and development. *American Political Science Review*, 87(3), 567–76.

Ong, L. (2006). The political economy of township government debt, township enterprises and rural financial institutions in China. *The China Quarterly*, 186, 377–400.

Ong, L. H. (2012a). *Prosper or Perish: Credit and Fiscal Systems in Rural China*. Cornell University Press.

(2012b). Between developmental and clientelist states: local state–business relationships in China. *Comparative Politics*, 44(2), 191–209.

(2018). Thugs and outsourcing of state repression in China. *The China Journal*, 80, 94–110.

Ostrom, E. (1990). *Governing the Commons: The Evolution of Institutions for Collective Action*. Cambridge University Press.

Paoli, G., & Wiles, A. (2015). Key analytical capabilities of a best-in-class regulator. Penn Program on Regulation Research Paper.

Pargal, S., & Wheeler, D. (1996). Informal regulation of industrial pollution in developing countries: evidence from Indonesia. *The Journal of Political Economy*, 104(6), 1314–27.

Pearson, M. (2011). Variety within and without: the political economy of Chinese regulation. In S. Kennedy, ed., *Beyond the Middle Kingdom*. Stanford University Press, pp. 25–43.

Pearson, M. M. (2015). State-owned business and party-state regulation in China's modern political economy. In B. Naughton & K. S. Tsai, eds., *State Capitalism, Institutional Adaptation, and the Chinese Miracle*. Cambridge University Press, pp. 27–45.

Peck, M. J., Levin, R. C., & Goto, A. (1987). Picking losers: public policy toward declining industries in Japan. *Journal of Japanese Studies*, 13(1), 79–123.

Pei, M. (2009). *China's Trapped Transition: The Limits of Developmental Autocracy*. Harvard University Press.

(2017). *China's Crony Capitalism: The Dynamics of Regime Decay*. Harvard University Press.

Perry, E. J. (2007). Studying Chinese politics: farewell to revolution? *The China Journal*, 57(57), 1–22.

Pflug, K. (2018). Impact of tightened environmental regulation on China's chemical industry. *Journal of Business Chemistry*, 15(3), 96–106.

Pils, E. (2014). *China's Human Rights Lawyers: Advocacy and Resistance*. Routledge.

Polanyi, K. (1957). *The Great Transformation* (Beacon paperbacks; 45). Beacon Press.

Post, A. E. (2014). *Foreign and Domestic Investment in Argentina: The Politics of Privatized Infrastructure*. Cambridge University Press.

Ran, R. and Han, D. (2014). Ruhe yong zhidu baohu shengtai huanjing? Huanjing zhili zhong de zhongyang – difang guanxi (How to use institutions to protect the environment? Center-local relations in environmental regulation). *Zhongguo Gaige Xili* Baogao (China Reform Report Series), 26.

Repnikova, M. (2017). *Media Politics in China: Improvising Power under Authoritarianism*. Cambridge University Press.

Revesz, R. L. (1992). Rehabilitating interstate competition: rethinking the "race-to-the-bottom" rationale for federal environmental regulation. *New York University Law Review*, 67(6), 1210–54.

Rithmire, M. E. (2013). Land politics and local state capacities: the political economy of urban change in China. *The China Quarterly*, 216, 872–95.

(2017). Land institutions and Chinese political economy: institutional complementarities and macroeconomic management. *Politics & Society*, 45(1), 123–53.

Roberts, M. E. (2018). *Censored: Distraction and Diversion Inside China's Great Firewall*. Princeton University Press.

Rodden, J. (2004). Comparative federalism and decentralization: on meaning and measurement. *Comparative Politics*, 36(4), 481–500.

Rohde, R. A., & Muller, R. A. (2015). Air pollution in China: mapping of concentrations and sources. *PLOS ONE*, 10(8), e0135749.

Rooij, B. van, Zhu, Q., Na, L., & Qiliang, W. (2017). Centralizing trends and pollution law enforcement in China. *The China Quarterly*, 231, 583–606.

Root, H. L. (1989). Tying the king's hands: credible commitments and royal fiscal policy during the old regime. *Rationality and Society*, 1(2), 240–58.

Rosberg, J. (1995). The Rise of an Independent Judiciary in Egypt. Ph.D. dissertation, Massachusetts Institute of Technology.

Rosencranz, A., & Jackson, M. (2003). The Delhi pollution case: the Supreme Court of India and the limits of judicial power. *Columbia Journal of Environmental Law*, 28, 223–54.

Rothstein, B. (2015). The Chinese paradox of high growth and low quality of government: the cadre organization meets Max Weber. *Governance*, 28(4), 533–48.

Rothstein, H., Borraz, O., & Huber, M. (2013). Risk and the limits of governance: exploring varied patterns of risk-based governance across Europe. *Regulation & Governance*, 7(2), 215–35.

Saffon, M. P., & Bertomeu, J. G. (2019). What/whose property rights? The Selective Enforcement of Land Rights under Mexican Liberalism in Mexico. In D. M. Brinks, S. Levitsky, & M. V. Murillo, eds., *Understanding Institutional Weakness: Lessons from Latin America*. Cambridge University Press.

Sappington, D. E., & Stiglitz, J. E. (1987). Privatization, information and incentives. *Journal of Policy Analysis and Management*, 6(4), 567–85.

Savedoff, W. D., & Spiller, P. T. (1999). *Spilled Water: Institutional Commitment in the Provision of Water Services*. Inter-American Development Bank.

Schlæger, J., & Zhou, J. (2019). Digital environmental monitoring in urban China. In J. Delman, Y. Ren, O. Luova, M. Burell, & O. Almén, eds., *Greening China's Urban Governance: Tackling Environmental and Sustainability Challenges*. Springer, pp. 131–49.

Scholz, J. T. (1984a). Voluntary compliance and regulatory enforcement. *Law & Policy*, 6(4), 385–404.

    (1984b). Cooperation, deterrence, and the ecology of regulatory enforcement. *Law and Society Review*, 179–224.

Scott, J. C. (1998). *Seeing Like a State: How Certain Schemes To Improve the Human Condition Have Failed*. Yale University Press.

Seligsohn, D. J. (2018). Corporate Concentration and Air Pollution Governance in China (Doctoral dissertation, UC San Diego)

Seligsohn, D., Liu, M., & Zhang, B. (2018). The sound of one hand clapping: transparency without accountability. *Environmental Politics*, 27(5), 804–29.

Shapiro, J. (2001). *Mao's War against Nature: Politics and the Environment in Revolutionary China*. Cambridge University Press.

Shearman, D., & Smith, J. (2007). *The Climate Change Challenge and the Failure of Democracy*. Praeger.

Shen, W., & Jiang, D. (2021). Making authoritarian environmentalism accountable? Understanding China's new reforms on environmental governance. *The Journal of Environment & Development*, 30(1), 41–67.

Shen, Y., & Ahlers, A. L. (2019). Blue sky fabrication in China: science–policy integration in air pollution regulation campaigns for mega-events. *Environmental Science & Policy*, 94, 135–42.

Shirk, S. L. (1993). *The Political Logic of Economic Reform in China*. University of California Press.

Short, J. L., & Toffel, M. W. (2010). Making self-regulation more than merely symbolic: the critical role of the legal environment. *Administrative Science Quarterly*, 55(3), 361–96.

Shue, V. (1988). *The Reach of the State: Sketches of the Chinese Body Politic*. Stanford University Press.

Silbey, S. (1984). The consequences of responsive regulation. In K. Hawkins & J. M. Thomas, eds., *Enforcing Regulation Law in Social Context Series*. Kluwer-Nijhoff, pp. 145–70.

Skocpol, T. (1985). Bringing the state back in: strategies of analysis in current research. In P. B. Evans, D. Rueschemeyer, & T. Skocpol, eds., *Bringing the State Back In*. Cambridge University Press, pp. 3–38.

Slater, D. (2008). Can leviathan be democratic? Competitive elections, robust mass politics, and state infrastructural power. *Studies in Comparative International Development*, 43(3), 252–72.

(2010). *Ordering Power: Contentious Politics and Authoritarian Leviathans in Southeast Asia.* Cambridge University Press.

Snow, D., Cress, D., Downey, L., & Jones, A. (2006). Disrupting the "quotidian": reconceptualizing the relationship between breakdown and the emergence of collective action. *Mobilization: An International Quarterly*, 3(1), 1–22.

Soifer, H. (2008). State infrastructural power: approaches to conceptualization and measurement. *Studies in Comparative International Development*, 43 (3), 231–51.

Solinger, D. J., & Jiang, T. (2016). When Chinese central orders and promotion criteria conflict: implementation decisions on the destitute in poor versus prosperous cities. *Modern China*, 42(6), 571–606.

Staats, J. L., & Biglaiser, G. (2012). Foreign direct investment in Latin America: the importance of judicial strength and rule of law. *International Studies Quarterly*, 56(1), 193–202.

Stern, R. E. (2010). On the frontlines: making decisions in Chinese civil environmental lawsuits. *Law & Policy*, 32(1), 79–103.

(2013). *Environmental Litigation in China: A Study in Political Ambivalence.* Cambridge University Press.

(2017). Activist lawyers in post-Tiananmen China. *Law & Social Inquiry*, 42(1), 234–51.

Stern, R. E., & Hassid, J. (2012). Amplifying silence: uncertainty and control parables in contemporary China. *Comparative Political Studies*, 45(10), 1230–54.

Stern, R. E., & Liu, L. J. (2020). The good lawyer: state-led professional socialization in contemporary China. *Law & Social Inquiry*, 45(1), 226–48.

Stern, R. E., & O'Brien, K. J. (2012). Politics at the boundary: mixed signals and the Chinese state. *Modern China*, 38(2), 174–98.

Stockmann, D. (2013). *Media Commercialization and Authoritarian Rule in China.* Cambridge University Press.

Strauss, J. (2006). Morality, coercion and state building by campaign in the early PRC: regime consolidation and after, 1949–1956. *The China Quarterly*, 188, 891–912.

Strauss, J. C. (2009). Forestry reform and the transformation of state capacity in fin-de-siècle China. *The Journal of Asian Studies*, 68(4), 1163–88.

Su, Y., & He, X. (2010). Street as courtroom: state accommodation of labor protest in South China. *Law & Society Review*, 44(1), 157–84.

Tan, Y. (2014). Transparency without democracy: the unexpected effects of China's environmental disclosure policy. *Governance: An International Journal of Policy and Administration*, 27(1), 37–62.

Tanner, M. S. (1999). *The Politics of Lawmaking in Post-Mao China: Institutions, Processes, and Democratic Prospects.* Oxford University Press.

(2000). State coercion and the balance of awe: the 1983–1986 "Stern Blows" anti-crime campaign. *The China Journal*, 44, 93–125.

Tarrow, S. G. (2011). *Power in Movement: Social Movements and Contentious Politics.* Cambridge University Press.

Teets, J. C. (2014). *Civil Society under Authoritarianism: The China Model.* Cambridge University Press.

(2018). The power of policy networks in authoritarian regimes: changing environmental policy in China. *Governance*, 31(1), 125–41.

Thompson, M. R. (2021). Pushback after backsliding? Unconstrained executive aggrandizement in the Philippines versus contested military-monarchical rule in Thailand. *Democratization*, 28(1), 124–41.

Thornton, D., Kagan, R. A., & Gunningham, N. (2008). Compliance costs, regulation, and environmental performance: controlling truck emissions in the US. *Regulation & Governance*, 2(3), 275–92.

(2009). When social norms and pressures are not enough: environmental performance in the trucking industry. *Law & Society Review*, 43(2), 405–36.

Thornton, P. M. (2009). Crisis and governance: SARS and the resilience of the Chinese body politic. *The China Journal*, 61, 23–48.

Tian, G., & Tsai, W.-H. (2020). The policy implementation strategies of county cadres: political instrument and flexible local governance. China Information.

Tilly, C. (1992). *Coercion, Capital, and European States, A.D. 990–1992.* Blackwell.

Tilt, B. (2007). The political ecology of pollution enforcement in China: a case from Sichuan's rural industrial sector. *The China Quarterly*, 192, 915–32.

Tilton, M. (1996). *Restrained trade: Cartels in Japan's basic materials industries.* Cornell University Press.

Truex, R. (2014). The returns to office in a "rubber stamp" parliament. *American Political Science Review*, 108(2), 235–51.

(2017). Consultative authoritarianism and its limits. *Comparative Political Studies*, 50(3), 329–61.

Tsai, K. S. (2002). *Back-Alley Banking: Private Entrepreneurs in China.* Cornell University Press.

(2011). *Capitalism without Democracy: The Private Sector in Contemporary China.* Cornell University Press.

(2015). The political economy of state capitalism and shadow banking in China (SSRN Scholarly Paper ID 2607793). Social Science Research Network.

Tsui, K. (2005). Local tax system, intergovernmental transfers and China's local fiscal disparities. *Journal of Comparative Economics*, 33(1), 173–196.

Tsui, K., & Wang, Y. (2004). Between separate stoves and a single menu: fiscal decentralization in China. *The China Quarterly*, 177, 71–90.

Tudor, M. J. (2013). *The Promise of Power: The Origins of Democracy in India and Autocracy in Pakistan*. Cambridge University Press.

van de Walle, N. (1989). Privatization in developing countries: a review of the issues. *World Development*, 17(5), 601–15.

van der Kamp, D. (2021). Can police patrols prevent pollution? The limits of authoritarian environmental governance in China. *Comparative Politics*, 53(3), 403–33.

van der Kamp, D., Lorentzen, P., & Mattingly, D. (2017). Racing to the bottom or to the top? Decentralization, revenue pressures, and governance reform in China. *World Development*, 95, 164–76.

van Rooij, B. (2002). Implementing Chinese environmental law through enforcement: the Shiwu Xiao and Shuang Dabiao campaigns. In J. Chen, J. M. Otto, & Y. Li, eds., *Implementation of Law in the People's Republic of China*. Kluwer Law International, pp. 149–78.

  (2006). Implementation of Chinese environmental law: regular enforcement and political campaigns. *Development and Change*, 37(1), 57–74.

  (2009). The politics of law in China: enforcement campaigns in the post-Mao PRC (SSRN Scholarly Paper ID 1368181). Social Science Research Network.

  (2010). The people vs. pollution: understanding citizen action against pollution in China. *Journal of Contemporary China*, 19(63), 55–77.

van Rooij, B., Stern, R. E., & Fürst, K. (2016). The authoritarian logic of regulatory pluralism: understanding China's new environmental actors. *Regulation & Governance*, 10(1), 3–13.

Van Rooij, B., Zhu, Q., Na, L., & Qiliang, W. (2017). Centralizing trends and pollution law enforcement in China. *The China Quarterly*, 231, 583–606.

Viscusi, W. K., Vernon, J. M., & Harrington, J. E. (2000). *Economics of Regulation and Antitrust* (3rd ed.). MIT Press.

Vogel, D. (2005). *The Market for Virtue: The Potential and Limits of Corporate Social Responsibility*. Brookings Institution Press.

Vogel, S. K. (1996). *Freer Markets, More Rules: Regulatory Reform in Advanced Industrial Countries*. Cornell University Press.

Vortherms, S. A. (2019). China's missing children: political barriers to citizenship through the household registration system. *The China Quarterly*, 238, 309–30.

Walker, K. L. M. (2008). From covert to overt: everyday peasant politics in China and the implications for transnational agrarian movements. *Journal of Agrarian Change*, 8(2–3), 462–88.

Wallace, J. L. (2016). Juking the stats? Authoritarian information problems in China. *British Journal of Political Science*, 46(1), 11–29.

Wang, A. L. (2013). The search for sustainable legitimacy: environmental law and bureaucracy in China. *Harvard Environmental Law Review*, 37, 365–440.

(2018). Explaining environmental information disclosure in China. *Ecology Law Quarterly*, 44(4), 865–924.

Wang, E. H. (2021). Frightened Mandarins: the adverse effects of fighting corruption on local bureaucracy. *Comparative Political Studies*.

Wang, H., & Jin, Y. (2007). Industrial ownership and environmental performance: evidence from China. *Environmental and Resource Economics*, 36(3), 255–73.

Wang, S., Paul, M. J., & Dredze, M. (2015). Social media as a sensor of air quality and public response in China. *Journal of Medical Internet Research*, 17(3), e22.

Wang, X. (1997). Mutual empowerment of state and peasantry: grassroots democracy in rural China. *World Development*, 25(9), 1431–42.

(2016). Requests for environmental information disclosure in China: an understanding from legal mobilization and citizen activism. *Journal of Contemporary China*, 25(98), 233–47.

Wang, X., & Herd, R. (2013). *The System of Revenue Sharing and Fiscal Transfers in China*. OECD.

Wang, Y. (2015). *Tying the Autocrat's Hands*. Cambridge University Press.

(2016). Beyond local protectionism: China's state–business relations in the last two decades. *The China Quarterly*, 226, 319–341.

Wang, Y., & Minzner, C. (2015). The rise of the Chinese security state. *The China Quarterly*, 222, 339–59.

Ward, H., Cao, X., & Mukherjee, B. (2014). State capacity and the environmental investment gap in authoritarian states. *Comparative Political Studies*, 47(3), 309–43.

Weber, M., Roth, G., Wittich, C., & Fischoff, E. (1978). *Economy and society: An outline of interpretive sociology*. University of California Press.

Wedeman, A. (2005). Anticorruption campaigns and the intensification of corruption in China. *Journal of Contemporary China*, 14(42), 93–116.

Weinberg, J. (2017). Bureaucracy as violence. *Michigan Law Review*, 115(6), 1097–1116.

Weingast, B. R. (1984). The congressional-bureaucratic system: a principal agent perspective (with applications to the SEC). *Public choice*, 44(1), 147–91.

(2014). Second generation fiscal federalism: political aspects of decentralization and economic development. *World Development*, 53, 14–25.

Wengle, S. A. (2015). *Post-Soviet Power: State-led Development and Russia's Marketization*. Cambridge University Press.

Wilson, J. (1980). *The Politics of regulation*. Basic Books.

Wong, C., & Karplus, V. J. (2017). China's war on air pollution: can existing governance structures support new ambitions? *The China Quarterly*, 231, 662–84.

Woo-Cumings, M. (1999). *The Developmental State*. Cornell University Press.

Woodworth, M. D., & Wallace, J. L. (2017). Seeing ghosts: parsing China's "ghost city" controversy. *Urban Geography*, 38(8), 1270–81.

Wright, T. (2010). *Accepting Authoritarianism: State–Society Relations in China's Reform Era*. Stanford University Press.

Wu, A. M., & Wang, W. (2013). Determinants of expenditure decentralization: evidence from China. *World Development*, 46, 176–84.

Xu, C. (2011). The fundamental institutions of China's reforms and development. *Journal of Economic Literature*, 49(4), 1076–1151.

Xu, X., Kostka, G., & Cao, X. (2021). Information control and public support for social credit systems in China. *The Journal of Politics*.

Yang, L. C. (2015) *Analysis of the Impact of Firm Closures on the Livelihood of the Local Informal Workforce* (企业关停对当地临时就业人员的生计影响研究), FORHEAD Report, Beijing.

Yang, D. L. (2017). China's illiberal regulatory state in comparative perspective. *Chinese Political Science Review*, 2(1), 114–33.

Yang, Y. (2021). The politics of inclusion and exclusion: Chinese dual-pension regimes in the era of labor migration and labor informalization. *Politics & Society*, 49(2), 147–80.

Yang, Y., & Gallagher, M. (2017). Moving in and moving up? Labor conditions and China's changing development model. *Public Administration and Development*, 37(3), 160–75.

Yashar, D. J. (2018). *Homicidal Ecologies: Illicit Economies and Complicit States in Latin America*. Cambridge University Press.

Yasuda, J. K. (2016). Regulatory governance. In C. Ansell & J. Torfing, eds., *Handbook on Theories of Governance*. Edward Elgar, pp. 428–41.

(2017). *On Feeding the Masses*. Cambridge University Press.

(2020). The other side of uncertainty: the perils of policy experimentation in post-reform China. Unpublished paper.

Zhan, X., Lo, C. W.-H., & Tang, S.-Y. (2014). Contextual changes and environmental policy implementation: a longitudinal study of street-level bureaucrats in Guangzhou, China. *Journal of Public Administration Research and Theory*, 24(4), 1005–35.

Zhang, L.-Y. (1999). Chinese central–provincial fiscal relationships, budgetary decline and the impact of the 1994 fiscal reform: an evaluation. *The China Quarterly*, 157, 115–41.

Zhang, X. (2017). Implementation of pollution control targets in China: has a centralized enforcement approach worked? *The China Quarterly*, 231, 749–74.

Zhi, Q., & Pearson, M. M. (2017). China's hybrid adaptive bureaucracy: the case of the 863 program for science and technology. *Governance*, 30(3), 407–24.

Zhong, Y., & Hwang, W. (2016). Pollution, institutions and street protests in urban China. *Journal of Contemporary China*, 25(98), 216–32.

Zhou, X. (2010). The institutional logic of collusion among local governments in China. *Modern China*, 36(1), 47–78.

(2017). The institutional logic of governance in China: an organizational approach. *SDX-Joint Publishing Company*.

Zhou, X., Lian, H., Ortolano, L., & Ye, Y. (2013). A behavioral model of "muddling through" in the Chinese bureaucracy: the case of environmental protection. *The China Journal*, 70(1), 120–47.

Zhu, J., Huang, H., & Zhang, D. (2019). "Big tigers, big data": learning social reactions to China's anticorruption campaign through online feedback. *Public Administration Review*, 79(4), 500–13.

Zhu, J., & Zhang, D. (2017). Does corruption hinder private businesses? Leadership stability and predictable corruption in China. *Governance*, 30(3), 343–63.

Zhu, J., Zhang, Q., & Liu, Z. (2017). Eating, drinking, and power signaling in institutionalized authoritarianism: China's anti-waste campaign since 2012. *Journal of Contemporary China*, 26(105), 337–52.

Zhu, X., Qiu, T., & Liu, D. (2022). Resisting public monitoring in authoritarian regimes: evidence from local environmental litigation in China. *Governance*.

INDEX

Figures are indicated by fig. and tables by tab.

CAMBRIDGE STUDIES IN LAW AND SOCIETY

Printed by Printforce, United Kingdom